VENUS ENVY

VENUS ENVY

Louise Bagshawe

ORION

The right of Louise Bagshawe to be identified as the author
of this work has been asserted by her in accordance with
the Copyright, Designs and Patents Act 1988.

First published in Great Britain in 1998 by
Orion
An imprint of Orion Books Ltd
Orion House, 5 Upper St Martin's Lane,
London WC2H 9EA

A CIP catalogue record for this book
is available from the British Library

ISBN 0 75280 460 X (hardcover)
0 75280 461 8 (trade paperback)

Typeset by Deltatype Ltd, Birkenhead, Merseyside
Printed in Great Britain by
Clays Ltd, St Ives plc

*This book is dedicated to
my mother Daphne and my little sister Tilly,
who could not be less like the mother or sister
in this book. Honestly.*

I would like to thank my wonderful agent, Michael Sissons, for all his encouragement on *Venus Envy* and for organising my whole working life with such effortless ease. I'd also like to thank the rest of the team at Peters Fraser & Dunlop and I.L.A. for being so fantastic; especially Tim Corrie and Fiona Batty. At Orion I am particularly lucky to have Rosie Cheetham as a witty and inspiring editor who always knows exactly the right thing for the characters and the story. I must also thank Susan Lamb for her terrific covers and marketing, and Louise Page (great party!) and Charlotte Hobson (great cover copy!) for their enthusiasm, which is much appreciated. My friends are very sympathetic when I am acting like a recluse as deadlines approach, so my thanks are due to all of them; particularly kind while I was writing this novel were Jacob Rees-Mogg, Fred Metcalf, Lord Alexander Hope and Peter Mensch.

Chapter 1

'Alan Pell's coming round in five minutes,' Keisha announced.

'Lucky you,' I said grumpily.

'Yeah.' Keisha preened, stretching her elegant black back like a prizewinning Siamese. 'He says there's a job going down at *Up and Running*.' She tugged her tiny Gucci cardigan disapprovingly round her polished-ebony shoulders and flung an expressive glance at my work station. Bits of clay and sweet-wrappers from my latest avant-garde creation littered my side of the room. 'Maybe if you carry on like that he'll recommend you for something at *Blue Peter*.'

'I'll clear it up,' I said gloomily. It did look like a reject from the *Play School* arts department.

'And yourself,' Keisha said not unkindly. She spoke in the tone of someone addressing a poor unfortunate fellow creature. 'I can lend you my black Ghost dress.'

'What's wrong with this?' I snapped.

Her glance at my tattered jeans and paint-spattered shirt was eloquent. My nails were broken, my hair was straggly, and my clothes were a style-free zone.

'He works in the record business . . . he knows lots of people in TV,' Keisha said temptingly. 'Interesting people . . . with money. And power.'

'I don't care about people with money and power!' I lied furiously. 'I only care about Oliver.'

My latest greatest love had just dumped me yesterday. By fax. From the set of his new movie, although obviously he hadn't had time to do it himself. I must be the only girl in the history of dating to be dumped by a secretary.

'Oliver was a loser. And so will you be, if you keep dressing like a refugee from the bypass protests,' Keisha insisted. She opened her wardrobe and pulled out a black scrap of nothing, immaculate in its dry-cleaner sheath. 'If you get this dirty you're paying for it.'

'How much was it?' I asked grimly.

Keisha blushed. 'Two eighty.'

'Two hundred and eighty quid?' I gasped. Keisha gave me heart tremors, the fortune she spent on clothes. Without wincing. She never had any money, but by God, she was flash. We're talking about a girl who once spent a month's dole cheques on an Armani jacket. Men only had to look at Keisha to go running to the nearest Prada store or Rolex outfit. Maybe she sold all the superfluous Rolexes to feed her designer habit. It was one of the mysteries of the ages, how she paid for it.

I felt guilty if I bought an M&S sandwich instead of making my own.

'I could take you down to Neville Daniels,' Keisha suggested cheerfully, 'drag you round to Liberty's and fix you up . . . we could get to first base with about three hundred quid.'

'Three hundred!' I gasped.

'Four hundred, maybe,' Keisha admitted.

I thought gloomily about that idea as I slipped on her dress. Four hundred quid would get me looking presentable. Great. And how was I supposed to find that, three months into London life with my parents still paying the rent, no boyfriend to pay for taxis or dinners, and a miserable future as a typist looming over me?

The door opened. It was Gail, my little sister, carrying a bunch of health-food bags and looking radiant and fragile in her pure wool organic dress. I still couldn't believe I was sharing a flat with Gail, but when push came to shove, I'd submitted to my parents' dictates. I was sharing this flat rent-free. I was taking the steady job in the City.

Two years ago you wouldn't have caught me dead here.

I was the great Alexandra, Wilde by name and wilder by nature. Failed in school – especially compared to Miss one hundred per cent A-grades Gail Wilde, but so what? I was creative. Making mud sculptures in the sandpit since I was about one, entered all the Young Artist competitions and won six national awards. I had a sunny life lined up as the next Dame Elizabeth Frink. Damien Hirst would have nothing on me. I scraped a C in Maths and English GCSEs, and went to Oxford. Not to do anything academic, as such. Bachelor of Fine Arts – painting and sculpting. With a little art history thrown in.

Oxford was too good to be true. I'd found *The Thornbirds* heavy going, let alone *Middlemarch*, and here I was in some Merchant Ivory film, punting down the Isis and eating strawberries in Christ Church meadows with Japanese tourists. All my friends were patronising, smug Student Grant types from *Viz*. I didn't care. I bought *Socialist Worker* and went on rent strikes. I was going to be like Vanessa Redgrave or Tony Benn – radical, but somehow still rich. Selling my mice and birds for a small fortune in smart London galleries.

All my mates laughed, but I had faith.

I was wrong.

Nobody wanted to buy my sculptures, and six months in bedsit land with cockroaches and broken radiators had crushed my spirit. I wasn't cut out for life on the streets. My bohemian director boyfriend, Oliver, had dumped me for a Californian Barbie doll the first job he got out there. I had no support except Mummy and Daddy. As I was finding out, a Bachelor of Fine Arts and a set of funky clay statues doesn't get you very far in the big city.

'God, you look tired, Alex-Palex,' Gail said annoyingly. She always used our baby nicknames in front of my cooler friends. 'Your b-complex vitamins need boosting.'

'Your face needs flattening,' I growled.

'Great dress,' Gail said airily. 'Pity about the rest of you. Oh, I hope you haven't nicked all the hot water, Keisha, my muscles are cramping, I'm sure it's extreme stress. Maybe I should try Prozac.' She gave her waif-like, doe-eyed reflection a smug glance and flounced into the bathroom. Gail was a hypochondriac and a health-food nut, but she got away with it because she was so fragile and lovely. Even her stupid organic clothes somehow seemed attractively rustic and simple. And, like Keisha, Gail had a job: she was an editorial assistant at *Organic Food Weekly*, making no money and waiting happily for Mr Right to come along and spirit her to a big Gloucestershire estate, where she could satisfy her need for nature by fiddling with a small herb garden, or something.

Gail also fancied herself as the next Martin Amis. She was writing something she called 'the Great Nature Novel', but refused to tell me the plot – like I cared! – in case I nicked it off her. She didn't trust me at all, which was ironic, since when I was at Oxford, Gail, who read sociology at Reading, used to come over all the time and date all the eligible men. Except Tom Drummond, who wouldn't give her the time of day, but I'll tell you more about Tom later.

Keisha was signing on when I first knew her, but her effortless self-confidence had got her into radio and then TV. She did things I would never dream of. Like driving her Mercedes coupé to the dole office, or making up her CV. Radio had needed experience, so Keisha calmly invented some experience. Now she was about to go for her first major job: Alan was putting a word in over at *Up and Running*, the BBC cult Saturday kids' show. Thousands of people went for the researcher posts there every year.

'When Alan comes over, will you write my letter, Alex?' Keisha wheedled.

I sighed. I wrote everyone's letters in this house. Letters of complaint, job applications, thankyou notes, the bloody lot. It was the only thing, apart from sculpting, I was any good at.

Great, I thought as I looked in the mirror. Gail was right: I didn't look cool at all, I was just plump, scruffy Alex wearing a smart black dress.

Tomorrow was my first day in paid employment. I was still dependent on my parents. I was boyless. I was a failure.

I was twenty-seven years old.

Keisha mistook my silence for anger. She should have known better, I never got angry with anyone. I had the spine of a jellyfish.

'Come on, hon, I'll get your hair fixed for you,' she wheedled.

I needed the help.

'OK,' I said.

The door buzzed. It was Alan Pell, looking sharp as a tack. Another urban star fresh from another promotion. They were all zooming down the fast lane while I was wrecked on the hard shoulder.

'All right, Keisha babe,' Alan said, looking her Gucci shift over admiringly. 'Hiya, Alex, hon.' He kissed me warmly on the cheek. 'You look really tired. Great dress though.'

'Thanks,' I said wearily. I racked my brains for some snappy comeback, but nothing.

Keisha locked in smooth pro chat-up mode. For such a class-A bitch, she can certainly turn on the charm when she feels like it. Alan was basking in the intense interest radiating from her chocolate eyes.

I stomped out of the flat and spent ten pounds on five Four-Play scratch cards. Then I went round to McDonald's and bought a Big

Mac meal with real Coke and extra fries. I won two pounds. I was just stuffing a great fistful of fries into my cheek when Gail, weighing bugger-all and with some smooth, tanned City type on her arm, walked past the window and gave me a cheery wave. The City type looked amazed. Gail was related to *that*?

I told myself tomorrow was another day.

Chapter 2

The radio switched itself on merrily. Bastard. Mark Radcliffe and Lard braying unfunny jokes into my shattered head. Then they put on Metallica. I dragged myself from my comfy, parentally paid-for white sheets and stumbled across the room to hit the off button.

'Rise and shine, rise and shine,' Gail yelled, poking her head through the door. She was wearing a wispy Lainey Keogh web cardigan today, over a neat silk jumper. 'It's seven already!'

'Seven?' I asked blearily. Did people really do this every day? It's against my religion to surface before ten.

'Yeah, hurry up, you'll be late,' Gail said bossily. 'Mummy wants you to make a good impression today. You know she pulled strings to get you this job.'

The sad thing was that this was true. With no formal qualifications, even this shitty job was really beyond me. But, rejoicing that their black ewe had returned to the middle-class fold, Mummy and Daddy had made phone calls all over the shop, cashing in goodwill chips from years of tennis tournaments and letting the local riding school hack over our scrubby field. I had a prompt letter from Personnel at Hamilton Kane, the private investment bank, offering me a job as second secretary to one Seamus Mahon, in Corporate Finance. Mrs Kane played women's golf with my mother once a month. Even though, since I was about to do this, I clearly had no guts at all, Mummy would still have them for garters if I failed her in any way.

'OK.' I headed for the bathroom, which was sealed tighter than Oliver Brown's cheating little heart.

'Keisha . . .'

'You can wait 'til I'm finished.'

'When . . .?'

'When I'm finished,' Keisha shouted superbly.

There was no way I was getting a shower now.

'You'll have to be quicker than that,' Gail said silkily, 'and there's no breakfast cereal left. Bronwen just got back and she's been on the grass all night and she had the munchies.'

Bronwen was our other flatmate. She was Welsh, lithe and supremely funky. A photographer's assistant, she went on fashion shoots all day and raved all night. She was on first-name terms with all the bouncers down the Ministry of Sound and knew more about drugs than our local chemist. Her clothes were so hip she made the *Face* look like *Woman's Weekly*.

I knew my life was radically changed if I was in the flat the same times as Bronwen. She sat in our kitchen, scenting the whole thing with acrid marijuana smoke so thick I felt I'd be spouting Beatles lyrics any second. She was wearing tight-ass white leather jeans and a pink Spice Girls T-shirt, with 'Girl Power' emblazoned across her impressive chest. Oh, why did everybody else in this place make me feel like Fergie, only less stylish?

'All right sister,' said Bronwen, '*bore da,*' then dissolved into giggles. She was certainly having a good time if she was dropping in Welsh phrases. Bronwen staggered over to give me a boozy hug, and before I could swerve away she'd spilt black coffee all over my carefully ironed blue suit.

'Oops,' said Gail, hugely amused. 'Better find something else to wear.'

I flounced back into my own bedroom and yanked open my wardrobe. My trouser suit was in the laundry, my navy dress had a toothpaste stain on it. It was amazing, I could almost hear my own blood pressure rising.

Keisha stuck her head round my door. She was a working fantasy in Nicole Farhi, with *Rouge Noir* Chanel lipstick and nail polish perfectly coordinated.

'Black dress. Only option,' she said succinctly. 'Black says – grace and strength,' she pronounced.

I tugged on my black jersey dress. It had a roll-neck collar and was quite forgiving to my unworked-out, McDonald's-loving bottom. Keisha was right, it was the only option. And in autumn it would have looked quite smart.

Except today was the fourth of August, and it was seven thirty, and it was already blazing hot.

★

7

Hamilton Kane was in Threadneedle Passage. I knew this very well. And right now the address was emblazoned on my overheated heart, because it took me forty minutes of frantic tramping and hyperventilating over my cruelly mismarked *A–Z* to find the bloody alley. I mean, have you ever tried asking suited City brokers for directions in the morning rush hour? Might as well ask a teeming piranha to stop and chat. The stares were incredulous. And the women were worse. One gorgeous female in Prada, with baby-blonde hair and pouting lips, snarled something that might not have been 'Fuck off, fatso', but then again, it might have.

'You're late,' the receptionist said coolly when I burst through the brass doors into a huge marble fantasy from *Wall Street*.

I panted and dripped in front of her. Three coats of Sure antiperspirant had, despite all its promises, let me down. However, in this dress the odds were stacked against it. My reflection in the dark glass behind her desk was red faced and sweating. My lipstick had already vanished and my under-eye concealer was glowing white like those sunblock streaks on Aussie cricketers.

'Sorry, it was the traffic and the—'

'We work to quite a tight schedule here, Miss Wilde,' the receptionist said nastily. 'You'll be reporting to Jenny, Mr Mahon's first assistant. Her office is on the fourth floor directly you step out of the lifts.'

'Thank you,' I muttered. I strode towards the lifts purposefully. Grace, Alex, grace and strength.

'Oh, and Miss Wilde?'

'You can call me Alex,' I said kindly. Ha, ha, score one to me, snotty cow.

'Very well – you've got a ladder in your tights, *Alex*.'

The lift doors hissed softly shut in front of my mortified face. The mirrored walls confirmed this was not just sadistic wishful thinking. Yes, Jacob could have climbed to paradise up the ladder in my new Fogal tights.

When the doors opened again I was stumbling bare feet back into teetering heels, one sweaty pair of ripped tights clutched feebly in my left hand.

A severe and impeccable matron in a Jaeger suit was standing in front of me with a thunderous frown.

'I am Jenny Robins,' she said crisply.

'Hi.' Desperately I looked round for somewhere to stuff the tights, but there wasn't anywhere, so I dropped them into my handbag. 'I'm Alex.'

Over the next two hours I learned several things. 1) I hate typing. 2) I can't spell – 'For goodness' sake, Alexandra, excited, not exited. Professor has *one* "f", I thought it said on your CV that you have a degree?' 3) Where the coffee machine is located; also, the stain freshly spilled coffee makes all over light beige carpet.

'Clumsy! Clumsy!' Jenny shrieked, when she rounded the corner and saw me on my hands and knees trying to wash the carpet in Fairy Liquid and Evian from the fridge.

'Sorry.' I felt near to tears. I was sweating buckets in my horrible dress, I was spilling things and ripping things like Mr Bean in a skirt. I couldn't even type well enough to be a secretary's secretary, and now I had spilled espresso on their carpet at the first attempt. 'It gushed out all boiling—'

'It's hot. Coffee is supposed to be hot,' snapped Jenny, 'and what on earth are you doing? That'll make it a thousand times worse . . . and *Mr Mahon's Evian*! Who told you you could open the executive fridge? Do you know how particular he is about his water? Really!'

I rocked back on my heels. In the gleaming front surface of the executive fridge I saw my own flushed face, with light-brown tendrils of fringe plastered wetly to my forehead.

At that moment the door opposite us swung open and a procession of heavyset bean-counters in Savile Row suits marched out. Most of them gave me amused or disapproving stares as they stormed past, mouthing off about 'equity derivatives' and 'December 50s' and the like. Her face a mask of horror at being so exposed, Jenny yanked me to my feet by the shoulder. She had a strength that would have done credit to a drill sergeant. Or alternatively, my mother.

As the last of the meeting rounded the end of our corridor, Jenny turned on me with a face that suggested I had just finished the shortest spell of employment Hamilton Kane had ever seen.

'Alll-exandra,' she began, my name rolling furiously off her tongue, 'I must say I have *never*—'

At that moment the door swung open again. A much younger, much taller man, in a flashy navy suit that looked like it came from Alexander McQueen or someone, a man with thick black hair that curled just below his collar in the most engaging manner, a tanned man with incredibly white teeth that were grinning at me in the most friendly way, and a pair of moss-green eyes that were twinkling at me like one of Keisha's gold watches, propped himself against the doorpost and extended me a firm hand.

'Miss Alexandra Wilde, is it yourself?' he asked merrily. His accent was as soft as Irish mist. I thought Celtic gold harps, I thought babbling brooks, I thought glossy-coated Red Setters bounding across Galway moors, or something like that. I also thought, my mascara is running and I want to kill myself.

'It is. Yes,' I stammered, and seeing Jenny's thunderous face, I added, 'uh, yes, sir.'

'Call me that, and I'll be turning around to look for my father. Mr Mahon, if we're being formal. But Seamus, otherwise.'

'OK,' I said miserably.

'*Mr* Mahon,' said Jenny, her face tight with emotion, 'I'm afraid Alexandra has—'

'Ah yes, I see the problem,' Seamus soothed her. 'What a bother that infernal machine is. The coffee comes out far too hot. Anyway, the cleaners'll get that out, Jenny, so I'll tell you what, you grab a mat to lay over the stain and that'll be grand.'

I must have looked like a death-chamber prisoner hearing the phone ring, because Seamus took one look at my face and coughed gently.

'And Jenny, do you have those letters done?'

'Well.' Jenny went back to her desk and picked up one neat sheaf. 'These are the ones I typed for you, the priorities.'

'Thanks.' He flicked through them rather intently for such a laid-back-looking guy. 'And the recruitment offers?'

There was a pregnant pause. It might actually have been expecting quads.

'Those,' Jenny said heavily, 'were being typed by Alexandra.'

She grabbed a much smaller, second sheaf of letters. Covered with angry scrawls in green biro.

Seamus flicked through my attempt at gainful employment. His lip twitched.

'Jenny, you're an angel, so you are,' he said, though unless he was thinking of the Angel of Death I'd like to know which one he had in mind. 'Why don't you get cracking on the Mandarin spreadsheets, while I try and explain all the madhouse rules to Alex, seeing as she's new to the team?'

I breathed out a deep sigh of relief. I still had my job. My father would not scream at me. My mother would not have to cancel her golf sessions with Fiona Kane.

Then I felt a wave of depression seize me as I realised what I was being grateful for these days.

'Very well, Mr Mahon,' Jenny snapped, and slunk back to her desk like a Dobermann cheated of its dinner.

'Come in, Alex. If it's OK that I call you Alex?'

'It's fine,' I said, wishing tremendously that he would give me five minutes to repair my face.

No sooner was this thought formed in my head than my boss stopped again, regarded me considerately and said, 'Only first you'll be wanting to dab that coffee off that lovely dress.'

I fled to the ladies' in one second flat, to face the greatest disaster area outside of central Bosnia. My runny mascara was giving me an 'eighties Goth vibe, my blusher had sweated off and my teeth were dotted with lipstick, from all that chewing my mouth in naked terror I'd been doing. Hurriedly I washed my face clean of all make-up products; better to go bare faced than court disaster twice. Then I tried to dry my sticky forehead with paper hand-towels. I thought about sticking my head under the hand-dryer to try for a quick blow-dry effect, but with my luck today Jenny would just walk right in and have a heart attack.

I gazed at the results. Neater, but still horrible. Black jersey dress and naked face reminiscent of a scrubbed, chubby schoolgirl. I yanked my clammy hair back from my forehead and tied it into a viciously tight ponytail that yanked up the skin at the corners of my temples.

Let's face it, I was just not cut out to be a corporate slave.

I ran back to Mr Mahon's office before he got up a search party for me. It was a daunting office, with floor-to-ceiling windows affording a magnificent view over the City of London. Various domes and spires peered serenely out behind New York-style skyscrapers. The office itself was peppered with enough computers to launch a NASA satellite and covered with enough Bokara rugs to please an Arab Sheikh. I wondered idly whether if I breathed enough of the air in here, would my own tiny bank balance grow any bigger? The flowers on his desk were the kind of twiggy, leafy affair that says 'designer florist'; the *Wall Street Journal*, probably flown in that morning, rested comfortably on his antique mahogany desk . . .

I gulped. My mistyped letters were laid out before Mr Designer Everything of the twinkly eyes. I was being weighed in the balance, in this Temple of Mammon, and I knew I was going to be found wanting.

What would Keisha do? Actually, at this point, Keisha would most likely light up a fag without asking, blow a stream of smoke in the boss's face and then swing her Manolo Blahnik heels up on his desk. Keisha, when she used to be a temp, regularly used to get up from her desk in the middle of the afternoon without a word to anybody and go and get her nails done. Nobody fired her, but then again, nobody would dare. Whereas I was the working world's equivalent of the seven-stone weakling on the bodybuilders' beach. I sort of begged to be reamed out.

Seamus Mahon leaned forward. I could see he was shocked by the web of green ink that represented my first morning on the job.

'Alex Wilde,' he said, 'now would that be any relation to Kim?'

'Sorry?' I asked blankly.

'Sure, you know her, so. "We're the kids in America," ' he whistled tunelessly. 'You look a little like her.'

Great. Now I look like a frumpy washed-up early 'eighties icon. Why not just say I look like Roseanne Barr and have done with it.

'No,' I said, as coldly as I could, but it washed right over Seamus Mahon.

'These letters, Alex. They're not actually spelled right.'

I blushed with mortification.

'But that doesn't really matter.' His Irish lilt was creamy as the head on a pint of Guinness. 'If you press –' he showed me a simple little thing on his keyboard – 'it'll check the spelling for you. And correct it. It's wonderful, what they can do with technology these days.'

'Oh,' I said weakly. Why, why hadn't Jenny told me that? My boss was clearly some kind of Nazi, longing for me to screw up so she could have this delectable creature all to herself.

Although, looking the way I did, the field was effectively clear for her anyway. I might actually have predicted something like this. I looked so fat, and so ugly with my unprotected face and no tights and clammy hair, I was bound to meet the most devastating man I'd ever laid eyes on. In fact, I'll tell you the surest way I know to flood your life with desirable men. Put on ten pounds, break out in spots and/or varicose veins, and have a hair-colouring disaster that leaves you with green streaks round your ears. Then Brad Pitt and Harrison Ford lookalikes will suddenly appear magically from every corner, like the mice coming out of the mouse organ in *Bagpuss*.

'I'll remember that,' I said.

'How about I call one of the computer boys and ask him to help you round all the shortcuts? Jack?' he asked, punching up a few numbers on his space-phone. 'Could you come up here and talk to my new assistant? Show her the ropes, like.' He listened to the other end whilst smiling engagingly at me, then laughed. 'That's right enough, there, Jack. I'd say she is. Now you take very good care of her, you hear? She's new. And she's Fiona Kane's pet project.'

He hung up. Embarrassment flamed through me. Great, just great, so everybody knew I was here because of the spurious golf-club connection.

'Thanks, Mr Mahon.'

'I thought we said Seamus,' he reproved me, smiling kindly at me as I fled his office.

And that was it. High-powered suits and skirts ran back and forwards through our corridor all day, paying homage to Jenny as she ushered them into the inner sanctum. Clearly Danny Boy was a very powerful, sought-after whizz-kid type. His clout was proven by the nerd who rushed up the stairs and was waiting by my cubbyhole the second I got back, explaining all the word-processing functions to me in patient, idiot-proof language. I tried hard to pay attention, I really did. I mean, if you had a boss like Seamus Mahon, you didn't want to be letting him down.

At six o'clock the door to the inner sanctum was still firmly closed. I wouldn't be getting any more of his time tonight.

'You can go home,' Jenny said acridly, 'and I expect to see you here in good time tomorrow and I expect you to be appropriately dressed. *With* tights . . . and,' she added in a low hiss, leaning forward, 'behave properly around Mr Mahon.'

'He's wonderful, isn't he?' I said dreamily.

The look on the old bag's face suggested she'd just sucked ten unripe lemons.

'Well,' she said heavily, '*Mrs* Mahon is a wonderful lady. Such style. Such poise. Good night, Alexandra.'

Chapter 3

Married. Of course he was married. My heart, I'm afraid to say, plummeted right into my boots. I know that's pathetic, after five minutes' acquaintance, but I really felt like I was being robbed. Wouldn't all the scripts say Seamus should be mine? I mean, when you really feel you've hit bottom. When you're chained to the rock and the fire-breathing dragon is crawling round the next hill – or in my case, when you've given up any pretence at talent and you're reduced to taking jobs from your mum and dad, *and* moving into a flat with your annoying, incredibly beautiful little sister – and the white knight turns up on his charger to rescue you, isn't it fairly understood that the said white knight should be single?

You couldn't have hit any more bottom than me that Monday morning. Well, I suppose you could, technically, you could be selling the *Big Issue* outside pubs in Camden and carrying a can of Tennant's and a filthy dog on a string. But to be honest, I felt like I was at bottom. With the typing, and the lateness, and the dress, and the mascara, and the tights, and the coffee. And the Evian. And then to have Seamus so soothing, putting a mat over the stain and protecting me from Jenny and so forth. Plus, being all flash and successful. With those eyes. And that voice.

The whole thing was like a big neon sign from the Gods of Romance. Never fear, Alex! Cease to worry about film directors' secretaries dumping you by fax! Do not dwell on the rejection slips the London art galleries sent you by the busload! Dismiss from your mind how you had to grovel to your mother, and pretend to enjoy trying on the tweedy Jaeger suit with the padded shoulders, also the cerise Laura Ashley ballgown, circa 1987, with the enormous bow at the back, or the silver puffball skirt with black velvet dots! Yes, all those worries are over now, for here is Prince Finn MacCool to save you!

But of course not. I should have known better. Seamus was just the final twist of the knife.

Ha, ha, ha, he's taken, Cupid was sniggering, just like every other decent man on the face of the earth.

'It does seem like that,' Gail agreed when I bitched about it later over our communal supper. I was eating a brown bread salad sandwich in a determined attempt to lose weight. Gail had brought home vegetarian sushi, and Bronwen was sound asleep on the sofa in the drawing room, thereby preventing us from watching *Brookside*. 'You shouldn't eat bread. It's processed.'

It was indeed so disgusting I couldn't even be bothered to argue the toss. Have you ever tried eating a salad sandwich? Cardboard with grass in it. But it was the supper of choice of a super-skinny, blonde whippet of a girl I used to be at school with, Elspeth, who once ran screaming through the halls when we tried to catch her and forcefeed her a Smartie. Just one Smartie. Her legs were so thin they didn't even meet at the knees, I mean there was daylight all the way down. Whereas I used to indulge in the great school teatime trick of getting more than one cookie per girl by breaking two cookies and heaping the pieces on my plate and saying they were one cookie. And I had the body to match. So now, whenever I'm really low, I start eating the salad sandwiches as a sort of foodie hair shirt. The great thing about them is they're so loathsome, you're never tempted to pig out on them. 'Can I tempt you with another salad sandwich?' I mean, you don't hear that at dinner parties across the land, do you?

But Gail was warming to the theme.

'I suppose it must seem like that when you're twenty-seven,' she said, as if trying to get her mind round the concept of being that old. 'In Japan, they call girls like you Christmas Cake.'

'Why's that?' I asked, feeling I wouldn't like the answer.

'Because they're stale and on the shelf, and after the twenty-fifth no one wants them,' she told me, laughing gaily.

Sometimes I could just throttle Gail in her dainty homespun dresses. It was even worse because it was true. It certainly felt true. No man wanted me, not once he'd a chance properly to try me out. Rolling back past Oliver, there was Gerald, who'd left me for a scoutmaster, Peter, who'd been apprehended by the police for GBH and aggravated assault and who was now doing five to ten in Pentonville, and Justin, whom I had actually, briefly, been engaged to at Oxford, before he dumped me six weeks into the engagement saying he needed space and would ring me in a couple of days, before, predictably, never ringing again.

Justin did me a favour, in fact, by breaking my naive little heart so thoroughly that Peter, and Oliver, and even Gerald were just a walk in the park. Being left for a man was certainly humiliating, although it provided me with the answers to Gerald's insistence that I go on diets and crop my hair very short, and his refusal, despite these aesthetic improvements, to go to bed with me. But it still wasn't as humiliating as Justin getting married, barely two months after his declaration of need for space, to a particularly clingy, horsy type named Hannah whom I'd known slightly and always loathed. Hannah was fond of tinkling laughs and flicks of her long hair, and loudly saying things like, 'You know, we all *talk* about so-called feminism, but we're really all longing for some darling man to pay the bills and give us lots of babies.' Hannah was the heir to a few hundred acres of Shropshire, so paying the bills wasn't too much of a concern. However, she did get a darling man, mine to be precise. What I got was a sleep disorder and panic attacks for a month, as well as lots of lovely phone calls from old friends ringing me up to congratulate me when they saw 'Recently married' appended to Justin's name in the frequent interviews he gave to the *Telegraph* and *Mail*, as a new, ambitious Tory MP. I suppose it wouldn't have suited him to be married to a would-be revolutionary like me.

Justin cured me of that nonsense, anyway. I decided soon after *Hello!* did a spread on him and Hannah that all the world were bastards, and I had better look out for number one. Not that such robustness did me any practical good.

'You must have heard of Dolores Mahon,' Gail went on mercilessly.

'Not 'til today,' I groused.

Gail reached for her *Tatler* and flicked unerringly to the big spread on the Krug champagne party. There, sipping premier grand cru with Tiggy Legge-Bourke and Joan Collins was the said Dolores. She had longer legs than a Derby winner, she carried herself like a ballerina and she had frothing platinum-blonde hair spilling winsomely over the shoulders of her pink Chanel suit.

'I think those diamond earrings really suit her,' Gail mused, 'don't you?'

I said nothing. It wasn't fair. Couldn't his wife at least have been a raging old boot, so Seamus and I could have spiced up the desert of my future days with a little forbidden flirtation? Wasn't that what offices were for? That, and making free phone calls. Bronwen had reminded me about the free phone calls before fainting on to the couch. And they were a perk indeed.

The door opened and Keisha strode into the room. Somehow her Nicole Farhi appeared to be even less wrinkly than it had been this morning. I was hit by a waft of delicious scent as she approached – not her personally blended French fragrance: that came a poor second to the glorious aroma of Kentucky Fried Chicken and a huge bag of fries.

I dropped the rest of the salad sandwich and slavered. Pathetically. Keisha was a beautiful girl, but get between Keisha and her chips and she turned into the killer bitch from hell. She had that black girl confidence, she never gave a damn about her weight and probably as a result she was always slim and stunning. How did she do it, how, how? She never went running and she unremittingly tucked into Chicken Kiev and burgers and Kentucky and chocolate. She smoked like a factory chimney and she ate entire loaves of warm garlic bread with her salad.

Tonight, though, she reached into her grease-stained brown paper bag and tossed me a packet of chips.

'I thought you might need these,' she grunted.

I was touched. Stunned. For Keisha, that was quite something.

'Alex really screwed up, and now she has a crush on her boss, Dolores Mahon's husband,' Gail said gleefully.

Keisha gave her a pitying look. 'I suppose you can borrow my blue Donna Karan dress tomorrow,' she said casually to me.

I was filled with relief. 'Just while I get the suit dry-cleaned and stuff,' I promised.

Keisha's face had all the world-weary cynicism of a Tory cabinet minister's wife. I supposed I should be grateful to Gail: it was only because she annoyed Keisha even more than she annoyed me, that I was being loaned this TDO, as Bronwen had dubbed them, Top Designer Outfit. Keisha's wardrobe divided neatly into TDOs, MDOs (medium – into this category went her Ghosts, her Emporio Armani and her Equipment) and SDOs (sale). Gail had basically tricked Keisha and Bronwen into moving in by being sweet and uncritical when they were seeing the flat, not mentioning the words 'organic' or 'pulses' or 'b-complex' or any of that nonsense. In fact she had passed herself off as the cheery, ethereal yet hardworking type anybody would be happy to share their place with.

And then Keisha and Bronwen had got used to the big space and pretty location, combined with the Wilde parent-subsidised rent rates, and then, of course, they were trapped.

After all, Keisha needed her money for the T, M and SDOs. And Bronwen needed her money for Class A and B pharmaceuticals. And, to be fair, also for drink, fags, taxis home from gigs and clubs, air fares to Oasis gigs in Scandinavia, that sort of thing. Keisha never had to pay for any of that. She wouldn't dream of leaving the house with cash. She was a bit like the Queen: an attendant male would always pay for everything, first-class air tickets, dinners, champagne, taxis, the lot. I felt awkward if the guy bought two rounds of drinks together, but Keisha's men never seemed to mind. Rich or poor, they did their duty without a murmur.

When I suggested that it was the 'nineties, didn't she think she should pay, Keisha looked at me like I'd lost my mind.

'Are you insane?' she demanded. 'If I'm going out, Al, I don't open my purse. Simple as that.' At which point she would strike up an imported American Marlboro Light, you know the ones with the stylish white tips, and that would be the end of the matter.

If we're honest, we all envied Keisha this ability. Keisha was a splendid creature, a pure dominant female. She thought of herself as a princess, so therefore so did everyone else.

I tried it, before you say anything. I tried standing in front of the mirror in a borrowed TDO and flouncing and giving my reflection cold, disinterested stares. But it didn't really work. I'd invariably have smudged eyeshadow or a creeping bit of cellulite at the fold of the knee or something.

Anyway, *you* try thinking of yourself as 'all that' when you're unemployed, jilted at the altar, or almost, deserted for a bloke and dependent on your daddy when you're twenty-seven?

It would have been hysterically bloody funny, if it wasn't happening to me.

Still, 'Things can only get better', as New Labour had yelled all the way through the election.

'Thanks, Keisha,' I said humbly.

'Don't sound so humble,' Keisha said briskly. 'You didn't get fired, did you?'

'No.'

'Well, then, you're gainfully employed. How much is your salary?'

I told her. Keisha did some sums in her head and announced, doubtfully, 'Seventeen five.'

Seventeen and a half thousand pounds! It sounded like a fortune.

Gail sniggered. 'We've all got to start somewhere.'

'There's plenty of money in the City,' Keisha said staunchly, 'I expect Alex will learn loads.'

I tried to feel better about the whole thing. Hell, I was still employed. And maybe such things as promotions and so forth were not out of the question. My mind drifted back to green-eyed Seamus of the soft voice and easy manner. Never mind Jenny, he was my *ultimate* boss, wasn't he? And he'd be the boss from heaven, even if he was married to Heather Locklear.

Maybe he would even take me out for mentor–protégée lunches, and pay for everything without being prompted, like all Keisha's men. A dark rebel part of me sometimes wondered if Keisha's men were so obliging because they were romantic, or because they were scared? I wanted a man to pay for everything just because he was a gentleman. Not that that happened very often. In fact, the few times I remembered it happening were with Tom.

Tom Drummond.

Ah yes, I forgot to tell you about Tom. Which is not to say that I'd forgotten Tom. Who could forget the only man on God's green earth to prefer me to my sister?

Yes, you read that right. Tom Drummond, one of my best friends at Oxford, and a would-be boyfriend, had been hit on unmercifully by my sister in all her fragile, sixth-form sexy schoolgirl glory. He had been treated to the naturally honey-blonde hair, the eight stone, five six frame, the crop tops and sprayed-on jeans that had preceded the current wispy jumper phase. And he had been wholly indifferent. In fact, he had once said to me, 'It must be hard, Alex, for Gail, with such a beauty as her big sister.' This in tones one hundred per cent irony free.

It had driven Gail mad. She reckoned all the eligible beaux were hers by right. Especially a boy like Tom, who was heir to some great creaking pile or other in Gloucestershire, and was going to join the

Army for a couple of years. Tom was sensationally upper-class, but he was nice with it. He listened patiently to all my socialist rants about banning foxhunting, then went out with the Christ Church beagles regardless. He thought Classic FM was a hopelessly vulgar modern station. He was the kind of man who would walk on the outside of the pavement when taking you home, who would open every door and pull out every chair, not just for his girlfriend but for every woman in the party. I thought Tom was a great laugh, even if he was one of the enemy. He would listen patiently to all my woes with various boyfriends – not saying much, except to suggest he go round and knock the stuffing out of them.

Our friendship had even survived his asking me out, in a fumbling sort of way, and me giving it a try, and it not working out. I mean, our tastes in life were just different. He liked the opera and Maggie Thatcher. I liked Arthur Scargill and Joy Division. He used to drink vintage port, whereas I was popping 'e's in disused quarries at four a.m., unthinkingly setting myself up for later panic attacks and misery.

Plus, there was the physical thing.

I realise I've lost your sympathy now. 'Looks aren't everything,' I can hear you say, and 'Where did your pretty boys get you, then?', and you certainly have a point there. But what can I tell you? I'm a hopeless romantic, I need the blood to stir and the heart to beat, not in a panic attack way, but in a squirmy, delicious, oh my God I can't think sort of way.

And Tom was fat.

I know, I know, far be it from a woman, one of the great sisterhood of fat-oppressed, weight-watching females, to castigate a man for a touch of the Robbie Williamses, but I mean, Tom was *fat*. Seriously overweight. What use they could have for him in the Army, apart from a ballast balloon, was anybody's guess. Maybe Intelligence: he was reading Applied Mathematics and he certainly had tons of it. However, I just couldn't get past the lard. We clicked mentally, but that's only half the story, if we're all honest. When I tried to see myself in bed with Tom Drummond, all I could do was shudder.

Gail said haughtily that *she* saw his inner beauty, but I'm afraid what she saw was an inheritance of several million quid and the Royal Enclosure at Ascot for the rest of her life.

For things like that, Gail would overlook the odd stone or two.

Thinking of Tom, I felt a guilty pang. I hadn't kept up with him, after college – somehow I was unable to face his pity, when relating the story of my artistic failure. I still sculpted, but so what? That was going nowhere fast, or maybe it had already arrived there. Last time I had seen Tom I was still sending off my sculptures to galleries, I was still bright eyed and bushy tailed, full of hope and defiant youthful enthusiasm. We'd had a brilliant, chatty lunch, at which Tom had three helpings of treacle pudding, and refused to let me pay for anything.

He spent ten minutes in the driving rain hailing me a taxi, and when it had discharged me at my destination, the cabby waved away my twenty quid.

'The gentleman paid for wherever you wanted to go, miss,' he grunted.

I wondered what Tom would say about Seamus. It would be great to have his advice. But Tom would surely tell me to stay well away. Married was as good as dead, in Tom's book.

Ridiculously old-fashioned creature that he was.

'I'm going to bed, I want an early night,' I announced, leaving them to try and dislodge Bronwen from the sofa before the start of *Friends*. I was totally shattered, and I wanted to look rested and beautiful, or should I say professional, for tomorrow.

After all, I was a working woman now.

Chapter 4

The next morning things were going to be different. Oh yes they were. I'm not such a hopeless case as all that when I've got good enough motivation.

I set my alarm for six thirty. I know, but desperate times call for desperate measures. And my patience was rewarded right away, with a Keisha-free bathroom, and no sound in the whole flat, unless you count the lilting strains of Bronwen grunting that she was a firestarter, a twisted firestarter, hey, hey. We had at least trained Bronwen to use her Walkman when she arrived back from clubbing at five a.m. It beat the early wake-up calls at maximum volume telling us that football was coming home, or that we were her Wonderwall, or whatever catchy tune was top of the hit parade that week.

Triumphantly I dragged my sleeping corpse into the shower and proceeded to give myself shock therapy. I meant to start with a cold shower, but that resolution lasted all of fifteen seconds. No wonder they get so many public schoolboys in the Forces. Since she'd been so mean, I also stole some of Gail's expensive Nexxus shampoo; it was cool because the bottle was white plastic, so she couldn't draw little lines on it in black ink to mark where she'd left it, like she did with all her bottles of spirits and scent, the mean cow. Amazingly enough, I did actually start to wake up and I set to like Posh Spice, plucking my eyebrows and shaving my legs and slapping on the body lotion and towel-drying my hair before starting on with the hair-dryer.

We'd put the hair-dryer in the bathroom in the hope that Gail would drop it in the bath by accident and electrocute herself, but so far, no luck, even though she went for those pseudy candlelit affairs with the organic body soak that costs twenty quid a pot, so you can't see what you're stepping on. Maybe it was the jet take-off roar of the dryer that gave its presence away.

It certainly gave my presence away.

Keisha was banging on the bathroom door in two seconds flat, as I sat there smugly, drying my hair, plucked and prepared like Mummy's prize Christmas turkey. Now the tables were turned!

'Get out, get out, get out, *get out!*' she screamed. It certainly had more of a ring to it than my timid enquiries as to when she might be finished, etc.

'I'll get out when I'm ready,' I said haughtily.

Keisha's voice turned menacing. 'You can get out *now*, or you can give me back my Donna Karan,' she said heavily.

I was back in my own bedroom in ten seconds. Oh well, can't win 'em all. Can't win any of them, when you live with this crowd.

Gail came in blearily to find me as sleek and shining as I'll ever be, carefully applying Nude Lip Gloss with matching Liquid Liner, Fresh Cream Blusher, Time-Off Hideaway Concealer and Crack the Whip Long-Lash Mascara.

'It won't do you any good, you know,' she said nastily, 'Dolores goes to the Dorchester Spa three times a week. *And* she works out at the Harbour Club.'

'I wasn't thinking of Dolores,' I replied defensively.

This was true, as I was thinking of Seamus.

I told myself I only wanted to look respectable. OK, pretty *and* respectable, but that was positively it. After all, he was married, and looked a real Liam Neeson type, or even Liam Gallagher, the heartbreaking playboy who dates every woman in town, but once they get married, they turn sick-makingly uxorious and faithful. I mean, what is it about the name Liam? Is it some kind of Irish luck charm? I should be grateful that Seamus was called Seamus. Even if I still wasn't in with a chance.

Could you believe that Dolores? As fragile as a Georgia peach, as pretty as Claudia Schiffer. Nobody could compete with the perfect body, the TDOs that were even out of Keisha's reach – Dolores would scorn Keisha's TDOs, she would say things like 'Oh, *prêt-à-porter*, how frugal,' since she would go for the real *haute couture* and have seamstresses in Paris and London moulding costly fabrics to her slender body. She would have the front row at all those mobbed-up designer shows. She would . . .

Never mind. Let's just say I felt no compunction about looking my best. I was about as much a threat to Dolores as Manchester City were to Manchester United.

Seamus was taken. I told myself this firmly. He was taken by a Patsy Kensit lookalike, so real women, as opposed to goddesses, would have no chance. Men who had the *Wall Street Journal* flown in every day from New York did not date real women. Who could blame them? They didn't have to. I mean, if I looked like Dolores Mahon, would I condescend to date some geezer from the local chippie? Nope, it would be Johnny Depp and Mr Darcy off the telly or forget it, boy.

Maybe Seamus would have some good-looking single friends.

I pulled on Keisha's Donna Karan super-carefully to avoid getting foundation on the collar. Best to start as you mean to go on, namely alive.

I slipped my feet into low heels and then I was ready. Oh, how I wanted to wear high heels, my new ones from Office that were so high it was like walking on stilts, for comfort is all very well but who cares about comfort when you can have an optical illusion that slices pounds of fat from your legs? But no, this was work, sorry to say, and even I could not justify teetering into the office like Naomi Campbell on that runway. Jenny would be on the phone to Mrs Seamus Mahon before you could say Code Red.

'Tony is coming round this evening,' Gail announced, sending dagger glances into my bedroom. 'So you'd better have that lot cleared right away.'

The cause of her ire was my latest sculpture, the one I'd been working on when Alan Pell came round. It was another owl.

'I haven't finished my owl.'

'It doesn't look like an owl, it looks like a squashed hedgehog,' Gail snarled.

'Yeah, man, or a wonky surfboard that curves a bit in the middle,' Bronwen chipped in. She bounced into my room with a merry expression and a chemical glitter in her eye that suggested she'd have many more happy hours before she finally went to bed. She was chewing gum like some sort of beautiful ruminant, a determined cow or goat or some such. Any minute now she'd be giving us all big hugs and telling us she really loved us, sister. Also she would start talking crap and continue blithely until the drugs wore off and she slumped into a depressed, irritable 'e'-hangover that would then last for days. It was a tough call which mood was more annoying.

'Hey, man, you look stunning,' Bronwen breathed, but she'd think the same thing about Cilla Black in this humour, so I ignored her.

'It's not meant to be an owl, it's meant to be the idea of an owl,' I explained.

'Well, it's my idea of a mess,' Gail snapped, 'and I don't want Tony seeing it.'

Tony was her latest bit of trouser, a beefy, rugby-playing, red-braces-wearing City trader. He laughed loudly at her attempts to get him to switch to tofu salads and soya milk, so he wasn't all bad. But the plus column was still fairly short, in my opinion. He was ruddy faced at twenty-nine, and thought that Michael Howard had been a dangerously soft touch. Bronwen and Keisha wondered what Gail could possibly see in him. I reckoned it was his cherry-red Ferrari.

'Tony will have to put up with it.' I heard myself go dangerously silky. Amazing, the way I could summon up the old backbone where my art was concerned, but under no other circumstances. Maybe it was because statues meant something to me, still, after all the misery and failure. This one had come to me in a dream last week, a pale shape ghosting through the blackness, and I'd jumped out of bed, wide awake at four a.m., to start the first sketches.

'Humph! You know you promised Mummy you'd forget all that nonsense,' Gail flounced.

Keisha strode in commandingly. 'I agree with Alex. It's a very nice buzzard,' she said defensively.

Gail sniggered.

I grabbed my genuine leather-imitation briefcase, an important part of every career girl's armoury, if you asked my mother. I hated the damn thing but if I ignored it Gail would just blab to Mum, and anything was better than that.

It may be pathetic to be scared of your parents at twenty-seven, but you haven't met my parents. And my parents were paying the bills.

So I grabbed the briefcase. It was neon pink.

'Men like a woman to look feminine, darling!' Mummy had insisted loudly, dragging me to the counter. 'This will grab their eye! You don't want to look the same as all the other girls, do you?'

No danger of that.

I hoped I could shove the nasty thing right under my desk when I got in to work, where it could stay as lost as the Ark of the Covenant until the end of time.

'And I've got some more news,' Gail added. 'Someone's taken the flat across the hall!'

We all paused in our last-minute application of female protective camouflage – scent, hairspray, tights – to listen up. This *was* news. The flat opposite ours, the only other flat on the top floor, was one of the smartest in Belsize Park. You could see right into Zoe Ball's apartment from the bedroom. It was three times as big as ours and was rumoured to have a sunken bath and in-house cinema screen.

'And guess who it is?' Gail asked proudly, enjoying our suspense.

It wasn't often we were hanging on her every word.

'Snowy!' she announced proudly.

Keisha and Bronwen looked blank, but my face was a picture. I could see myself in the mirror gaping like some landed fish, or Bronwen when she was 'on one'.

'Olivia White?' I asked, horrified. Olivia White, hence 'Snowy' (nobody ever accused Catholic schoolgirls of being original), had been one of Gail's friends at school. She was impossibly beautiful and always rowing with everybody. She refused to do any work, as I recall, and accused the teachers of jealousy over her looks when they tried to suspend her. Nobody wanted to expel her, because she had been orphaned aged three in a car crash. Brought up by a long-suffering old aunt, Snowy had milked this early tragedy over and over again during our schooldays and it always worked. She was supposed to be a major bitch. I didn't mix with the fourth-form girls, so I didn't care.

I was horrified, really, at the thought of Gail having reinforcements.

'She was *such* a sweetheart at school,' Gail said airily. 'You'll love her, Keisha, she gets thirty per cent off at Gucci, and she's supposed to know all the big promoters, Bronwen, she says she can get you backstage passes to any gig you want.'

'She sounds great,' Keisha said.

'She sounds brilliant!' Bronwen enthused, chewing wildly.

I stomped gloomily off to work.

I can't deny it was a better start than yesterday. This morning the receptionist looked almost mollified, apart from cruelly obvious stifled grins at my neon briefcase. I could see her struggling not to say anything, but she lost the struggle. Obviously I did not rate the cool professionalism everyone else got walking through these doors. Receptionists were probably not encouraged to be chatty at Hamilton Kane, but she doubtless figured I wouldn't be around long enough to cause any problems.

'What is it, top of the range at Strawberry Shortcake?' she sniggered.

'You're showing your age,' I shot back. 'It's My Little Pony these days.'

'Avoided the tights problem by not wearing any?' she retorted.

'Actually, I've got two pairs in my bag, I'm going to change in the loo,' I batted back.

'Well, you'd better get a move on. Jenny Robins has been in Mr Mahon's office for half an hour already,' she said, winning the match on points.

I darted into the loos and put on my tights with a nerve-racking combination of speed and caution. Damn. I wasn't sure how long I could keep this organised stuff up.

Still, I thought modestly, I didn't look bad. Tummy pulled in with Tummy-Buster support tights that made it hard to breathe, but which did let the dusty pink Donna Karan jacket drape forgivingly over my torso. Foundation, nude lips and blushers and concealers and mascara all gave my face that un-made-up look that takes hours to perfect. Scent was still wafting from my pulse points – 'A woman should place her scent where she wants to be kissed,' said Coco Chanel, but somehow despite me dousing myself everywhere except my armpits, nothing usually happened. I also left my toes out. Maybe it is very erotic, but it now calls forth pictures of a) David Mellor or b) Fergie, and thus is sent to Forbidden Sex Prison along with all fetishes and men that need to call you 'Mummy' before they can come.

I clip-clipped on my low heels, pretending to be that woman from the Kenco advert, only younger, and got in the lift for Seamus's floor.

I stepped out prepared to receive Jenny's congratulations.

'Ah, there you are,' she snapped, 'finally arrived, I see, well, we've got a *lot* of work to do today and you can start with the filing.'

She reached behind her and lifted a huge pile of files on to my desk. Then she lifted a second pile. And then a third.

'The filing room is down the hallway,' Jenny said briskly, 'and I've put the colour-coded date/time system on your clipboard. There. It's really self-explanatory. Don't get it wrong, every item of correspondence is vital, you never know when the SEC or the SIB might want it.'

I looked blank.

'Come on, Alexandra, the *SIB* supervises the SFA and IMRO.

27

They're our SROs. Or is it RPBs? Come along, girl, don't stand there gaping like a moron!'

'But what about Mr Mahon?' I asked timidly, feeling my lip-gloss get duller by the minute. 'Won't he need his letters typed, or something?'

Jenny gave my washed, made-up, scented self a quick once over. Something like frosty amusement registered on her face.

'Never you mind about that, young woman,' she said. 'Mr Mahon is away at an investment presentation all day.'

Bastard. Bastard. Bastard. Sorry about that, had to clear the system, it was just that five straight hours of filing had taken its toll on me. When Dante wrote the *Inferno*, he didn't mention filing in the lower circles of hell. He must have been having an off-day. Compared to filing, typing letters was a joyously exciting magic carpet ride through a Disney universe of love and laughter. Filing at Hamilton Kane involved carefully spreading out incomprehensible documents all over the floor and then trying to put them neatly into cardboard wallets suspended by little metal hooks in identical drawers. Only I couldn't get them to fit in the little wallets, I didn't understand the colour-coded labels (sample Jenny instruction:)

Blue is for October filings preceding Discovery motions on the fifteenth, but make sure Due Diligence motions from the seventeenth to twentieth inclusive are in Turquoise Sub-File

and I wasn't sure which drawer was which, as after a while they started repeating the colours. The screaming boredom of this task was broken only by the fact that I crushed two lovingly tended nails, manicured at great expense only last week, Jenny screeching at me – 'No! that's not the Magenta file, Alexandra! Any fool can see that's Cerise!' – and the repeated excursions to the photocopier machine to make copies of special documents.

Seeing my teary face, one of the other assistants took pity on me after I started sobbing as the copier ate two priceless documents. I swear, I will never say catty things about secretaries again. Just because one dumped me by fax. And I am the slave of another one.

'You feed them in like this,' Melissa said kindly, 'and they don't get stuck. You must be Alex Wilde, yeah? Lucky you, to work in Seamus Mahon's office.'

'Yeah,' I said dreamily, bucking up a little.

'You get to work with Jenny Robins! Everybody loves Jenny.'

I stared at her. Obviously working here was dangerous to your mental health. Less than two days at work, and it had already started to affect mine.

Jenny came in at five p.m., when I was exhaustedly knocking off for the day, and surveyed my workload with a total lack of satisfaction.

'You'll have to finish the rest tomorrow. Things don't file themselves, you know.'

'No, Miss Robins,' I said, biting my lip.

'I'll take care of Mr Mahon while you're busy in here. At least you can't make spelling mistakes when you're filing,' she pointed out with irrefutable logic.

'Well, that's all right, then,' I said bitterly.

Chapter 5

It was a nasty time. Seamus Mahon was away at conferences and vital lunch meetings. Back home, the house was filled with a succession of men calling for Keisha (media and celeb types), Bronwen (disco-dancing madheads bearing drugs), Gail (Tony and his high-earning friends) and me (meter reader, irate bank representative).

Across the hall, the builders were merrily knocking things down and playing Brian Ferry at top volume, while Bronwen and Keisha purred over the thought of Snowy. They were a whole lot nicer to Gail. I'd have thought they could have shown a little backbone, but Keisha would sell her soul for a Gucci discount. After all, where Gucci leads, Joseph is sure to follow. And as for Bronwen, ask her the three most beautiful words in the English language, and she will say without hesitation, 'Access All Areas.'

Gail let me know about it too. She flashed me looks of triumph as she sat there with her captive audience, extolling her mate Snowy White.

So there was nothing to do except go to work.

But I couldn't get the *Reservoir Dogs* vibe about this fact. For a start, I had no threads (Keisha's Donna Karan being a never-repeated, once-in-a-lifetime offer). For a second, I had no motivation. The glorious Seamus was gloriously absent morning after morning. I ask you! I started to burn with resentment. How dare he show up on day one, like a glimmering mirage of lemonade in the desert, and then vanish into thin air! 'AMAB,' I would mutter under my breath around the office, 'bloody AMAB,' which was Bronwen's cunning code for All Men Are Bastards. Something we said so often it was good to have a shortcut. And thirdly, Jenny Robins was clearly a sadist.

'I'm going to be on-site with Mr Mahon,' she would announce importantly, 'so you will be answering his calls today.'

I had spent one afternoon doing that and paled in fear. Answering

Seamus's phones was a job for a world-class traffic controller, not a klutz like me. You had to rack 'em, pack 'em and stack 'em while you took their incomprehensible messages, decided which ones to forward to the mobile – which they all insisted on, and woe betide me when I got it wrong – fax *out* the right documents, and sort the ones spewing *in*, whilst holding the phone with one hand and writing messages with a pen cramped between your toes. Or something like that.

I would have cried but I didn't have time.

I got it so wrong the first day I'd hoped Jenny might insist on doing it herself henceforth.

'You've got to learn, Alex.'

'Where will you two be on-site today?' I asked, preparing to set the speed-dial.

Jenny smiled. 'Corfu.'

So I did it. I answered the phones and scrawled the messages and filed the files and faxed the faxes. After a while it even got less terrifying and just settled into boredom. I never took a lunch hour, just ate a sandwich on my desk when anyone could be bothered to get me one, or bought something from the lunchtime office hawker who came round with a big basket full of goodies for sale. By the time it got to me, the goodies usually consisted of:

1 bruised apple

1 brown banana

1 soggy cheese and pickle bap (spilt orange juice flavour).

I then would miss lunch and spend an irritable afternoon with hunger screeching audibly in my gut, like the Shreddies advert.

At any other time I would have quit. I was seriously thinking about quitting when I got a phone call. Or more accurately, took a phone call.

'Mr Mahon's office.'

'Is he there, please? This is the Carrefour Trust calling.'

'I'm afraid he's not available at the moment,' I said, slightly less bored than usual, since something about the voice was pricking at my memory lobes. Low, masculine and well modulated, an accent that the wideboys in here were always emulating and never quite getting right.

There was a fractional pause on the other end.

'Who am I speaking to?'

'His assistant,' I said warily.

Another pause, then politely, 'That wouldn't by any chance be Alex Wilde?'

'Tom!' I almost shouted. I forgot I didn't want him to know what had become of me. I was so happy to hear a friendly voice.

'So, you decided to go into the City, eh?' Tom was asking. 'Very wise, I should think, get a bit of life experience to feed into the art . . .'

I let that generous assessment stand uncorrected.

'So what are you doing?'

'This and that,' Tom said vaguely. Tom was the type of man who thought it was vulgar to get too specific. 'I expect you're loving it at Hamilton Kane, Alex . . .'

That was enough. The floodgates opened. Poor Tom, he called to talk about high finance and instead got me practically blubbing at him down the receiver. And with infinite patience, he didn't hang up or suggest that we talk later, maybe one Sunday in the year 2000.

'You can't quit,' Tom said firmly when I'd finished.

'Why bloody not?' I demanded.

'Because you're not the quitting type, Alex. It'll get easier. You'll learn something. And you'll have some money of your own.'

'Money doesn't buy happiness,' I said sulkily.

'No.' He sounded rather heavy. 'But it does buy independence.'

We rang off, promising to meet up for lunch so he could insult New Labour as much as he wanted. Another one of those things I would never get round to doing, like putting up the picture-hooks in my bedroom, or visiting the National Gallery. But I didn't quit. I would never have heard the end of it.

I was sitting at my desk morosely typing out the analyst's report on Dyson Electrics when a large shadow loomed over my desk.

'I've nearly finished, Miss Robins,' I muttered through clenched teeth. God, the woman wanted blood. She was like that sergeant in *An Officer and A Gentleman*, screaming at Richard Gere that he wanted his Drop On Request. I had ink-stains on my palms, it had been another missed-lunch day, and I was caught in the grip of a crushing tension headache.

'Now why would you want to be calling me that?' a soft voice inquired.

I looked up to see Seamus Mahon glancing merrily down at my one-handed typing technique.

'It's easier this way,' I said defensively.

'Sure, and it's very original,' Seamus said sweetly, 'just think, if you lop your left hand off in a freak gardening accident, you'll still be able to come in to work.'

I smiled slightly. But only slightly. Maybe he was standing there in a slouchy suit with those glittering green eyes, cracking jokes and generally improving any view, but I wasn't fooled. Any moment now he would shimmer away and leave nothing but a huge pile of paperwork and a teasing waft of aftershave.

'We'll have to be giving you an efficiency award.'

'Ummm,' I grunted.

'Maybe we should be giving you one of those anyway. All the work you've been doing while I've been away. You never told me you were Wonder Woman in disguise.'

At this I really did start to perk up. I couldn't actually believe it. Somebody had just given me a compliment; bothered to thank me and told me I was doing a good job. Wonder Woman? Invisible Woman, more like. Or Incredible Shrinking Ego Woman. A bit of a grin slipped out before I could stop it.

'There you go, gorgeous,' Seamus Mahon said happily, 'I was thinking the weather forecast was indefinite gloom and now it's all sunny.'

I caught the eye of Jenny Robins across the desk. Her back had stiffened and she was sending a world-class death stare in our direction.

I resisted the impulse to give her a jaunty wink.

'Now I haven't had a chance to get to know you at all,' Seamus said decisively, 'and it's highly important to be acquainted with everybody on the team. Isn't that what Alex Ferguson says to Manchester United?'

'Er . . .'

''Course it is. And you and I are part of a team,' Seamus added, waving one bronzed hand at our surroundings as though to somehow make me feel that the nuclear bomb site that was my cubbyhole, and the immaculately gleaming universe that was his inner office, were in some way connected. 'And I'm betting you haven't had any lunch.'

'I don't really have time for lunch,' I said very reluctantly. Jenny's death stares were increasing in intensity. I knew I'd be paying for this later today.

'Nonsense. If you don't eat your concentration wanders, biological fact,' Seamus said slowly. Really, his voice was like warm brandy on a St Bernard, thawing you out and bringing you slowly back to life. He was looking at me so intensely I couldn't stop a raspberry blush spreading right across my face. His eyes were locked on to mine.

Rudolph Valentino had nothing on this guy.

'Jenny, hold the fort for an hour or two, could you?' Seamus ordered, raising his voice peremptorily. 'I'm taking Alex out to lunch.'

We exited the building via a back entrance I'd never seen before, where a monster black limo was waiting.

'I thought we'd go to the Pont de la Tour,' Seamus said, holding open the door for me, 'if you've no objection?'

'None at all,' I said, pretending that I got asked to swanky Conran restaurants every day of the week.

When we arrived the waiter greeted Seamus with fawning deference and led us to a marvellous table outside in the sun, overlooking the river. Then he made the mistake of handing me a menu. The descriptions of the delicious, non-soggy-bap meals were just too much. My stomach set off a volley of cannon fire that could have caused a security alert in Downing Street.

I flushed crimson.

'Well now,' said Seamus with supreme unconcern, 'it's nice to hear a girl with a healthy appetite for a change.'

He ordered for us both. Large helpings of everything. 'Sure, and then we'll try the chocolate soufflé with the ice cream, why not? And bring me some sticky toffee pudding while you're at it. And for drinks . . .'

'Oh, *drinks*,' said the waiter, as though this was a dangerously novel idea, 'let me just get the wine waiter for you, sir.'

I cringed, but my boss was having none of it.

'I don't want to wait for the wine waiter,' he said icily – it was amazing how his voice could go from balmy to freezing in the blink of an eye – 'so bring me champagne first, then that white Bordeaux, number 567.'

'Very good, sir,' said the waiter, in magnificently haughty tones, to tell us that it wasn't.

I loved it. First we were bunking off Hamilton Kane and now we were giving orders to waiters! Waiters, who terrify me only a little less than shop assistants. The ones who seem magically to know you've got no money when you're trying to have a quiet window-shop in Prada, who come up to you and go, 'May I be of assistance, madam?' and 'What exactly were you looking for, madam?' or the killer, 'What price range did you have in mind?' until they've totally spoiled your pipe dream and you have to slink out of the shop, pretending to be fascinated by your shoes.

'I can't be shown up by the likes of him when I'm out with such a pretty girl as yourself,' Seamus Mahon said to me with a gorgeous grin.

And my heart didn't flutter at all. It sounded like he was flirting, but he couldn't really be flirting. Because he was married to Dolores. And he was out here with me.

I'd learned my lesson. I'm a terrible one for the daydreams on the first dates, not that this was a date. You know how drowning people get those past life reviews? Well, I get future life reviews. It happens every time I meet a new man. I've married him, decided on the number and names of the children and picked the house before he's shaken hands.

Sometimes I've also divorced him. I can't even get things to work out in my own daydreams.

A future life review involving Dolores and a tragic bus accident was hovering around the front of my consciousness, but I batted it away with a mighty effort.

A different waiter materialised smoothly with two chilled splits of champagne.

'Good luck to you, Alex Wilde, and the horse you rode in on,' Seamus said. 'Welcome to the team.'

'Thank you.' I smiled and tried to look brisk, à la Jenny Robins. 'Why don't you tell me about it, Mr Mahon? All I know so far is how busy you get.'

'For the last time, my name's Seamus – if we're not in the office. Famous Seamus,' he grinned engagingly. 'I'm a pretty big shot around these parts, kiddo.'

'So I gathered.' God, his smile really was devastating. I couldn't help it, little tendrils of lust were crawling all over my tummy.

'If you don't want to talk sweet nothings,' Seamus said, sighing and handing me a huge piece of warm bread, which he first slathered in herb butter, 'I suppose I'd better fill you in on the set-up around our way. They first poached me for Hamilton Kane from Goldman Sachs in New York . . .'

And he was off. Courses came and went, delicious wine – I wasn't used to anything better than supermarket plonk you could clean your ovens with – was daintily sipped, and then gulped as my resolutions to drink lightly and eat like a little bird, in the manner of Dolores, Kate Moss and suchlike, went south, and still Seamus was talking. His luscious eyes shone with enthusiasm as he described this major deal, that hostile takeover, all of which he had been instrumental to. 'I shouldn't mention this,' or 'If I have to be honest,' he'd say, but then he'd have to tell me anyway.

My hunger pangs were melting but so was my stomach. Oh God, what a man, I thought, he's probably the most successful bloke in the whole City.

'Do you know Tony Meadows at Barings?' I butted in. Couldn't resist mentioning Gail's boyfriend. Just to check.

He looked slightly put out at the interruption, but then gave me a blistering smile. 'Never heard of him,' Seamus said flatly. 'Your man's probably some junior sales grunt. I know all the big shots there.'

Junior sales grunt! Ha, ha, ha, ha, ha! I thought triumphantly.

I was thrilled to be at Hamilton Kane now. Thank God I hadn't quit, I thought. One for Tom Drummond! Now I would get to be in the wake of a man like Seamus! It was better than working for a rock star.

'Do you have any nice single friends?' I blurted out. Then wished I'd swallowed my own tongue. Why couldn't I just say nice things like, 'Please pass the Evian'?

Seamus leaned forward as he waved his platinum American Express card for the waiter.

'Now why would I want to be introducing a beautiful girl like you to that shower?' he asked with a slow wink.

This was totally disconcerting, I thought, as my heart started to hammer in the most unbusinesslike way.

'Well, you're certainly very successful . . . Seamus. Your life sounds great,' I stammered.

A flunky duly materialised with the bill and bowed low as he took the card away on a silver salver. Seamus waited until he'd gone, then looked quizzically across at me.

'Money doesn't buy you happiness,' he said slowly. 'Work's been good to me . . . but I'll tell you the God's honest truth, Alex, my marriage is terrible.'

Chapter 6

'S-sorry?' I stammered. I wasn't sure I had heard it right.

Seamus sighed again. His dark eyes flickered over me, hardly taking in the neat burgundy dress or well-brushed hair. I'd come to some arrangement with my appearance now. I wasn't the Wild Woman of Borneo, but then again, the Long-Lash Volumiser mascara and Very Cherry lipstick had also gone the way of all flesh. Who's got the time? I did pass depressing numbers of Keisha-like super females, the investment banker warrior queens with their Dior suits and professionally applied cosmetics, sometimes also with a baby strapped to their backs in a smart papoose, but those women lived on another planet from me. They were all part of the big World Conspiracy to make me feel small and inadequate, as they rushed past conquering three worlds before breakfast and then going home to their male-model husbands on the dot of five thirty.

Seamus was having to make do with me and my slapped-on concealer under the eyes.

'I shouldn't have said anything,' he murmured. 'A trouble shared is a trouble doubled. Now why should I be burdening you, Alex Wilde, with my problems?'

His problems!

'I envy you, and that's the truth. A gorgeous young girl like you, out with all her suitors each night of the week, breaking hearts all over the place . . .' His voice trailed to silence as he scribbled a signature on the gargantuan bill.

I got up, wishing violently that lunch was about to start, not finish.

'Oh no. It's not like that at all,' I babbled. He'd got it the wrong way round – didn't he know that I was the one whose heart was permanently parked in the repair garage?

'You don't need to be pretending to be lonely just to keep me company,' Seamus said kindly. There was a misty look in his eyes. Like the Andrex puppy if someone kicked it very hard.

'Er . . .' I began, but he cut me off.

'Now, I shouldn't have said anything. Very unprofessional, but you've such an open face,' Seamus whispered as he led me from the restaurant. 'I feel I can trust you. Isn't that the most stupid thing you ever heard?'

His driver held the door open for me, tipping his cap a little in salute. I felt like Demi Moore. I gazed eagerly at Seamus to see if he wanted to unbend any more, but he leaned forward curtly.

'Back to the office. And hurry up, I've got a three o'clock.'

He looked straight ahead as the car purred through the streets. I was lost in admiration, what a guy: he could be so brave, just switching it off like that.

When we got back, Seamus walked straight over to his office to meet up with some bowing Japanese bankers. I watched out of the corner of my eye as he inclined his neck very properly and said something nice in Japanese. The two men exchanged glances. They were clearly as impressed as I was.

'Have a nice lunch, Alexandra?' Jenny Robins asked as I dawdled back to my desk.

'Ummm,' I said happily.

'Good. Then you'll be full of energy for these,' she said, dumping a huge pile of filing in front of me.

Bloody Jenny kept me out of Seamus's way for the rest of the day. No sooner had I finished the bloody filing than it was down to the copier room with me. When I resurfaced from that, coughing out dust mites and bleeding paper cuts from every finger, I saw the lovely Seamus hanging around outside his door. Was he sending furtive looks in my direction?

I caught myself. Just because he was sad and lonely, didn't mean he wanted me.

But what about all that 'gorgeous,' and 'pretty' stuff? my optimistic side asked hopefully.

Forget it, snarled Cynicism and Realism. He's just being polite. You are a coffee-making machine, a photocopying slave, a filing flunky. And he is a big rich prince with a poet's eyes. In your dreams, sister.

Cynicism and Realism won hands down.

Although Optimism nearly came back with a late equaliser, when Seamus stopped at my desk at six o'clock.

'Can I give you a lift home, at all, Alex?' he asked charmingly.

'Sorry, Mr Mahon,' Jenny bustled in, before I could jump at the chance, 'Alexandra hasn't finished her spreadsheets, she's going to be a good while yet.'

'Ah, of course, Jenny,' said Seamus, all businesslike. I was out of my mind if I thought he might be interested in me! He was a nice attentive boss because that's the sort of guy he clearly was.

I slunk home feeling very mixed up. So no change there, then.

'We have to get this place tidied up,' Gail announced with authority.

'Why?' Bronwen demanded, lifting her head from her copy of the *Face*.

'Look at it!' Gail screeched. 'This is no way for Snowy to see us!'

I had to agree that she was probably right there. Magazines scattered all over the floor. Crisp packets and crumpled Bounty wrappers from last night's Chocolate Run – a major feature of flat life, we went on the Chocolate Run most evenings, stocking up from the shop across the road. If God wanted us to be thin, he wouldn't have put a newsagent's across the road, would he? Mr Patel had a fine selection of Fuse bars and Bountys, Fruit and Nut and Twixes and anything else your heart could desire. The Chocolate Runner often took an agonising ten or so minutes deciding which ones to have. Keisha would say 'Whatever,' when asked for her preference, and then would always want what I chose.

'You said two packets of Buttons.'

'Well, I don't want them. I want your Topic.'

'Well, you liked Buttons last time.'

'Well, you never asked me if I wanted a Topic.'

And so forth until I had surrendered the Topic. She could be bloody annoying, could Keisha. And she would never lower herself to do the Chocolate Run. Last time, I had come downstairs from the shower, hair sopping, wrapped only in a towel, to find Keisha, fully dressed, sitting on the sofa pouting that I wouldn't go out on the Run.

'I'm naked, I'm soaking and I'm barefoot.'

'Well, put some shoes on and get dressed,' said Keisha reasonably, 'or use a dressing gown, no one's going to care.'

'You're dressed!' I spluttered.

'Oh, I don't know, Al,' Keisha said snottily, settling back into the sofa with a world-weary air. 'Sometimes you're really selfish. And lazy,' she added firmly, before I could say another word.

However, fair's fair. Keisha's room was the only part of the flat that didn't look like a bus had recently passed through it. As well as the wrappers, our drawing room boasted three KFC buckets (empty), six wine-glasses (empty) and four Happy Meal containers (full, because Bronwen had dreamed up some chemical scheme for feeding all London's homeless children and then forgotten about it when she passed out).

Previously, I hate to admit, I would have been at the fries in those Happy Meals, but now I had Seamus to think of. He wasn't going to be interested, but it wouldn't hurt to look nice. Just in case.

'Who cares about Snowy?' said Bronwen, but her heart wasn't really in it.

'Two words,' said Gail heavily. 'Reading. Festival.'

Bronwen was out of that chair faster than I ran out of the office doors each evening. I levered myself up to help her, and even Keisha consented to fetch the Hoover. It was bad enough that we were all here slaving for Olivia White, but it would be worse to have her laughing up at me in her superior way. Bin liners were produced and kitchen sprays dug out from where they'd been gathering dust. With all of us blitzing the problem, it didn't in all honesty take that long, but we'd never normally do anything like that together. Not unless we were giving a party, and specially gorgeous men were coming round. Then we got as houseproud as Monica in *Friends*, screaming at each other over the coffee stains and the dried spaghetti strands stuck to the table legs.

It's actually much better to go to parties at some other poor bastard's house. That way you can spill the wine and be sick and play that trick with the fountain of champagne glasses which always goes wrong, with total impunity. Not to mention, if you ever get really hammered and cop off with some ginger-haired Chris Evans lookalike, you can get silently up in the morning and tiptoe away. Not like letting them back to your own place, when they invariably lie sprawled across your bed like the Living Dead, refusing to notice all your gentle coughs and hints about breakfast and the time and suchlike.

I'd heard this from mates mostly. Things like that never happened to me at parties, because even the Chris Evans lookalikes weren't desperate enough to go for me. And also because I didn't really like the idea. Sex with no strings attached is one of those things that's great in theory, but I'd really rather leave to other people because it might make me sick. Like hang-gliding.

'You know, Al, you're really frigid,' Keisha used to tell me, returned from one of her evenings out on the prowl. She said she used to enjoy what she called 'a little poke', just for curiosity's sake. But Keisha was always leaving her rock star/movie star/media mogul/ sporting legend with a broken heart and a big dent in his bank balance. I thought she had a commitment problem. She was looking for something too, not that she'd admit it.

'You are. You always want to fall in love and ride off into the sunset,' Bronwen agreed.

'But life's not like that,' Keisha said wisely.

'It *is* like that,' I replied staunchly.

'Well,' said Gail, delivering the *coup de grâce*, 'not for you.'

We set to like the four dwarves for Snowy. Only it wasn't so much 'Whistle While You Work' as 'Out of my way, you fucking bitch'. But we meant it nicely.

'This your bloody KFC?' Gail screeched at Keisha.

'So what's this, you *slut*?' Keisha roared back, holding up two empty cartons of wholemilk four-grain goat's milk yoghurt, kiwi fruit flavour, with teaspoons stuck to their insides.

I was standing there in my clay-spattered dungarees, bin liner in one hand and empty box of Marks & Sparks red in the other, when the doorbell rang.

'It's the pizza,' Gail said gleefully, for we'd ordered in for tidying provisions.

It wasn't the pizza. It was Snowy.

'Gail,' she said sweetly to Gail's squeal of excitement, pressing her back in a ghost of a hug, as if afraid she might get homespun wool stuck on her nail polish.

Snowy looked fabulous. Not in my most disgruntled nightmares had I expected this: Olivia White standing there in what looked like a cream silk Versace shift, gathered at one shoulder with a gold clasp in the manner of a Greek goddess. Her lips were slicked with something massively expensive; her face, even close to me over Gail's shoulder, was flawless, her perfect pores tiny. As was her nose. Snowy's once distinguished Roman job had vanished under some skilled scalpel, leaving behind only a tiny, fairy little nose that looked as though she never needed to blow it. Behind our open door I could see piles of Louis Vuitton monogrammed luggage in the hall. I hoped it was a fifty-buck Hong Kong rip-off, but somehow I doubted it. Snowy's earlobes were groaning under two rocks of sparkling ice big enough to sink the *Titanic*. Her skin was buffed and tanned and she was so bloody thin she was in danger of disappearing down the plughole every time she took a bath.

She probably bathed in asses' milk or champagne. Or dissolved pearls or—

'Gail, do introduce me to your friends,' Snowy was purring. 'I'm Olivia White.' She held out one slender hand to Bronwen, who shook it almost mesmerised.

'I'm Bronwen Thomas,' Bronwen said, then blurted out, 'I hear you can get backstage passes and that.'

Snowy smiled graciously. 'Mmm. What were you thinking of? Reading? No problem, I'll get you some biked round tomorrow.'

'And this is Keisha,' Gail said triumphantly, shooting I told you so looks at me.

'What a gorgeous shirt,' Snowy said. 'Clements Ribiero, isn't it?'

'It is,' Keisha agreed with a small smile.

'I can get you wholesale at Harvey Nicks. Or Harrods – Mohamed Al-Fayed's such a dear sweet friend . . .'

Keisha's reserve evaporated. I felt a bit jealous, actually. Snowy was already bonding to her like Superglue.

'And Alex . . .' She gave me a faint smile, but didn't bother getting too close. She surveyed my dungarees and bin liner and scrunched-up hair and tired face. 'You look just the same as ever,' Snowy said.

'I like your nose job,' I retorted.

Childish, but it made me feel better. Snowy stiffened a fraction, then gave us a grin so white you needed sunglasses. God, her teeth were bleached white as an American soap star's.

'Thank you,' she said. 'I see the body as a work of art.'

I looked down at my own squidgy midriff, thought about my beige teeth and pale skin and non-gleaming hair, and tried not to despair.

Of course Seamus hadn't meant it when he called me pretty! There were women like Snowy and Dolores in the world. Girls like me were just there to make up the numbers.

Bronwen and Keisha were now looking at me, waiting for a snappy comeback, but my venom had deserted me. Dorothy Parker would have been ashamed.

'I'm going to go and work on my sculptures,' I said defiantly.

'Oh, your sculptures,' said Snowy pleasantly, 'of *course*. You must have sold thousands by now and be really famous.'

There was a dead quiet in the room.

'Alex works in the City,' Keisha said defensively.

'Alex is a secretary's assistant,' Gail butted in.

I seethed inside as Snowy digested this little tidbit.

'Oh,' she said sympathetically, 'so that's why you've got so many . . . laugh lines already, it must be the stress.'

'And what do you do?' Bronwen asked eagerly.

'Me?' Snowy gave a tinkling little laugh. 'I *party*, darling, what does it look like?'

We spent a wonderful girly evening together. No really, it was marvellous. Snowy and Gail treated Keisha and Bronwen to fabulous stories of my happy schooldays. Like the way I would never get any letters unless they were from my granny. Or the time I was attempting to serve a tennis ball and knocked myself out cold in the middle of the forehead.

'And really, Alex was such a loner,' Snowy laughed, 'always hanging out in the pottery room, all her blouses always had mud on them.'

'True,' Gail said eagerly, 'and do you remember how she always hung out with Ellen Jones?'

Ellen Jones! Ellen had been my only friend at St Mary's, if you can call it that. Ellen and I didn't have much in common. She wasn't too bright and even plumper than me. But we were both Norman No-mates, as the other girls would say, so we hung out together. I was always grateful for Ellen on Valentine's Day.

It's funny, how people bang on about Christmas and the suicide rate and they never say a word about 14 February. Each year I dreaded it more and more. The red roses that flooded the lobby, beautifully wrapped in tissue and ferns and white frothy babies' breath, teddy bears and chocolates and phones ringing off the hook. And the girls running barefoot down the corridors, flinging themselves on their beds squealing. 'Look what Crispin got me, Vanessa!' 'Isn't Robin so *sweet*!' 'Oh, it's real silver, Tim's so darling!'

The dorm mistress was never troubled with post, flowers or anything else for me and Ellen on Valentine's Day. We stayed in our rooms under siege, pretending to study and slagging them all off for being bimbos. We were utterly miserable. I would gladly have swapped the odd A-minus in pottery for just one card, no matter how spotty or speccy the sender. And poor Ellen felt even worse, not even having talent to console her. Once, on 11 February, I caught her by the post box in the hedge outside the school, her jumper snagging on a blackberry twig, as she attempted to stuff a gift-wrapped box of chocs, addressed to herself, through the slot. I talked her out of it. Everybody knew her handwriting and Snowy White would have been merciless.

'Ellen was all right,' I said grumpily.

'Just as well,' Gail laughed, 'since no one else wanted to hang out with you.'

'Gail, did you realise you've got a huge zit on the end of your nose?' asked Keisha sweetly. 'It must be too much tofu.'

But they were still hanging on Snowy's every word.

'I'm going to bed,' I announced, getting up and leaving the table. I don't think anyone even noticed.

Chapter 7

I flung myself into my work.

OK, then, I flung myself into my drudgery. Filing. Typing. Coffee Making. Faxing. Photocopying. There was a massive variety of different things to be done, and each one as boring as the last. On the other hand, it was a routine. I knew where my life was going (nowhere). I got into a desperate sort of rhythm. Waking up a few seconds before my alarm clock. Jumping into the shower with a commando-like ferocity that dared the others to make a fuss – Bronwen would still be bopping in her bedroom at that hour, and Gail didn't need to be in her office until quarter to ten, and nor did Keisha, for she'd landed that job at *Up and Running* and the BBC didn't want her until mid-morning.

'Your letter worked, I've got an interview,' Keisha said last week.

Then, being Keisha, she went into one of her infrequent bouts of workaholism and came up with a pretend running order for the show. It was a slam dunk.

I danced round with her and bought her a cheap bottle of sparkling wine, but I felt like a top grade ratbag because it made me feel so miserable.

It's tough to be happy for your mate when your own life is going downhill faster than an Olympic skier.

One morning I caught myself daydreaming about winning the lottery – like, would I march straight into Jenny's office and blow a big raspberry in her face, or would I work one last day in this hellhole, showing up in a limo and pink Chanel suit, and do my typing in fingers dripping with diamonds?

That's when I knew it was all over. I was living the same life, doing the same scuzz work, and dreaming the same dreams as the whole rest of the world. I was nothing. Zero. A big fat zip. I would have won the Brownie badge for ordinariness in a heartbeat.

I used to fantasise about the six months I had spent in the fleapit in Hackney, before I'd given in and taken my parents' 'Live in our flat, live by our rules,' so-called generous offer. However, they weren't very frequent dreams. Not even this numbing boredom could make that roach-infested dump seem romantic.

So I switched to sculpting. It could still happen, I told myself. You were born to do it. You could get discovered by some avant-garde Japanese scout . . .

But I couldn't make that one sound convincing, even in a daydream.

So, I'm sorry to report, it was all down to Seamus.

I was supposed not to be thinking about my boss, but what could you do, when he was there every morning in his slouchy, daring-coloured suits and flashy ties, with all the City boys laying the full-court press on him, and his rakish body moving about, and his aftershave and his dreamy greeny eyes . . .

Jenny never let him near me. Oh, she was subtle about it. She would quite often send me into his office.

'Take this cup of coffee in to Mr Mahon, could you, Alexandra?' or 'These papers need Mr Mahon's signature,' or 'Here are Mr Mahon's hotel vouchers for Prague.' All innocent, like, there you go, you *can* see the big man, little girl.

The problem was, she always sent me in there when he wasn't alone. There'd be some junior Hamilton Kane quant in there, eying me up as I completed my mission.

So I'd say, 'Here you are, Mr Mahon,' or 'Sign here please, Mr Mahon.'

What sparkling dialogue, eh? Oscar Wilde couldn't have done any better!

Oh, and a 'quant' is City speak for a 'quantative analyst', or 'number cruncher' in English. I was getting fairly up on the old jargon by now. I was a bit of a veteran.

'If they recruited one called Mary, they could call her Mary Quant,' I suggested to Jenny, and she actually smiled, so she clearly was human and not some fiendish robot after all.

Anyway, the luscious, pouting Seamus would say, 'Thank you, Alex,' politely, but like I wasn't even there. Like you thank the newspaper man for your change.

In fact, have you ever noticed how polite we English are as

47

shoppers? My weekly basket of cheap wine, frozen ready burgers at ten per cent off and a packet of discount strawberries, usually a false economy because the bottom layer's all bad, goes something like this: put down the basket. 'Thanks.' 'Thank you,' says Dwayne on the checkout listlessly. 'Six pounds fifty, thanks.' 'Thank you,' I say, handing over the tenner. A bit reluctantly. 'Thank you,' he says, snatching it from me. 'Thanks,' he says, handing over three fifty. 'Thank you,' I say, pocketing it, grabbing my carrier. 'Thanks,' says Dwayne.

God knows what it must be like in Japan.

Of course in Keisha's case not a word is ever exchanged. Even taxi drivers don't launch into their life stories. Nobody would dare.

It wasn't all boredom and frustration in the office, though. Sometimes it was embarrassment and annoyance, too. This sprang mostly from Kevin Harvey in Admin. Kevin held the title of Administration Clerk. He was actually the oldest postboy the world has ever known. Thirty-five, with thinning sandy hair he used to comb in wet strands across his bald patch, a pudgy body with breasts that needed a Cross-Your-Heart, and a nice line in cheap, see-through white shirts, always dark with sweat despite the air-conditioning.

Kevin was sweet on me. As my mother and Jenny liked to put it.

He lingered at my desk. He handed over each of Seamus's letters individually, very slowly. He tried out different 'manly' scents every day (Superdrug Super Saver Fresh Pine, Old Spice or Bad Boy Rum being favourites). He used to try and impress me with his big schemes.

'I've an idea for Federal Express,' he said one day.

'That's nice, Kev,' I said, burying my nose in my papers.

'Coloured envelopes. The ones they use now are so boring.'

'I'm busy right now, Kev,' I said witheringly.

He flushed. 'Sure, right. I'll see you tomorrow – same time, same place, huh huh huh.'

Jenny scowled at me after Kev's overloaded cart had trundled round the corner. 'Poor man! You needn't be so foul to one of God's fellow creatures, Alexandra.'

'Well, I don't want to encourage him,' I said sulkily. She needn't make Kevin sound like a kitten with a broken leg.

'You could try being kind. Looks aren't everything,' Jenny retorted. It was about the most personal thing she'd ever come out with. Why should I care what the old boot thought? But I did venture down with my soggy bap to the post room at lunchtime, God knows why. Kev was thrilled to see me. So then I felt sulky and guilty, and lunch with Kev became a once-a-week deal.

'That's a nice girl, Alexandra,' Jenny said approvingly.

And I'm sorry to say I was secretly quite pleased. As I was when she praised my typing. Or my answering, or anything really.

'You're getting quite . . . competent,' Jenny told me briskly. Well, you take your praise where you can get it.

This morning I'd been bashing away at the PC when Personnel rang up to tell me Jenny was off sick. For a second I felt worried about her. What was wrong with me? I was going bonkers.

'It's only flu,' Personnel said reassuringly, 'but she wants to knock it on the head. So we're sending somebody along from the typing pool downstairs to take over your work. Jenny wanted you to handle her stuff.'

'Fine,' I muttered, a prickly flush of anticipation spreading halfway up my back before I could stop myself. I hoped they would rustle up some sixteen-year-old gum-popping kid with a punk haircut, so I could yell at her about her appearance and send her to the filing room for a change, but no, I got Rhoda Black, a fat frumpy matron with a boxy green suit and a typing speed that took my breath away.

'Could you possibly do these for me, and get this line?' I asked nervously. My command authority was sorely lacking, when it came down to it.

'Is that all?' Rhoda asked contemptuously, examining my pile of letters as though she needed a microscope to see them.

'Well, maybe these,' I suggested daringly, offering up some reports and a couple of spreadsheets that would have taken me days to get through.

Rhoda sniffed. 'They don't work you up here, do they?'

I ignored her. What did I care, when I could dash off to the ladies' for a slick of nude lipstick and a reapplication of my concealer? I was getting promoted, if only for the day. That meant Jenny's immaculately neat desk and only taking calls from important people. And, more importantly, it meant Seamus. Estimated Time of Arrival: five to nine. Just enough time to settle myself in, spritz myself – well, douse myself from head to foot – in CK Be, and make a fresh cup of espresso, just the way he liked it.

He was bang on time. Amazingly enough. And he looked brilliant, wearing some off-burgundy suit with dark brown shoes and smelling of spiced oranges, his dark hair neatly combed back and sprayed, as though it might tumble out into wild curls at any minute if not subdued. He strode into the office clutching his briefcase, with a sort of corporate warrior swagger that made me go all weak at the knees.

Oh how I longed to wind the clock back just a couple of hours. Just long enough for me to steal some of Bronwen's make-up and beg Keisha to lend me a TDO. Even an MDO would do. Rather than the neat, sexless suit from Next in pebble-grey wool mix I was sporting drably.

Seamus's first glance at me out of those deep green eyes was one of – annoyance?

'Where's Jenny?' he almost barked.

'Er, got the flu,' I said.

'Bugger. That bloody woman's never around when I need her,' Seamus said sharply.

It was my impression that Jenny practically camped in this office, but . . .

'Is that my coffee?' He took it from me, downed it in a single gulp, then grimaced wildly. 'Jesus, Mary and Joseph! That's not how I like it! Don't you know I take the bloody stuff decaffeinated?'

What's the point of decaffeinated espresso, I wanted to say, but bit it back. I was afraid my voice might wobble into tears if I said anything. And who'd want to cheek him in this mood? He might fire me!

Poor Seamus must have had a really atrocious morning!

'I'm sorry—'

'Get me another one and bring it into my office,' he said without looking at me, picking up a sheaf of faxes from Jenny's desk.

Then he went into his office and slammed the door.

I got up and went to the coffee machine, pretty automatically. Tears were prickling in the back of my throat but I swallowed them down determinedly. I wasn't going to let fat Rhoda over there see me blubbing. I'd never hear the end of it from that minx on Reception if I did.

I made sure to knock on his office door before going in.

'Come in, sure you'd think I'd got all day to hang about,' shouted Seamus, as I hastily fumbled with the knob and ushered myself inside.

'Sorry about that,' I said falteringly, setting the proper version of the coffee down in front of him.

'Who's doing your stuff, if that lazy cow's away?' snapped Seamus.

'Rhoda. Personnel sent her up,' I told him, 'she's very good.'

He unstiffened a fraction. 'At least it's not some temp bimbo. They always screw everything up. And leave early.'

I wondered wildly if Keisha had worked for him in her previous incarnation.

'To get their hair done,' he added. It sounded like Keisha. I made a note to ask her some time.

'Do you think you can handle Jenny's stuff? My appointments and everything?'

'I think so, Seamus,' I said boldly.

He looked up at me sharply. 'Hey, it's Mr Mahon in the office, you never know when someone might walk in.'

'Ummm. Yes. Sorry,' I said. I felt like a complete fool. I was as red as a radish. It was such a slap round the face. For a moment I almost got angry. There was no need to be such a—

'Hey.' Seamus was looking at me more carefully. His eyes looked at the hem skimming my knees, the calves balanced neatly on their low heels. He gave himself a little shake and a sort of thoughtful expression crossed his brow. 'That's a nice suit you're wearing, Alex.'

'Thank you,' I muttered, slinking off to the door. His phone was buzzing outside and I wanted to get to it as soon as possible.

'And I'd say it's a new lipstick, too. It's very pretty.'

I hardly dared let that register as I dived on the phone, chirping, 'Good morning, Mr Mahon's office, may I help you?' as sweetly as I could.

Why do men always call women weathervanes? Seamus was changing tack as often as Madonna changed image. Anyway, his first meeting was due in ten minutes. I knew there would be no idle chit-chat after that.

I was totally shattered by three p.m. It wasn't so much the work – Jenny left everything so organised there was nothing for me. It was the tension. Seamus had morphed into a smiling, charming executive the moment the first visitors from Germany arrived. I, on the other hand, had to worry my guts out about getting it wrong – smudging my make-up, spilling the coffee, mixing up the teas and coffees and peppermint infusions. I took messages with my face aching from smily politeness. I even managed to cope with the hotshot Singapore trader who rang and screamed at me that I was a clap-ridden whore. 'Fuck off, fuckface,' though tempting, would not have been the correct reply.

It was a miracle, but I thought I'd made it through without any serious errors.

At five p.m., I ventured to take Seamus in another cup of decaf and a selection of Charbonnel & Walker chocolates from the executive fridge.

To my amazement, he was sitting – sprawling out – on his cream leather couch, doodling cartoons on the front of his *Wall Street Journal*.

'Ah, she comes bearing coffee like an angel of mercy,' Seamus said sweetly. 'Or maybe a fairy. Are you a fairy, Alex Wilde?'

'Not last time I looked,' I said, confused, handing over the grub.

'Perfect. And chocolates,' he approved, 'she knows how to keep up a man's blood sugar. And other things too, I'll be bound. Although we'll not talk about that now.' And he gave a rich laugh.

I was amazed. I half expected him to apologise for before, but he said not a word about it. Instead, he was gazing up very intently at my face. I thought I might have lipstick on my teeth.

'That's a gorgeous foundation you're wearing. What is it?' Seamus asked.

I blushed with pleasure. 'I'm not, actually.'

'That's your skin?' Seamus asked, lifting his dark eyebrows. 'Like a peach, so it is. You must use awful expensive moisturisers.'

Did Boots No. 7 qualify? Probably not, but it was nice to hear it, at any rate. I felt my tension melting away and my smile blossom like a lotus on a lily pond. 'I hope everything was all right today?'

'Ah, you did a grand job. Grand,' Seamus said genially. I looked back nervously to where the red light was winking on my phone, but he waved away my worries. 'Let the other girl pick that up. It won't be anyone important, now the market's closed.'

'OK.' I shifted from foot to foot, wondering if that was my cue to wish him a good night and grab my jacket.

'Alex. Will we go out and grab a bite of dinner?' Seamus asked.

It was so unexpected I didn't say anything for a second. Then I stammered my thanks just as fast as I could get it out. I've always been a cool customer that way.

'How about the Ivy? Covent Garden? Yeah, that's the one, be a good girl and go make the reservation,' Seamus decided, not consulting me, but then why would he? Expensive London restaurants were a closed book to me. Hell, *cheap* London restaurants were a closed book. 'We'll eat at eight. Suit you?'

'Sure.' I grinned up at him happily, jumping to my feet to follow him out the door. First cocktails in one of the many post-market City bars, then a leisurely limo ride to the West End . . .

'Where do you think you're going?' Seamus asked, sounding slightly annoyed.

I stopped short. 'Aren't I following you?'

'Ah . . . no, it's best if we meet up there later. Don't want to be seen hanging around together. It's terrible for your career, darlin'.'

I nodded eagerly. 'OK.'

'You just book us in, we'll have a great old time. I can't wait,' Seamus said softly. Then he handed me a green slip of paper.

'What's this?'

'My dry-cleaning,' Seamus said amiably. 'I've got to run off, but if you bring it along to the Ivy I'll load it straight into my car. Don't worry,' he reassured me, 'you won't be sitting there with a bunch of suits draped over your lap.'

I laughed uncertainly.

'See you, sweetheart. Looking forward to it,' Seamus said. Then he exited his office and looked blandly at me as Rhoda waddled past with a pile of documents.

'Good night, Mr Mahon,' I said loudly. He nodded and headed for the lifts.

Wasn't it thrilling?

Chapter 8

I stood in the dry-cleaner's office clutching a heavy pile of suits. His bill was fifty pounds, but the attendant waved it away.

'Mr Mahon is a *very* good customer. He can pay us when he comes in next. I don't suppose you have the money on you.'

It wasn't a question. I wished I could pull out a fistful of fifties and tell her to keep the change, but the only fifties ever to be found on my person had 'pence' stamped across the bottom.

'Are you one of Mrs Mahon's new maids?'

'No,' I said furiously. What, did the woman keep a fleet of servants, like the Queen? And did I look like a skivvy?

'I didn't think so.' The attendant gave me a wintry smile. 'She's such a stickler for grooming.'

I flounced out as best I could, with clingfilm wrappers crackling against my skirt. Great. Now I wasn't even polished enough to be Dolores's skivvy.

'*Work's been good to me . . . but I'll tell you the God's honest truth, Alex, my marriage is terrible.*' Seamus's words kept drifting back to me as I staggered back to my car. Poor Seamus, I thought sympathetically, having to slave away all day just to keep his wife in maids and *haute couture*. It was flattering that he wanted to talk to me . . . talk, obviously, would be all he wanted to do . . .

He'd said he thought he could trust me. Just like that, at our first lunch. Seamus would be that kind of man, the type who leaps before he looks, that wild Celtic streak in him carrying him away. He could see behind the Tipp-Ex and the filing cabinet. He could see the depths of my artistic soul. No man could have a face that meltingly sexy and *enjoy* working in an office. But since he was forced to do it, he was naturally great at it.

I was looking forward to dinner. It had been a royal pain in the ass, begging the *maître d'* for a reservation that wasn't at either six p.m. or ten thirty. At first the guy was closed tighter than Keisha's chequebook, but then, in desperation, I dropped Seamus's name and a miraculous cancelled booking materialised out of thin air.

It gave me a thrill. A tiny squeeze between the legs. To think of eating with a man whose name worked better than 'Open Sesame' any day.

It took me forty minutes to find a parking space in Covent Garden. I was just beginning to fantasise about driving a Sherman tank with diplomatic plates, so I could squash the BMWs that were clogging the kerbs, when a haughty-looking blonde in a low-slung Bentley pulled out of a prime slot right in front of me.

'Cheers,' I yelled, waving madly from the grimy windows of my clapped-out Mini.

The elegant blonde head whipped round and smiled graciously. My heart dropped. It was Snowy.

'Darling,' she said, pulling up beside me. 'I was just on my way back with a few goodies for Bronwen and Keisha.'

I could see All-Access laminates swinging from her dashboard, and a small white bag with 'Prada' stamped across it. Her car was immaculate inside as well as out. I felt bitterly ashamed of my old banger and tiny paycheque.

'Did you get me anything?' I asked.

'Hmm.' She nodded. 'A pot of La Prairie moisturiser.'

That stuff cost about a hundred quid a jar. Women in the pages of Jackie Collins novels used it. I smiled as gratefully as I could – no need to be a bitch, if Snowy was making this much of an effort.

'It's got the world's best anti-ageing system. So maybe it can help you,' she added spitefully. 'Oh no, is that his dry-cleaning? What kind of a jerk makes his secretary pick that up? He'll be getting you to send flowers to all his girlfriends next.'

'I don't mind picking it up.'

'So I see . . . whatever floats your boat, Alex. Oh,' she looked prettily down at her tank Cartier watch, 'must dash. Meeting a pal in Knightsbridge.'

'Anyone I know?'

Olivia looked at me through narrowed lids swept with plum and gold and gave a little snort of laughter. 'Shouldn't think so, dear, unless you spend a lot of time in the Gulf of Oman . . .' then she sat bolt upright, as if catching herself, purred, 'Later,' and pulled away smoothly.

Anti-ageing? God, I was only twenty-seven. I started peering at myself in the rear-view mirror for crows' feet, but the glass was too dusty and spotty for an accurate reading. Anyway, I said to myself as I jumped out, suits in tow, there were plenty of stunning babes far older than me. Cindy Crawford. Sharon Stone. Err, Helen Mirren. But where had the years gone? They seemed to have trickled under my feet while I was waiting for the lights to change to green. It seemed like yesterday that I was up at Oxford, full of fire and getting drunk on vintage port with Tom Drummond . . .

I snapped myself out of it as I got to the Ivy. How could I be depressed? I was about to have dinner with Seamus Mahon.

'Reservation for two, name of Mahon,' I announced imperiously to the waiter. That's a tough one to pull off when you're clutching six wire hangers with one index finger.

For a second nasty thoughts drifted through my mind. Like, what if he cancelled, what if they refused to let me in with the clingfilm accessories, what if he was hours late and I sat at a table for two twirling a breadstick and trying not to catch the pitying eyes of the other diners, who, because I'd been so obviously stood up, would doubtless include Mel Gibson and Richard Gere?

'Of course, madam. Mr Mahon is already here,' the waiter said.

Sweet relief washed over me like a soothing stream. I exhaled loudly. 'Could you put these in the cloakroom for me, please?'

'Certainly, madam.' He handed them to a flunky without batting an eyelid. 'Let me show you to your table.'

Seamus was sitting alone at a table half-hidden behind the most enormous bunch of flowers. As I approached he leapt to his feet, brushing the waiter away so he could pull out my chair himself. His eyes swept up and down my body. I hoped fervently that the pale pink silk dress I'd bought from Whistles about an hour earlier, for miles more than I could possibly afford, would please him.

'I hope I didn't keep you waiting too long,' I stuttered.

'I've only just walked through the door myself. God, what a beautiful dress, is it new?'

'This?' I shook my head violently. 'Had it for years.'

'Waiter.' Seamus signalled. 'Take these roses away. My companion's loveliness is putting them to shame.'

A rich wave of blushing swept across my cheeks. It got worse a second later when I realised that a great big price tag was protruding from the side seam of the dress and laying across the table. I whisked it hastily away, praying that Seamus hadn't seen it, but it was too late: his long fingers reached across and grabbed it before I could stop him.

'Two hundred pounds? Ah,' he laughed sexily, 'Alex Wilde, if I didn't know you better I'd say you were trying to impress me.'

'Women always say they've had stuff for years,' I muttered in a lame attempt at a last-minute save.

'But you bought something new, even if it was only cheap and cheerful. I think it's sweet.'

Cheap and bloody cheerful, my ass! 'Hmm,' I said, trying to flick my hair in a girly way like they tell you to do in *The Rules* and all the other 'how to catch a man the eighteenth-century way' self-help books. I am a sucker for all those books, even though they contain sadistic advice on how to accept bunches of roses and how to not return calls, which is fine if you ever get roses, or indeed calls to not return.

Seamus grinned at me. Then he gave me a slow wink. I was embarrassed and spellbound all at once. I didn't know whether to be bothered or flattered. It was that familiar confusion. It was heady. I hadn't had a sip of wine as yet, but I was starting to feel drunk.

'Will we have something to eat? I'd like the braised lamb and how about the steamed scallops with ginger?'

'Sure,' I said dreamily, although I didn't really like ginger.

'And a bottle of the number twenty-eight.'

'And a Diet Pepsi.'

'Ah no, not a Diet Pepsi,' Seamus said, flashing me a teasing smile, 'she doesn't want that, it'll take the flavour off the fish. Well,' he added once the waiter had melted away, 'it's good to see you, Alex, without a computer screen in front of your nose. You're looking quite the loveliest thing in the place.'

'Thanks,' I said, wondering if he'd looked in any mirrors lately.

'Who's the lucky man? No, wait, let me guess. He's an astronaut. A prince of Spain. An international master criminal, with minions to slit your throat and dump you in the Thames if you leave him.'

I shook my head, smiling broadly. As if! 'No boyfriend.'

'You're never . . . a *lesbian*?'

'No!' I blushed.

'Pity,' he said, grinning back at me. 'But then the thought of that would be liable to give me a heart attack. I could have you done for murder of a poor lonely old man.'

'You're not poor or lonely or old,' I said feebly.

The wine arrived and Seamus poured it lavishly into my glass, just taking a splash for himself.

'You're not drinking?'

'Not too much. It hurts your memory, and why would I want to forget an evening with the likes of you?'

'Er – perhaps Jenny will be better tomorrow,' I said brightly, trying to get off the subject. He was probably just making polite small talk.

'Well, maybe she will and then again maybe she won't. The question,' Seamus added as if to a small child, 'is will I be able to survive another day in the office, tortured by your brown eyes, and no way to get near them?'

My heart skipped a beat. I didn't know that could actually happen, but it was so surprised it stopped for a second. Then it was racing away down the line like a thoroughbred greyhound. I gasped, 'What?' but then the food arrived, and Seamus leant back discreetly and waited for the coast to clear. Then he leant forward and looked me over. It was so sexy. It was as if he had Superman eyes and could see clean through to my new lacy Knickerbox bra.

'Now you're an intelligent lady and you've no hearing problems. So why are you asking me to repeat myself?'

'But you're married,' I said. To a Dior-clad sex goddess, I didn't say.

Seamus snorted bitterly. 'Only in name. We don't get along. The passion has died, she lives for shopping. I'm of the opinion that without passion, you might as well be dead.' He grabbed my hand fiercely. 'Without passion, it's all worth nothing.'

My skin crackled at his touch. I could have lit a fag with the sparks in his eyes. Oh God, Oh God, it was too good to be true.

'Why don't you get a divorce?'

'Me? Good Catholic boy? My mammy would drop dead on the spot. And anyway, there's the children. The issue of my issue,' he said woefully. 'Ah, I shouldn't be burdening you with all this yearning.'

Burden me, burden me! 'That's OK,' I said gently. I pushed my fish round my plate and fortified myself with the excellent wine. Seamus was eating heartily, unburdening his soul in between large mouthfuls of lamb.

'I've been looking for someone like you all my life,' he said intensely. It was amazing, I started to blossom under his stare. It was like I was the only girl in the room. The only girl on the planet. The way he was looking at me like he wanted to eat me alive. 'Someone who I can talk to and not feel so guilty, or unhappy. Someone I can trust to understand. Someone who . . .'

'Who's an artist, like you are inside,' I suggested helpfully.

He looked at me weirdly, then went on, 'Yeah, maybe I guess. Anyway, someone to talk to, and it certainly helps when you're as beautiful as you are. Although maybe not. Maybe it actually *doesn't* help.'

'Why not?' I whispered.

'Because I can't concentrate. I should be thinking about talking things through. And I'm after thinking about something else entirely.'

I swallowed dryly.

'I'm thinking about those soft cherry lips of yours, and what it would be like to kiss them. How it would feel to have you in my arms. Just to have the warmth of human comfort again, after all these years.'

'All these years?'

'My marriage is as dead as St Patrick.'

'Seamus,' I began, scrabbling about for something to say.

He held up one tanned hand. His wedding ring glinted in the candlelight. 'Don't say it. Don't shatter my dreams just yet. Just let me sit here and look at you, before you tell me you could never be interested in a sad old goat like myself.'

'But I am!' I burst out. 'Interested! I mean, not that you're a sad old goat or anything. Not a goat . . .'

'Just sad and old?' he enquired, green eyes twinkling merrily.

'Not old at all. I think you're gorgeous,' I said warmly.

'Do you now,' he said, smiling softly. My breath was catching in my throat. But then he turned to his lamb and attacked it with gusto.

We ate pudding and coffee and then split. Or rather Seamus ate pudding. I was desperate for some warm lemon tart but didn't dare, in case he thought I was a greedy pig. I ordered a champagne sorbet but couldn't manage more than a couple of spoons. Too many butterflies were squirming in my stomach for me to do anything as positive as eat. Seamus had changed the subject to utterly unimportant things, like the economy and football. I was uneasily wondering if I'd failed some kind of test by admitting everything to him.

'You eat like an ant,' he approved when he'd finished his chocolate fudge cake. 'Will we get the bill?'

'Ummm. Thanks for a lovely evening,' I managed miserably.

'What do you mean by that? Is the evening over?'

'Isn't it?'

'Not unless you're after breaking my heart,' Seamus said, and the sun was out again behind the clouds. He tipped the waiters lavishly and they loaded his suits into his bright red Ferrari, so I didn't even have to worry about the clingfilm any more. Seamus held open every door and helped me into my jacket, opened the car door for me and everything.

'Rose for the lady, sir?' asked a grubby bloke with a sheaf of tired-looking red roses. 'Quid each.' I froze. Men always told these blokes to bugger off, when the girls were always hoping they'd buy one and give it to them.

'Here,' Seamus said, extracted two twenties from his wallet and pulled the entire bunch out of his arms. Then he leant across and presented them to me with a flourish.

'Wow,' I stammered weakly.

Seamus leant forward and waved me into the car. 'Come on, my lady, your carriage awaits.'

We sped through the traffic. Seamus drove so fast he could have got a job as one of those maniacal New York cabbies, no problem. Cars seemed to melt away as we screeched by them. There was only a fraction of a second for me to clock all the envious glances of the boys and girls in their Ford Escorts.

We pulled up outside one of those standard-issue, highly expensive white terraced houses in Kensington, the kinds with steps and pillars flanking the porches.

'This is the London flat,' Seamus said expansively as he slipped a key in the lock. 'Just a little *pied-à-terre*.'

He led me up to the first floor and another, solid mahogany door. The flat may have been small but it looked blisteringly expensive: all modern creams and white leather sofas. There were framed photographs of naked women and a big red splodgy canvas over the fireplace, a right dog's dinner if you ask me. Which he didn't.

'You see these photos? They're by Herb Ritts ... he's a very famous photographer, these are original Ritts prints.'

'So you can be putting on the Ritts,' I joked.

He gave me a bit of a cold look. 'And my picture ... a Gardolfo, cost me twenty thousand. You're not standing in the right part of the room – come here, you can see the light on it better.'

He manoeuvred me into a pool of light, so now I saw the sun on the red splodge. 'Umm, very nice – uh, dramatic,' I said, trying to sound convincing. I've never seen the point of the modern art world. But it's never seen the point of me, so that's only fair, I suppose.

'Come here,' Seamus said softly, 'you little minx.'

He pulled me to him and kissed me. And I know I ought to be saying that fireworks exploded across the sky and the world stopped spinning on its axis, but actually I started worrying about my knickers. They were clean, but they were a bit grey at the same time. Now Seamus was going to see them. And had I shaved carefully this morning, or were my legs full of prickly stubbly bits like John Wayne's chin?

'I'd say I'm thinking what you're thinking,' Seamus whispered.

I doubted it. Not unless he was desperately wishing for some KY Jelly. I mean, I was turned on – I must be, right? – but I wasn't particularly *ready*. In the physical sense. Well, let's face it, it was so long since I'd made love there were probably cobwebs up there.

'Come on, darlin',' Seamus murmured sweetly. 'Enough talk.'

And he led me into the bedroom.

Chapter 9

When I woke up I didn't know where I was. It actually took me a good five seconds to get it right, the little computer in my head trying to process unfamiliar data, like tidy room, air conditioning, crisp sheets, man in bed.

Ah. Man in bed. Me and Seamus.

I felt a little thrill as I remembered it. Making love to him. It was kind of quick and violent, but like he said, he was a lonely man, trapped in a loveless marriage. No wonder he couldn't wait. I puffed a bit and gasped and he looked satisfied, like a cockerel. Or one of those pigeons you see in the spring puffing its chest out.

'Ah, that was grand,' he said, breathing hard through his nose. 'You're lovely, so you are, Alex.' He pulled me to him and held me tight against his chest, his arms wrapped round me in a bearhug like he never wanted to let me go.

'Mmm, it was great,' I whispered. I hadn't come, of course, nothing like, but then you don't, do you? I'm convinced that *Marie Claire* and *Cosmo* must be read by nymphomaniacs with different body chemistry to me. When you're anxious for him to enjoy himself and hoping he can't see the cellulite at the back of your thighs, and sucking in your stomach and trying to grind about seductively, the chances of you coming are nil. Zero. Zip. Nada. I don't care: the emperor has no clothes! I am convinced that this 'orgasm from sex' nonsense is a just a modern myth, like Swinging London, designed to make you feel inadequate because you're not a part of it.

But I've never admitted it to my girlfriends. Just in case I'm wrong.

I mean I'm not frigid. I've had some bloody good orgasms in my time. It's just that there's never been anyone else in the room.

The discussions girls have about orgasms are a dead giveaway. First, everybody pretends they have them at the drop of a hat. (Or pair of knickers.) It's the one area where female honesty sort of breaks down, like the sexual prowess of your current partner. Only after he's history do you ever get the full story. And only if a man's around do girls ever get honest about sex . . . like a man says, 'I can tell if she's faking it,' which is the cue for all the girls to snort and laugh derisively and go 'Yeah, right.' Then the man asks you what you mean and you're trapped, so you explain that faking it is actually sex manners – 'A courtesy to your partner,' is how Keisha once put it – but fortunately, in your current relationship, you don't have to fake it at all. You say the last bit with a totally straight face. After all, it doesn't do your cred any good to admit to your mates that your man is less exciting than watching *Frasier* repeats.

Blokes would always wonder why a woman would sleep with a man if she's not having orgasms. To them it would all be a bit pointless. But that's planet bloke for you, just like men think that the reason to go out to dinner is to eat food. Obviously, the reason to go out to dinner is the conversation, and most girls couldn't give a bugger if the fare was hot dogs and beer, so long as he's making puppy dog Droopy eyes over the paper pint glass. And the reason for sex is to be held, to cuddle afterwards, to go to sleep with the smell of sex and testosterone all round you, and to wake up before he does because you're too excited to sleep, and watch the sun play on his eyelids. Right?

In fact I find orgasms a bit embarrassing. To have one I need to think of some awful things. I mean, I would die a billion deaths if Seamus knew what I was thinking when I finally did shudder into some sort of peace, quietly in the bed beside him.

Anyway, moving swiftly on . . .

There he was, lying next to me, looking so sweet and pretty, like a sort of elfin king, like Oberon, with his dark curly hair and his thick black eyelashes. While I was mooning over them they flickered open and focused on me. And those red lips curled into the sweetest smile, and then he said,

'Christ! Is that the time! It's bloody half-six!'

My face crumpled. Seamus leapt out of bed, leant over and gave me a quick kiss. 'Sorry, darlin', didn't mean to startle you. Can I shower first? I'd better leave before you do, we don't want to set the tongues wagging away in that nest of vipers.'

'Sure,' I said briskly. *Be brisk. Be brisk.* Men hated clingy women,

I'd learnt that much. 'Hurry up, won't you, I don't want to be late myself.'

Seamus grinned approvingly at me as he legged it into the bathroom. 'Good job you got me those suits back, Alex Wilde, or I'd be into the office smelling of you.'

Then he jumped into the shower room and slammed the door.

I sat on the bed, wondering what was wrong with this picture. Of course we had to get up and go to work, we couldn't have bunked off to feed the pretty ducks in Hyde Park. This wasn't the Greatest Film Moment of All Time, the bit in *Pretty Woman* where Edward leans over Vivien waving a Platinum Amex in her face, cooing, 'Wake up! Time to shop!' No, Seamus was a big wheeler dealer and the market waited for no man.

A horrible thought struck me in the face like a wet kipper.

My Whistles pink number was laying scrunched up on the floor. Unlike Seamus, I had no dry-cleaning conveniently here to solve the dress problem.

'Seamus!' I yelled through the bathroom keyhole.

'I'm trying to shower, love!' he shouted back, exasperatedly.

'I'm going to have to go home – I've got no clothes,' I yelled.

The water hissed off and Seamus stuck his dripping brown curls through the door. God, he looked adorable, like a sleek baby otter or something.

'Quick, be off with you,' he said lightly, 'you'll be terrible late in otherwise.' Then he leant forwards and gave me a drippy kiss on the cheek.

I struggled into the pink dress and rushed out of the door. Fortunately there was a taxi finishing his night shift right outside – who wants to wait on the Tube platform in the clothes they clearly wore last night, eh? I was too panicked to think about anything except getting home, leaning forwards on the back seat of the cab as though that would somehow make it go faster. I daren't say anything, the cabby was in a foul mood and would have deliberately started driving slower just to bug me. What would I wear? My blue suit? Too sexy? Something really dull, I decided. I caught a glimpse of myself in the rear-view mirror – red eyes, tangled hair, grey bags under the eyes big enough to take on holiday. Shit. Shit. I wasn't even going to have time for a shower, let alone pick up my own bloody car from Covent Garden.

I thrust a handful of notes at Mr Happy and bounded up the stairs, four at a time, to meet Gail coming out of the door in a floaty little cotton number, looking like the girl in the Timotei advert.

'You look like shit,' was her friendly greeting.

'Hey,' said Keisha, sitting curled on the sofa watching the *Big Breakfast*, 'someone got lucky last night, then?'

'Big party at work. Hen night,' I lied. Somehow I was wary of telling them everything. Somehow I felt Keisha wouldn't really understand.

'Sure,' Keisha muttered.

'Sex, sex, sex,' Bronwen sang happily, murdering the Beatles, 'Sex is all you need, sex is all you need.'

I ran into my bedroom and slammed the door, pulling off one outfit and pulling on another. Emergency measures were called for: thick make-up, greasy hair ripped into submission with brush and pulled back in a scrunchie – how I longed to be a Muslim chick and get a neat white headscarf, would they buy an Islamic conversion? probably not – and half a bottle of Dune to give me that seashore freshness, as opposed to that 'all night in man's arms with no wash' fragrance. The result wasn't too bad. Considering the material I had to work with.

So why did I feel so much like crying?

I obsessed about this all the way down to Bank station. Seamus had been sweet, hadn't he? Kissed me in the morning – I mean, he didn't have any time. But I was upset. He hadn't even suggested a quick one. And he'd taken the first shower, the bloody bastard. He didn't really care.

'AMAB, AMAB,' I hissed under my breath, 'bloody AMAB, All Men Are Bastards.'

What if he thought I was lousy? Too fat? Too cold? Too poor? Too unkempt? Too – well, let's face it, there were many candidates for what I could have been too much of. Or not enough. I was angry at Seamus, but that didn't stop me thinking it was still all my fault.

I marched into the office doors like Boudicca on the warpath.

'Man trouble?' asked the girl on Reception triumphantly.

I ignored her and shot straight upstairs. Jenny was back and there was a huge pile of new filing on my desk.

'You're better,' I said lamely.

'You're late,' Jenny observed. 'You look tired. You haven't been gallivanting about, I hope?'

'Chance would be a fine thing,' I said glumly.

'Well, Mr Mahon is – oh, hello, Mr Mahon.'

My heart stopped. There was Seamus, walking towards Jenny, looking immaculate, a friendly grin on his face. He gave me the briskest smile this side of an NHS nurse. 'Hi, ladies.'

'Hi, Sea—er, Mr Mahon,' I stammered.

Seamus glanced at me in a thunderous frown, then turned his most dazzling smile on to Jenny. 'So you're better, Jenny, it's not been the same without you. Why don't you come into my office and we'll go over the trip to Seville.'

The two of them turned away from me without a backwards glance. I was left alone at my desk with nothing but my files for company, and of course the flashing phone, already lit up like NATO headquarters in World War Three.

He didn't love me.

He didn't care.

I was useless in bed.

I listlessly flicked through my latest *Hello!*. Sure enough, Dolores Mahon was there, this time attending Ulrika Johnson's launch party for her biography. She was wearing what looked like a far more expensive and flattering version of my pink Whistles dress.

Outside my window it was raining. I picked up the phone dully. 'Good morning,' I said robotically, 'Hamilton Kane.'

Seamus was stuck in meetings all morning. Jenny was the only person he let near him. God, I just wanted to get out of there, to break down and start crying.

Keisha rang at eleven. 'You looked like death warmed up when you came in.'

'Hey, thanks for sharing.'

'What's the matter, was he that bad? Better to find out right away. And anyway, he's married.'

'Only technically,' I said sullenly. 'And you can talk. What about David, and that solicitor, and the copper, and You Know Who . . .'

Her latest had been a very famous, very married World Champion boxer who had waited outside her *Up and Running* office at seven a.m.

one Saturday morning, with the pathetic excuse that he wasn't waiting for her, he was just up training.

'Yeah. Well, never mind about that. We're all going to a big party on Saturday night. In Kensington, for Versace . . . Snowy fixed it.'

'Oh,' I grunted, the flicker of excitement that had sparked sputtering out.

'You can come, you'll find someone better than Seamus.'

I blinked back thick tears. Better than Seamus, right, Brad Pitt was going to be there and think how much prettier than Gwyneth Paltrow I was.

'Sure, why not.'

The phone trilled again. It was Snowy. 'Tell me you are coming, darling . . . I'm sure Keisha will lend you something to wear.'

'You hardly need me there.'

'But I do! You'll add some originality to the mix.'

'I will?'

'Oh yes, darling, all the people there are usually rich and glamorous, or beautiful, it can get very samy after a while. Do bring that director chappie, Oliver – oh, sorry, didn't last, did it? Well, anyway, do bring your man, it'll probably be a lovely change for him – must go, booked in for a facial . . .'

Great. So I was going to bring the poor, non-beautiful, non-glamorous colour to the event. And a man Snowy assumed would be a bricklayer or an accountant or something.

The phone went again. I nearly said, 'Piss off, Snowy,' but stopped myself just in time.

'Alex?' asked a familiar voice. 'Alex, is that you? Tom Drummond here. How are you?'

'I'm just great, Tom,' I said chirpily, and then I burst into tears.

Tom made me go outside and ring him from a payphone, so he could call me back. 'You are entitled to a lunch break, Alex. Honestly.'

I poured out the sorry story, or some of it anyway. Between sobs, I heard Tom being sympathetic. Not girly, but sympathetic.

'You're just too much of a romantic, Alex, you want the hearts and flowers all the time. Give the guy a chance . . . he'll probably ask you out again,' Tom said calmly.

'But he didn't want to go to work smelling of me.'

'He's not married, is he? Or you work with him?'

'Of course not!' I said indignantly.

'Oh good – for a second I thought you were going to be back to your old tricks.'

'What old tricks?' I demanded. At least being annoyed meant I wasn't snivelling any more.

'You know, Alex, the way you always fall for these charming bastards who don't value you, and make you feel small. You have fantasy crushes on fantasy people.'

'That's not true!' I said. Seamus was real, wasn't he? How much more real could that wavy black hair be, that lilting voice, that passionate stare!

'Well,' Tom sighed, 'what about that ludicrous director with the pink ties and the hair that needed cutting?'

'Oliver was an artist.'

'Nothing wrong with Oliver that a bloody good flogging and six months in the Marines wouldn't cure,' Tom grunted, as though he would personally like to be in charge of the flogging. Then he sighed again and devoted twenty minutes to making me feel better about myself.

'We *must* meet up for lunch,' he said when he'd finished.

'OK.' I actually wanted to go, I found. Tom was such a laugh, and he would be shovelling food into his mouth at such a rate that I would be bound to feel slim by comparison.

'Next week?' Tom asked hopefully. 'Don't suppose you're free?'

'I'll check my diary and give you a bell,' I managed, without cracking up. Free! My diary was as empty as Sister Wendy's love life.

I slunk back into the office and worked on my files. Tom made me at least feel things weren't my fault, but it didn't really help, how could it? The fact was that Seamus had been cold this morning and he hadn't talked to me all day.

Towards the end of the day Jenny came to find me.

'You must have done all right with Mr Mahon yesterday. He didn't have any complaints today.'

'No?' I asked eagerly.

'No,' said Jenny, 'he didn't mention you at all. Why do you look so depressed? Dear me, you've been very irritable today, Alexandra. Do you feel quite well?'

'Never better,' I said gloomily.

Jenny gave me a long stare. 'He hasn't been upsetting you, has he?

Mr Mahon I mean. He can be . . . bothersome. You know you can talk to me about it, if you wish.'

And do you know, I had an insane urge to confide in her. Actually to spill the beans. To Jenny Robins!

'He's been fine,' I told her. 'Really.'

'You do a good job, Alexandra,' Jenny said to my amazement. 'Don't put up with any nonsense. Anyway. Better get back to work. I have to leave early.'

'You do?' I said, gutted. I didn't want to face Seamus on my own. What would I say? He clearly didn't want to know.

'Yes, but Mr Mahon has said he can handle his own phones for the last ten minutes, so you just finish up in here.'

It was a godsend. When Jenny left, I stayed barricaded in my fortress, filing. Sometimes I would glance up and see Seamus watching me from inside his own office, as he talked into the receiver. I made sure I looked away. I didn't slink back to my own desk until I'd seen his driver arrive to take him off to the airport.

The tension drained out of me as I walked back into the office. No point being tense. Or excited. Everything was monochrome and it was going to stay that way for ever.

I arrived at my desk and stopped dead.

There was a single red rose laid across my computer keyboard. And a note.

'Can't wait to see you again. Keep thinking of me. Your not so secret admirer.'

God, isn't it good to be alive?

Chapter 10

It was wonderful. It was worth the wait. After he came back from Seville the next afternoon – bearing a bottle of Chanel No. 19 for me – Seamus acted like a dream come true. He sent Jenny off round the building so he could stand by my desk and talk. He smiled at me with that thousand-watt grin whenever the coast was clear. And he sent me e-mails: 'Can't imagine why I didn't think of this before.'

God, it was so weird to get little love letters in flashing neon, with 'bc' blinking at the side. Blind copy. Nobody could see what he was saying. It was like James Bond.

'Meet me at the flat tonight. We'll order in. P.S. Bring some clothes.'

He didn't go over the top. No sly glances when there were others around. But whenever he passed my desk, and saw the single red rose propped in a plastic cup, he winked. A gorgeous, slow wink that made me want to squirm on my chair.

I could barely work. I was so excited.

'Who's the rose from?' Kevin the postboy asked, crestfallen.

I could see Jenny hovering around, waiting for my reply. She kept glancing at Seamus, sealed inside the sanctuary of his office.

'Tom Drummond,' I replied, quick as a flash.

Jenny perked up. 'Tom Drummond? Of the Carrefour Trust? He's a *very* eligible young man. Lucky you, Alexandra, you must be the envy of all the girls in the City.'

'Oh, Tom's just a friend,' I protested, to Kevin's great joy and Jenny's disapproval. She gave my red rose an eloquent glance. Friends don't send those. But what did I care for her sniping? I was going to see Seamus tonight.

He was waiting at the flat when I got in. Delicious smells wafted from the kitchen: grouse, buttered spinach, blueberry and raspberry slump with French vanilla ice-cream.

'Take-away usually means Pizza Hut,' I breathed.

'Not when I'm eating with a beautiful girl,' Seamus said merrily, spooning warm blueberries into my mouth. I was still only able to manage a few bites. I was quivering with excitement, like a teenybopper at a Boyzone gig. Waves of lust were pulsing through me. I stoked the fires with his very expensive plum brandy. 'I've wanted to do that from the first moment I saw you . . . put something into your mouth.'

'Hmm,' I gasped. My nipples hardened up like I'd just stepped into a cold shower.

'You've got such kissable lips,' Seamus told me. Then he leant forwards and traced the line of them with his fingertip.

I got daring. I pressed my lips back on his fingers. Flicking over them with my tongue.

Seamus breathed in sharply and pushed his finger inside my mouth, so I sucked it, nervously because I've always thought that was kind of stupid.

Seamus went crazy. Like someone had flicked on a switch. He jumped up from the table, grabbed my hand and pulled me towards the bed. So fast, I didn't have time to stop it. To say, 'Hey, slow down, baby.' Or 'Maybe we could kiss each other's neck, very slowly.' I didn't want to spoil the moment.

He was in the throes of passion! You can't ruin a man's throes of passion. Or he throws you over. Like Justin Roberts, my ex-fiancé: I'm sure his darling wife Hannah never told him to cool it just a tad.

At least I wasn't worried about my knickers. On the way home to change I invested in some new silky scraps. And a tube of KY Jelly from Boots. Buying that was half-cool and half-embarrassing – like, yes! I *am* having sex! But also, yes! I do need lubrication!

What the hell, I've told you my theory on orgasms. At least I was a bit turned on now. Maybe Seamus could be the one, I thought dreamily as he scrambled out of his clothes. Even in the height of lust, he still stopped to fold them carefully over the back of the chair. Maybe Seamus could be the man to make it happen for me . . .

But it wasn't going to be tonight. He didn't last very long, but since sex isn't the big deal everybody pretends it is, maybe that didn't matter.

Afterwards he rolled me over on to my tummy and curled his arms round my neck, gazing romantically into my eyes until I thought I was going to die of pleasure.

'I've been waiting for you for ever,' Seamus said, 'never, never leave me.'

All that week was so perfect. Seamus gave me keys to his flat.

'How's that for commitment?' I boasted over the spoils of the chocolate run.

'Crap,' said Bronwen through a mouthful of Walnut Whip. 'He just wants the sex on tap.'

'Totally agree,' Keisha said coolly.

'You're just jealous,' I replied snippily. Seamus also gave me a mobile phone, so he could ring me without talking to Keisha. Keisha might start asking how Dolores and the kiddies were, just for the hell of it. She loved stirring things. I didn't want anyone to get in the way of this marvellous romance.

'I can't believe he prefers you to Dolores,' Gail said, annoyed. It was a triumphant thrill to have Gail jealous of me! What a change!

'He's trapped in his marriage. For the sake of the children,' I explained eagerly.

Keisha snorted. 'Oh, please, girlfriend. The guy is a class-A jerk. You need to get another pair of glasses, those rose-tinted ones are getting grimy.'

I ignored her. Seamus was typing out Yeats poems and 'bc'ing them to me on the computer. We met most nights and sometimes at lunchtime. It was all so dramatic, I felt like my soul was on fire.

The best thing about it was, I no longer felt left out. I was Cinderella now and I was going to the ball! When you're single, the whole world seems to divide into couples. They plague London, like pigeons or bluebottles. They stand in the doorways of pubs, lip-locked on each other for hours. They neck in the cinema when you're trying to watch a film. They even ruin nice Sunday walks in the park, sprawling on the grass with their cheap bottles of white wine, looking like the most romantic thing since Romeo and Juliet.

And they say 'we'. All the bloody time. 'What are you doing over the weekend?' 'We're taking the kids to the seaside.' 'We're going down to the country.' 'We're going to stay in and have mind-blowing sex all day and night, broken only by declarations of eternal love, while you sit on your own moping.' OK, I made that last one up, but that's what it sounds like.

Next to 'we', 'I' sounds so pathetic.

Not very liberated, but that's just how I feel.

But now I was part of a 'we'. I could think about 'us'. And my 'we' didn't incorporate a criminal, a homosexual, a faithless fiancé, or a cheating American bastard. So that was a nice change. Seamus gave me presents – perfume he liked, sexy lingerie. We ate on our own all the time, in sweet out-of-the-way places, or in the flat.

I was in heaven.

'So what are you going to wear to the party, darling?' Snowy asked us on Saturday morning.

She'd come over with a bottle of vintage Perrier-Jouet, 'To get you in the mood.' To show off, I thought sourly, but the other girls all loved it.

'Purple dress from Granny Takes a Trip,' Bronwen said simply. 'Bovver boots.'

'Nicole Farhi suit,' Gail announced.

'Alexander McQueen jacket, Galliano dress,' Keisha said superbly, trumping everyone. For Versace, she would bring out the big guns. And besides, Lennox Collins, the Star Boyfriend of the moment, would probably be there since he loved flash designer stuff. All the boxers got it for free. Keisha would spend three hours in the hairdresser's this afternoon, just so she could shine next to the deep red suits Collins always wore to match his fiery red hair and blue eyes.

'I'm going to be boring. A little Gucci silk number,' said Snowy, in the smug voice that said it probably cost more than we made in a year. 'And you, Alex? What will you be wearing?'

'My new Joseph suit,' I said proudly. Seamus had bought it for me, it was a funky thing in shiny brown leather with flat front trousers. I'd dropped five pounds since I started seeing him, through not being able to eat.

'This'll encourage you to keep it off,' Seamus told me, grinning. I blushed. I knew I had been a greedy pig in the past, but that was going to change. Even on the chocolate run I now made the others get me a Halo or a Flyte. I was determined to get to Dolores-style levels of thinness, not that Seamus slept with Dolores, but even so.

'You must make good money in your typing job,' Gail said bitchily.

'I'm getting a raise soon,' I lied.

'Hey, do you think a purple – er – hippy thing is *quite* the right outfit?' Snowy asked Bronwen.

'Dick likes it,' Bronwen said defensively.

Dick was the big love of Bronwen's life. They'd been going out for two years now, and she longed for him to ask her to move in with him. We thought he was a total loser: he was as straight as Bronwen was screwy and a real user. Dick was a bank manager, with a nice, neat little flat in Bayswater and a shiny blue Volvo. He had Bron over all the time, cooking for him, cleaning his house and ironing his shirts like some sort of daily help, except that she had to fuck the boss as well. Dick liked Bronwen to do more and more wild stuff, which she hated, but did anyway. He wanted her to go out to dinner in short skirts and no panties, or wriggle out of her bra while they were in a cab. She had to watch porno movies with him and ring him up from her office and talk dirty to him.

'It makes me feel so filthy,' she told me sometimes, tears prickling her eyes. 'Really cheap.'

'Tell him to go fuck himself,' Keisha said furiously. Keisha wasn't the best person to talk to about Dick, because she would a) suggest she call some Yardie gangsters she knew to go round and beat the shit out of him or b) get enraged with Bronwen herself for being such a wimp.

'I love him,' Bronwen sobbed. 'We had such a fight. He told me he'd met this girl and he wanted her to come back with us. I said no way, and he said, how did I know I wouldn't like it if I've never tried it?'

'He's sick. Please tell me you said no,' I begged.

'I did, I couldn't face it.'

Keisha stormed off in disgust before she said something really bad.

'I wanted to please him so much,' Bronwen sobbed, 'but I couldn't do it, do you think I was being a selfish bitch?'

'Is that what he said?'

'He said it was his major fantasy. If I loved him I would do it.'

'Oh, Bron,' I said, pulling her close for a hug. 'You can do so much better. You could have anyone. Look at all the boys that turn up here for you.'

'But I don't want them, I want Dick,' she wept.

What an appropriate bloody name, I thought but didn't say. I mean, what could I tell her? Dick was as good for her as syphilis, but how could I advise her? One ex in prison, another living with a man . . . at the time you know they're screwed up, but only in your head.

And what woman listens to her head when her heart is talking?

Dick the dick was going to be there tonight. I hoped he would treat Bronwen properly, and not just use her as the antidote to his staid boringness.

'I'm going to meet you there. I'm going round to Tony's for cocktails first, and he's bringing me into town,' Gail said triumphantly. 'I just wish I could get him to switch to organic champagne.'

She was going great guns with Tony. Evidently his income level was satisfactory for her: she liked the BMW and the townhouse and his plans for a country cottage next year. I was pleased for her. However much she bugged me, she was my sister. I wanted her to be comfortably married, since that was what she wanted. For myself, however, without those delicious butterflies and heart palpitations, it was all worthless.

'Well, some dear friends are sending a limo for us,' Snowy said sweetly. At which Gail looked a bit annoyed, since she couldn't back out of Tony's BMW now.

We arrived at the hotel nicely lubricated. Snowy had delicately chewed half an 'e' with Bronwen, and the two of them were glassy eyed and giggling madly. They needed to be, I thought sourly, with these bloody Arabs leering at us on the back seat. The limo was long and white and tacky, big enough to have its own postcode, and four of Snowy's friends, swarthy guys in very expensive suits, were sprawled across the leather. One of them laughed a lot and said, 'Preeety, preety,' all the time. The other one had his clammy hand parked firmly on Snowy's knee, and even though you could see the sweat stain on her Fogal tights, she didn't attempt move him off her. A third was pawing at Bronwen and being slapped away like a bothersome fly, but Bron was high and didn't scream at him to drop dead, like she should have done.

Keisha and I were left to deal with the last little charmer, a pudgy bunch of dough with a few dark strands combed across a glittering bald forehead. He muttered things in Arabic and giggled in a pitch so high you'd assume someone had sliced off his balls, except for the way he kept trying to kiss us. Although after my first squeal of repulsion he mainly tried to bother Keisha. The first time, she scowled, 'Fuck off, Fatso.' The second time, she poured her chilled champagne over his lap. So he sat there looking like he'd wet himself, giggling madly and just staring at us.

'Wanna share a cab home?' Keisha asked me.

I nodded fervently.

'Oh, darlings, you're so boorring,' Snowy drawled, sniffing a thick line of cocaine off the back of Prince Charming's hairy hand.

I was double glad to get out of that car. Snowy waltzed in with her retinue of leering men, smiling full-watt at the doorman as he scrambled to lift aside the rope for her. He checked my invite, probably a bit disappointed to find it valid, and then deigned to let us follow her.

The party was already in full swing. I recognised a bunch of faces from the *News of the World*: a couple of *EastEnders*, Dannii Minogue and Tara Palmer-Tompkinson. Definitely a b-list crowd. But what the hell, I was thrilled anyway. So many designer colours and tight little black numbers; about the only person who really stood out was Bronwen. Keisha moved off in search of Lennox, and Bron and I settled in to get plastered.

Funny how you don't notice how much you're drinking at swish parties. The silent waiters are always ghosting past and refilling your glass once it's a centimetre shy of the brim. So you're gulping it down but it only feels like you've had one drink. Well, that's my excuse, anyway.

Twenty minutes into it Bron and I were well away.

'Look at that,' I sniggered, pointing out a blue-rinsed matron in one corner wreathed in feathers. 'Twenty crows did not die in vain.'

'Or that.' Bron giggled madly at Peter Stringfellow and the young woman draped over his arm, wearing nothing but sheer plastic with butterfly motifs plastered over tits and crotch. 'Is it OAPs' day out? Or maybe someone told her it was fancy dress, and you were supposed to come as a condom.'

'Well well well,' said an obnoxious voice from somewhere above my ear. 'What are you two ladies whispering about, bless you?'

I gave Dick the dick a wintry smile. Bronwen looked up like she'd been electrocuted. Her misty-eyed adoration made me want to puke.

'You girlies, always giggling in corners with your female secrets,' Dick said patronisingly. 'All about boyfriends and babies, I expect?'

'Sort of. We were actually talking about period flow. And men with premature ejaculation,' I snarled.

Dick paled while Bronwen shot me an imploring look.

'Come on, Bron,' he said cursorily. 'Alex is doing her ball-busting thing again. No wonder you don't have a boyfriend.'

'That's where you're wrong, actually. And a man who can have his balls busted by a woman wasn't much of a man in the first place!' I shouted after them, but Dick had dragged Bronwen into the crowd.

'On your own again?' It was Gail, waltzing past with the beefy Tony on one arm. He got ruddier and ruddier whenever I saw him. 'You really ought to try to mix more.'

Annoyed at being caught by myself, I thrust through the crowd looking for Keisha. I found her about ten seconds later, puffing on a fag under the shade of a giant palm tree festooned with golden bells.

She looked upset. OK, she looked very slightly, almost undetectably to the naked eye, perturbed. But that meant serious trouble.

'What's the matter with men?'

'Why don't you ask me something simple, like the recipe for world peace?' I asked.

'Bloody Lennox. He wants me to move in with him.'

'The bastard.'

'No, Alex, God, get real. He says he hates it that I've got other men. He wants us to be together more often.'

'Just tell him that you're not ready for that kind of commitment.'

'I did. He said if he wasn't enough for me I could fuck right off.'

'How poetic. Look, Keisha—'

'I don't want to talk about it. I just want to know why they can't just go with the flow. Men, they all want to trap you, it's just all or nothing.'

Keisha shook her lovely head and got up, stomping off towards the exit. I sighed but didn't follow her. She hated people around her in this mood.

Snowy glided up to me. 'Darling! Have you seen who's here? Seamus Mahon!'

'Really?' I lit up like the Christmas lights on Oxford Street.

'Yes,' Snowy purred, 'he's just over there. Kissing his wife. Aren't they the most adorable couple?'

Chapter 11

I didn't panic.

For at least thirty seconds.

I kept calm. I told myself, don't overreact. Don't react at all. That's what she wants you to do, the glossy-haired witch.

'You must have got the wrong guy,' I said shakily.

'No.' Snowy arched an eyebrow. I wondered if she knew – I mean, I hadn't told her, but Gail sucked up to her like a vacuum cleaner.

'Seamus is in Paris,' I announced. 'He's got an important meeting tonight.'

'Clearly not as important as polishing his wife's tonsils,' Snowy purred. 'I mean, that *fabu*lous creature in the silver Prada shift is definitely Dolores, I'd know her anywhere – such a sweetheart – and they *told* me the man with her was her husband.'

'Can't be. She must be having an affair,' I stammered.

Snowy laughed. 'Get real, Alex! She'd hardly tongue-wrestle another man in front of *le tout Londres*.'

'What?' I snapped.

'The whole of town, darling! No, that's a married kiss, isn't it thrilling to see passion can last past the altar?'

'What does he look like?'

'Hmmm – skinny, black curly hair. Can't see the face, because it's plastered on to Dolores. Rather tacky brown suit, looks like an Ozwald Boateng. Bit of a dandy . . .'

'Seamus isn't a dandy,' I said, sick with fear because it did sound a lot like him.

'Well, come and see. You tell me,' Snowy laughed. 'If Dolores *is* having an affair, what juicy goss that would be!'

For a second the fear was replaced by a wild hope. Seamus had sworn to me he was going to Paris, because I'd been asking all week if we could go out tonight. And Dolores Mahon having a snog in front of the cameras – God! Wouldn't that be grounds for div—

I stopped dead. No grounds for divorce there. You didn't get divorced for a lip-lock on your own husband.

Dolores and Seamus were right in front of me. She was shimmering in silver like some immaculately groomed, wafer-thin mermaid. And Seamus, *my* Seamus, the love of my life, my saviour, was standing next to her. His mouth locked on hers. One hand caressing her waist, the other absently stroking her high, pert little ass. His body language was so entwined with her they might as well have been Siamese twins.

'Well?' Snowy asked silkily.

'Mmm, yeah.' Amazing how my voice could work when my brain was closing down. 'That's the boss man.'

Seamus took his mouth off Dolores for a second, but he was only coming up for air. In a gesture that twisted my guts around my heart like a rope, Seamus took Dolores's head in his hands, her platinum curls bubbling over his fingers, and covered her lips in tiny, butterfly kisses.

He does that to *me*, I thought in outrage. That's one of my favourite things he does! I could hardly believe it myself. It seemed everything was happening in a sick sort of slow motion.

I didn't hear Keisha come up behind us until she tapped Snowy on the shoulder. 'Mohammed says he's been looking for you.'

'Must dash, Alex, love, but I'll be back – you can introduce me to Seamus, and I'll introduce you to Dolores.' Snowy giggled. 'Fair swap?'

Keisha's hand tightened on my shoulder. 'Look, I said he was a bastard. Better to find out now.'

'Better to find out now? To see my baby practically fucking another woman?'

'Alex.' Keisha sighed. 'She's his wife. *You're* another woman.'

Now I was crying, not delicate little tears, great big heaving sobs and salty floods gushing down my cheeks and streaking my foundation. 'But he's meant to be in Paris. And his marriage is dead.'

'I wouldn't be writing up the tombstone, hon,' Keisha said softly.

I caught a glimpse of myself in one of the mirrored pillars. Thank God my mascara was waterproof, but my eyes were as red as a rabbit's and my make-up was striped like a Brighton deckchair. My nose would have done Rudolf proud. And at that moment, something clicked in Seamus's head, because he sort of froze, and then turned his gaze towards us very slowly.

He saw me. Emotions swept across his face. The first was horror, the second was guilt and the third was panic.

Dolores looked down at him. 'Sugar,' she whispered loudly, 'who's that girl making an exhibition of herself? Do you think she's drunk?'

Keisha was opening her mouth to deliver God knows what, but I kicked her in the shin before she could get it out.

I wanted to scream. To hit her. To hit him. To have the earth swallow me up, to run away – something, anything – but I couldn't move. I lay there like a hedgehog caught in the headlights. Paralysed.

Then Seamus said, 'Come on, darlin',' and dragged Dolores away through the thickness of the crowd.

Keisha pulled me into the bathroom and flung tissues at me. 'Quick, mop yourself up.'

'I can't,' I sobbed, 'I want to go home.'

'Not a chance.' Quite brutally, Keisha started dabbing away at my cheeks. 'What make-up have you got?' She rummaged around inside my handbag, but produced only a concealer and some lipstick.

'I left it at home. Can't I use yours?'

'Oh, good one,' Keisha said sarcastically, patting her own ebony cheek. 'Somehow I don't think my Iman Dark Mahogany is going to be a match. We'll just have to make do.'

She painted and dabbed and restored my face, if not to attractiveness, to some semblance of decency.

'Seriously. I can't take it.'

'Well, you're going to seriously have to. You're not giving him the satisfaction. And what would Olivia White say?'

That decided me. Feeling like I wanted to puke, I headed out into the throng, muttering Shakespeare. ' "Once more unto the breach, dear friends, once more; or close the wall up with our English dead . . ." '

'Come again?' Keisha demanded. 'Here, drink this.' She grabbed a kir royale and thrust it into my hand. I stiffened. I could see Dolores again; one arm firmly threaded through Seamus's elbow, she was dragging him in my direction. I didn't want to look, so why was I staring? It was like some awful road accident you just couldn't take your eyes off.

'Laugh,' Keisha snarled. I gave her the Look of Death. 'Laugh,' she insisted, as I ignored her. Dolores was bearing down upon us like a Sherman tank.

I burst into a peal of laughter, almost spilling my champagne.

Keisha had tickled me unmercifully at the side of my stomach. Cheating cow. But now Keisha was giggling, watching me try to save the champagne, and the two of us actually were cracking up.

'Hello, Seamus,' said Keisha loudly before I could stop her, 'I'm Keisha, Alex's flatmate. She's told me so much about you.'

'She has?' asked Seamus, looking frightened. 'Er – this is my wife, Dolores. Alex works for me. How's yourself, Alex?'

You'd have thought that would be it. I'd puddle, I'd break down, I'd weep like a weeping willow watching Gareth Southgate's England penalty whilst chopping an onion.

But you'd be wrong.

Something else about being a woman. You find you have reserves of strength in front of your enemies. How dare Dolores Mahon look so bloody smug, with her servants and her *haute couture* and *my Seamus*? I thought furiously. I was buggered if I'd let her see me upset. I could almost feel my sinews stiffening. *Hey*, I thought nastily, *I've been fucking your husband, so you can wipe that smile off your face.*

OK. OK. I know I've lost your sympathy now, but I'm trying to be honest and that's what I thought, at the time. They say violence doesn't solve anything, but they're wrong there: it would have made me feel a hell of a lot better. I wanted to jump up and slap that careful make-up job right off those sculptured cheekbones.

'I'm great. I just split up with my boyfriend, earlier.'

'Some men think they can get away with anything,' Keisha added, staring at Seamus very hard.

'Oh, don't be too hard on him,' said Dolores sweetly. 'Maybe he has an explanation.'

I couldn't look at Seamus, but my heart did a skip a beat when he added urgently, 'I'm sure he has.'

'Alex doesn't have time to listen to his explanations,' said Keisha superbly, 'she's going out with Lennox Collins.' And before I could splutter anything in protest, Keisha smiled brightly at the Mahons and dragged me into the throng.

'Now you can leave,' she said proudly. 'And on Monday, you just ignore him. Do what you do.'

'You're kidding, you think I'm going into work on Monday?'

Keisha looked at me like I was an alien from the Planet Zog. 'Don't be a jerk, of course you are. God, Alex, you're such a drama queen. So you had a bit of a horizontal jig with an asshole, well, welcome to the club!'

'Look, he said he had an explanation,' I said limply. I braced myself.

'An *explanation*!' Keisha roared. 'Suuure, honey, let me save you some time! The *explanation* is that he wants to screw his wife and his secretary at the same time. You can't even give him points for originality.'

'He sent me poems on the computer. He was so romantic – didn't I tell you how we fed the ducks in the park?'

'Well, excuse me. I was wrong, he's obviously Prince Valiant come to save you.'

I shut up. Because secretly, that's exactly what I thought he was. Keisha just didn't understand that Seamus was special. And if he said there was some explanation, then there was. I trusted him. That's what love's all about, isn't it? Trust.

We threaded our way through the crowd, looking for Bronwen. She should have been easy to spot, in her clumpy boots and purple concoction. I sniffed the air for the pungent whiff of grass. But no luck.

Snowy was laughing in a corner, surrounded by men. Her nipples were winking through the pure silk of her dress. Mohammed and his pals looked absolutely entranced.

'Someone's having a good time,' I scowled.

'Well, Snowy's a party girl,' Keisha said neutrally. 'Come on. Let's get out of here.'

We took a night bus home.

Keisha dragged me upstairs and made me change before I started crying. 'No point getting your suit filthy, at least you got one good thing out of the bastard,' she said. That set me off again.

'He's not a bastard. I bet she made him do it.'

'Oh yeah, she made him jump all over her. Alex, he's seen around town with lots of women.'

'What do you mean?' I said with horror.

'I saw him in Quaglino's with this very slim brunette. She was wearing an Azzedine Alaïa. Really stunning plum thing with a V-cut neck and—'

'I don't care about the dress!' I shrieked. 'Maybe it was a business dinner.'

'I dunno. Do people hold hands and play footsie during business dinners?'

A dreadful memory ghosted up at me. A vague sighting of a stunning girl with a Louise Brooks bob, waving goodbye to Seamus outside our building.

'And I saw him in Harvey Nicks last Tuesday. Buying underwear,' Keisha added, 'sorry.'

Last Tuesday he was meant to be in Hull. For a conference. He hadn't given me any underwear later.

'Why didn't you tell me?' I gasped. Dancing visions of Dolores-like babes, with every hair colour down to punk green, except my own mousy shade, gripped my heart. How many of the sleek, moneyed bitches there must be in the world. With more exciting jobs than mine. Younger. Thinner. Better in bed.

'You didn't want to hear it,' Keisha said flatly.

This was true. I didn't specially want to hear it now.

'He sounded pretty upset tonight,' I ventured, stammering.

She laughed. 'Yup. Definitely gutted.'

'So maybe he wants to tell me that he'll change his ways, that he'll—'

'Oh right. And Gazza's going to become a feminist,' Keisha spat. 'I'm going to order a pizza.'

'Double cheese. Spicy pork. Pepperoni and anchovies and prawns,' I said morosely. Desperate times called for desperate measures.

The pizza arrived, and Keisha lit up a stream of fags and opened one of her boyfriends' magnums of champagne. She had bought it for his birthday and it was sitting in our fridge, waiting for a special occasion.

'What's he going to say?'

'Who gives a fuck?' asked Keisha, as she poured the champagne into a Mr Tickle mug. 'Cheers.'

We got companionably hammered. There's really nothing like a bottle of wine and a pig-out with your girlfriends. Or girlfriend. Snowy was on the Peruvian marching powder, so she'd probably hit Browns after the party where she would of course be swept upstairs to the VIP room. Gail would be back at Tony's flat, cooking or tidying, arranging flowers and otherwise trying to show off her wifely qualities.

'AMAB. Bloody AMAB,' Keisha said, tearing apart another slice of garlic bread and slugging down champagne. 'Can you believe Lennox pushing me like that? I hate famous men.'

'You love famous men, as often as possible.'

'I hate them,' Keisha ignored me, 'they think they fine, girlfriend, and they want you to do all the work.'

Oh no, she was lapsing into black American street slang. Keisha got this from Ricki Lake and Sally Jesse Raphael. We would watch these together all the time before my cruel parents forced me into the workplace. Our favourites were the ones where black American women would shriek at each other. Keisha rocked back and forth on the sofa squealing and clapping her hands. 'My man be with me twenty-four seven, he be givin' me all the play, he don't be wantin' no two-bit hoochie with holes in her stockings!' 'Girlfriend, you be frontin' like that – he is sending me flowers, he be buying me flash rocks, 'cause I'm all that.' 'You be ten cents a pop and I got a dollar!' 'You be a ten-buck ho with a two-buck haircut!' It was hilarious. Some of these girls had their front teeth missing and others of them weighed two hundred pounds, and they were still screaming at the top of their lungs how fine they were.

Keisha would turn her blackness off and on as she wanted to. Normally she was colour blind, but show her a cute American black male and it was 'Hello, my brother,' before you could say 'Spare me.' She once got taken home to Mum by a Very Famous Footballer and his mum threw her out of the kitchen because she didn't know the first thing about creole chicken, yams or red beans and rice. It was a disaster.

'I don't cook, darling, people cook for me,' Keisha said superbly, but she had to dump the footballer because she was too embarrassed to go round to his house ever again.

'Why do you keep dating these losers?' Keisha slurred.

'Why do you keep running away from relationships?'

'I just want to have some fun. They keep pushing,' Keisha said miserably.

'Look, thas' no' true,' I objected. 'Yorra *woman*. Women want love.'

'Women – need – men – like – fish – needs – bicycle,' stated Keisha, poking me in the chest after every word.

'Women need men like fish need water,' I said, and then I burst out crying.

'He's no' worth it. 'Sss a scumbag,' Keisha said firmly.

I didn't say anything. I knew Seamus must have an answer. I held on to that. All that love must have meant something, the champagne was making that so clear!

The door creaked open. It was Bronwen, soaked to the bone and in floods of tears.

'He's left me. He made me pose for all these pictures with my clothes off,' she sobbed, 'and then he said I was a frigid bitch and he was leaving me anyway!'

Chapter 12

'Jesus,' said Keisha, suddenly sober.

I blinked at Bronwen. It was like a lance jabbing through the numbing fog of the booze. Pain came back, waving a spiteful hello – hers and mine: How selfish. For a second I was just glad nobody could read my mind: that my flatmate's telling me something like this and I'm thinking about Seamus and how badly I want him to be mine.

'He took me back home and made me get undressed – he was kissing me everywhere,' Bronwen sobbed. 'Then he – he – got out this camera. I said I didn't want to but he told me to relax, it was just for him, because he loved me and I was so gorgeous.'

Now I was not thinking about Seamus. Now I was angry, so bloody angry I could have put this asshole in thumbscrews. But it also struck me how someone like Bronwen would actually do this. It's one of the great shitty things about being a girl. They never mention that when they talk about the joy of motherhood and everything else. Or even when they mention labour and periods and thrush and the menopause. 'Being a woman means you will some day fall in love. This will surgically remove your spine from your body. You will talk tough but if push comes to shove you will also do absolutely anything to hang on to your man.'

'How many pictures?' Keisha asked flatly.

'I don't know,' Bronwen choked. 'Lots. It was so quick – he's got one of those big pro cameras with a flashlight and he was just clicking. So fast.'

'So why was he angry?'

'I kept trying to close my legs. He kept forcing them open, so I started to cry – I couldn't help it,' Bronwen wept pathetically. 'Then he got so mad. He went upstairs and took my stuff out of the bathroom and put it in a carrier bag. Made me give him back the keys . . .'

At this point she dissolved and couldn't say another word. Keisha went into the kitchen while I sat there rubbing her shoulders. Keisha came back with some brandy and made Bronwen swallow it, so she was coughing and choking, but it restored her a little bit.

'He said I was a frigid cow and he was tired of it. And I was too skinny for good sex anyway, he hated scrawny women. He knew – he knew I loved doing all those things really because I was that sort of girl and he was tired of me playing coy, so I could just fuck off. I begged him to stop and think about what he was saying, but he just laughed at me.'

She put her head in her hands. 'And then I told him to give me the film, and he laughed again and said at least it would be good to have something to show to his mates,' and then she sprang up and rushed to the loo, didn't even have time to shut the door before she was puking her guts out.

Keisha and I stared at each other. Ten pints of coffee couldn't have sobered me up any faster. I'd never been quite as close to Bron as I am to Keisha, but right now I felt like she was flesh and blood. I couldn't have been any angrier if this guy had done it to Gail.

We think we're so in control, us 'nineties chicks, that nothing like this could ever happen to us. Bronwen is a feminist like me – not an Andrea Dworkin nutcase, but into her independence and workplace equality. So how, *how* could she have been in love with this abusive bastard?

If Bronwen had dropped Dick, she might have been able to cope with it. We'd been trying to talk her into leaving him for six months at least. And sometimes we even got her to say yeah, she knew he wasn't treating her right . . . I'd hoped she was thinking about making a break. Cutting him off. There were enough guys ringing up hopefully for Bronwen all the time, but they were all from her world – straight fashion designers, photographers, models, bassists. It didn't take a shrink to see that there was some kind of screwed-up thing going on with Dick. Why would a girl like Bronwen, who looked like she'd time-travelled here from Haight Ashbury in San Francisco, circa 1968, go for a bank manager? Who drove a Volvo? And kept his pension fund up to date and his suits dry-cleaned? She must be looking for a father figure. Or stability, or some goddamn thing. But the trouble was, she'd picked a first-class perverted prick to fixate on.

I know. Thank you, Dr Alexandra Freud. But really, man. What did it say about Bronwen's childhood? I probably didn't want to know.

'OK, that's it,' Keisha said quietly. This was ominous, because when Keisha's quiet she's really dangerous. 'I'm gonna call Stella. Her cousin Rashid knows some boys who can sort this out.'

'Wait, wait,' I said hurriedly. I wasn't against the idea of some gangsters kneecapping Dick, as far as that went, but the idea of Keisha banged up in Holloway on five to ten for GBH wasn't that great. 'Let's call him and see if we can get him to see sense.'

'You're mad.'

But I was already dialling. He was number one on the speed dial on Bronwen's phone. And she was still in the loo heaving up everything she'd eaten in the last month.

'Yes?' The clipped tones maddened me.

'Dick, this is Alex Wilde. I live with Bronwen Evans.'

'Yeah, I know who you are. Forget it, I'm not taking her back. She's a whiny bitch, and it's over. You can tell her I said so.'

For a second I was too dumbstruck to reply.

'And don't bother calling here again, OK?' he drawled. 'It's none of your business. I don't need Bronwen hanging around like some godawful puppy and I don't want interference from her ball-busting friends. Good night.'

'Wait! You can talk to me or you can talk to the police,' I spat, and now I'd got his attention.

'What the bloody hell are you talking about?'

'About those pictures, you sick fuck,' I snarled, and it felt so good to swear at him, so good to get furious. 'Bronwen's going to press charges of blackmail unless you give us the film right now.'

'Nothing to do with blackmail.'

'That's not how we see it. We'd all testify against you. And make sure it got maximum publicity. Your bank would love that, wouldn't they, Dick the dick? Bank Manager was Sicko Pervert? Sounds like a *News of the World* splash to me, mate. It'd be good to see you humiliated, you wanker. Better to see you in the dock.'

'The police wouldn't be interested. She consented,' said Dick, but he sounded less sure of himself now. Almost scared, in fact. Keisha was watching me with rounded eyes, and she liked what she heard.

'That's not what she says. And I've got three witnesses here. And the police are very interested, sunshine. Guess who I've spoken to?

WPC Mary Baker and WPC Susan Embury. They run the sex-crimes unit round here. They hate blokes like you. Oh, and the DCI is also a woman. Eve Mensch. So, you fancy your chances, go right ahead.'

What a crock, but he was buying it. Women in uniform must be this guy's worst nightmare. He knew how any woman would react to this. I could almost hear the wheels slowly turning in his tiny hamster brain. 'If we come round now and you hand over every bloody thing, we'll forget about it as long as you stay away from Bronwen. Not for your sake. But we want you out of her life. You stink like your own bad breath.'

'OK.' He sounded as limp as his handshake.

'Good. We'll have a guy over in half an hour. Don't go anywhere, lover boy,' I said, and hung up on him.

'Wow, that was amazing. You actually sounded like you got some balls, girlfriend,' Keisha approved. She moved off to summon Rashid. I imagined that scene for a moment, this big, buff guy with muscles on his muscles and huge dreadlocks, banging on Dick's door. Rashid would crush his camera underfoot and rip the place apart. And Dick, who likes to dabble in the counterculture, would just plain shit himself when its avenging angels came down.

I went back into the drawing room to hug Bronwen, who'd come out of the loo now, her face as white as ice-cream. She looked like she'd been bled out.

'It's over, isn't it? And those pictures—'

'We're on that.'

'You're not going to hurt him?' and her face twisted with such concern for Dick that it broke my heart clean open.

'No, I promise. We're just going to destroy the negatives. Bron, please please see he was horrible to you.'

'I know, but I want him so bad.'

'Sex with him was lousy, wasn't it?'

'But only because we liked different things.' You can say that again, I thought.

'Bronwen, you were always coming back from his place in tears. I know you maybe don't see it like that, but it's true. He didn't make you happy.'

'I just want to turn back the clock, I want it to be the start of tonight, then things could be different,' she wept, and there was really nothing else to do except put her to bed with more brandy. At least she was out like a light. Crying does that for you: it wears you out faster than a marathon run. Bronwen would sleep the sleep of the dead now.

I mean, I should know. I'm an expert.

Keisha gave me a quick kiss and said she was going over to pick Rashid up. Someone should be there supervising who knew Bronwen's stuff. I agreed with that, so I was on my own in the flat.

About one hour later, I was still sitting on the sofa when Snowy came back in across the hall. Two male voices laughed as they followed her into her flat. I felt a stab of annoyance: nobody should be having a good time this evening.

In my own room, I thought about Seamus again as I turned out the lights. I halfheartedly resolved not to let him walk all over me, but I didn't really mean it. Maybe Keisha was wrong about those other women. She wasn't the one getting all his attention, she didn't know how he could make you feel. And it was totally unfair to compare him to Dick.

My last thought before going to bed was that I could win him back. He sounded panicked, right? 'I'm sure he has' – got an explanation? And if Seamus could prove he'd changed, well then. Things could be different.

Bronwen was better the next morning. Or at least she was together. She had that terrible listless look about her, you know the one, when your life has fallen apart but you still have to live it. She skipped breakfast. Food would be tasting like dust right now, and the world would be grey from sky to horizon.

'Are you OK?' I asked gently.

She shook her head. 'I'll get through it, though.'

'It's Sunday. Take the day off.'

'Can't. Got a shoot with Trevor Leighton today. Anyway, it wouldn't help.'

It wouldn't, so I didn't push it any harder. Keisha arrived back ten minutes after Bron had left, grinning madly.

'Girl, you should have seen it. He nearly fainted when I got there with Rashid. He hands over the film, and Rashid says, "Let's check the camera." So he gives that up and Rashid drops it on the floor and stamps it into pieces, goes, "Whoops." Dick didn't say a word,' Keisha pealed with laughter.

'I hope you went through the place with a fine-tooth comb.'

'We went through it with a bulldozer. Rashid smashed every-thing up. It looked like he'd been burgled when we left. The TV, the video . . .'

'Won't he go to the police?'

'You must be joking. He almost wet himself, he was so frightened. And Rashid wore gloves. He won't do shit. When we left, Rashid shook his hand and crushed so hard he moaned, there was this huge welt all along the side.' She chuckled, hugely pleased. 'I told him he was right, Bronwen was frigid, and that's why she'd bothered with him. Because his dick was so small she hardly noticed it, and he came so quick it was all over in thirty seconds.'

We smiled at each other.

The good feeling lasted almost the whole way to the office on Monday morning. When I reached Hamilton Kane I no longer felt twenty feet tall, the Avenging Angel of Womankind. Now I felt two feet tall. The dumb broad Seamus had screwed over. And I was late. But Jenny didn't seem to mind.

'I don't why you're even here, Alex,' she said in astonishment. 'Mr Mahon told me he'd given you the day off.'

'Oh.' I pressed my fingertips to my temples, my mind racing. Seamus must have assumed I'd be too upset even to come in. 'Yeah, he did say something like that. I forgot. I just don't want to get too behind.'

I saw Seamus inside his glass office, holding forth to some brokers. He paused for a second and looked at me, then gave me a rueful little grin like a boy caught raiding the chocolate tin.

I felt deflated. Didn't he care, didn't he realise how serious this was?

I sat down at my computer and switched it on absently. I felt a compelling urge to find out the truth, no matter how hard it was. I had a feeling that I wasn't going to like what I found, but I had to do it all the same. Like picking at a scab or scratching a gnat bite. It only makes it worse, but how do you fight the compulsion?

I tap-tapped on my keyboard. Pulling up dates and notes. Double-checking against my own desk diary. When he told me he was abroad, or away at conferences. I had eight dates to check with Jenny.

'Mr Mahon wanted me to log his movements for the travel office – was he away these nights, or am I going mad?'

Jenny scanned my list in amazement. 'You're going mad, Alexandra. Who on earth told you this? He went to Seville on the eighteenth and there is no Hull conference – why on earth would one of our partners be in Hull?'

Why indeed? I reddened. 'I'm so stupid, I've probably got the wrong month completely. Never mind.'

Jenny was watching me suspiciously now, but I couldn't care. We were on the net so the quants could check the press database for clues to companies they were tracking, but I was Sherlock Holmes in a skirt today. I typed in Seamus Mahon, Dolores Mahon and 'mystery'. You know, as in 'mystery blonde'. I was hoping it would come up with 'Please modify search terms,' computer speak for 'drop dead, loser,' but for once it didn't. 'There are forty-three hits.' Oh, my God, I said silently as I pulled up one gossip-column item after another. Seamus and the mystery brunette. Seamus and Dolores. Seamus and mystery companion seen exiting nightclub. Dolores ultimatums. Ecstatic reconciliations.

I couldn't hide from this, much though I longed to. Wonderful Seamus and horrible Dolores, horrible 'mystery companion'! He didn't just want his wife, he wanted as many women as he could schedule in! For one dizzy second I wondered if I myself was the mystery companion in any of these articles.

Oh sure. 'Seamus Mahon and mystery mousy secretary.' Doesn't have much of a bloody ring, does it?

Maybe I should have wanted to cry but I didn't. I just sat there feeling winded, like Rashid had punched me in the solar plexus. Then I had to scramble to dump the Seamus articles because Jenny was coming over to see if I was OK.

'Fine. Bit of a hangover,' I said morosely, offering her an excuse she could believe.

The phone bleeped on my desk, making me jump out of my skin.

'Alex, would you come in here for a minute?' Seamus was asking, so mildly I wanted to scream. 'I need a quick word with you.'

'I knew it,' said Jenny, staring coldly at me.

'What are you talking about?' I demanded, but she didn't say another word, and there was nothing for it but to walk across the room and knock on Seamus's door.

I told myself I was going to give him seven shades of hell.

'I hope you're not too cross with me,' Seamus said endearingly.

'Cross? You've lied to me: you've got other girls, and your wife—'

'Now, boys will be boys, so,' said Seamus, and he gave me his most dazzling smile. 'Don't tell me we can't work something out. I've got every faith in you, Alex Wilde.'

'You've . . .' I was so aghast I was just spluttering.

'Sure, I've every faith in you being reasonable. We're having so much fun. You like it and I like it, why would we ever want to pack it in?'

Chapter 13

It's a bit like hurting yourself really badly. Sometimes you don't feel the pain at first, because you're so numb with the shock. But you know it's coming.

'What do you mean?' I whispered. 'All those things you said . . .'

'I meant them all, sure I did. But you've got to understand,' he said, a bit prissily, 'I'm the type of man who loves women. I just have to be around them. I can't help myself,' and there was that little-boy shrug again.

I heard what he was saying. What the words were shrouding. He was telling me that even though I'd found him out, he didn't care. He was not going to change. And I could take him as he was or not at all.

The only future for me was as one of the harem.

I must have looked how I felt, because a spasm of worry crossed that pretty face. 'Alex, look. Now we can start a real relationship. Now you know who I am.'

'You're a lying bastard,' I said, and to my horror, a big fat tear trickled down my cheek. I dashed it away angrily but not before he noticed.

'I never actually said you were my only woman.'

'You said your marriage was dead.'

'Well . . . Dolores told me she wanted to try again.'

'Oh right, she just said that on Saturday night.' Even I couldn't buy that much bull.

'So? I'm up for free love, Alex. Monogamy just isn't natural. The difference between me and most guys is that I admit it,' Seamus said virtuously. 'Look, you can have another boyfriend as well.'

'Hey, thanks very much,'

'Don't you value what we have? We have a grand time together, you're a great laugh. All the romance in the world. And I love to hold you in my arms,' Seamus said, and his green eyes were soft and now he was twisting the knife in my heart. I wanted to drop to my knees and beg him to think about this, to think about how much I adored him, how wonderful we were together. To ask why he needed other girls. To promise that I would be all he needed in a woman. I'd get thinner, I'd borrow Keisha's clothes, I'd take *cordon bleu* cookery courses and instruction in Gaelic.

But you should be proud of me.

'It's over between us. I don't share blokes,' I said, and I rushed out of his office before the tears brimming under my lashes could escape and betray me.

Our flat was a bit of a downer. Bronwen came home sober and crying and went straight to her room. Keisha sat around chain-smoking and watching videos of Lennox. And I found I couldn't even cry. I just felt empty and withered, like an autumn leaf.

Gail got in around eight o'clock. She was carrying a stiff blue paper bag from Tiffany's and humming away.

'God, who died?' she demanded, flopping down on the sofa. 'Did anyone pop down to Planet Organic for me? I'm out of tofu, too. Look what Snowy bought me.' She pulled out a stunning silver necklace of interlaced stars. It was so delicate and romantic it made me want to start crying again. Nobody ever got me things like that.

'You'll have to make do with what we've got in the fridge. Keisha's split up with Lennox—'

'That wasn't a real relationship anyway,' Gail said in her superior way.

'Maybe not, but she's upset. And Bronwen broke up with Dick, and I've broken up with Seamus.'

'Oh.' Gail thought about this for all of five seconds. 'Hey, my door's open. I'm sure I left it shut. You haven't been in there reading my nature novel, have you? If you nick the idea I'll sue.'

'Nobody cares about your bloody nature novel!'

The phone rang. All three of us jumped at it. We were like Pavlov's dogs with a ringing phone. Well, it could be your man, right? Blokes can let a phone ring and ring. I've never met a woman who can go past two rings without giving in and picking up.

'It's Seamus,' Gail said grumpily, holding the receiver out to me. I grabbed it with no self-control whatsoever. Oh please say you see the error of your ways, please say you'll change . . .

'Alex Wilde. You sound as gorgeous as ever. How about letting me make things up to you? *Swan Lake* on Friday night, Covent Garden, champagne, the works?'

'And then back to the wife and kiddies on Saturday morning? Get real.'

'Ah, come on, babe. How long are you going to be like this?'

'The whole thing is just boring to me,' I lied.

'Maybe one day you'll be bored, and then we can forget it. But right now,' said Seamus, and lust was thick in his voice, 'you want it.'

He was right. That's the sad thing. Desire was clinging to me like rabid ivy. His voice was getting me slick between the legs and hardening my nipples into raisins. God, how great it would be to be a guy and just fuck without consequences. In all my relationships, sex would drive away the sadness. Even though I wasn't coming, his passion made me feel so good, so earthily female. It was the only time I felt we were talking the same language: not words but kisses, sweat and flesh, rubbing all the extraneous stuff away.

I wanted Seamus back. I didn't want to be alone in this flat, nearly thirty, with my lonely girlfriends. My work sucked, my career was non-existent. And I couldn't even make a success of love. Which I firmly believe every woman is born to.

'You can't always get what you want,' I told him and hung up.

How was I going to get through this? I had to go into that office every day and see him, looking so beautiful. God, what if he turned nasty? What would my mother say when she was out golfing with Fiona Kane? 'Thank you for getting that shitty job for my worthless daughter, but she got fired because she was screwing her boss.'

'I might split up with Tony,' Gail said importantly. I looked over at my little sister, her waifish beauty such a contrast to my lumpy, healthy looks. Gail is the kind of girl who never spends a day unescorted – the boyfriend is dead, long live the boyfriend. Men fall in love with her after one flick of her glossy hair. And the irony is, inside Gail is as robust as a troop of Horse Guards, whilst I am as fragile as a cobweb in the dew.

But men don't bother to look past the wrapping.

Still, anything was better than obsessing about Seamus, so I went along with it. 'What's wrong with Tony?'

'He's OK, but he isn't The One,' Gail said dreamily. I was

uncharitably thinking that maybe his country cottage wasn't really up to snuff, or perhaps his BMW was more than two years old.

'I thought you liked him.'

'Mmm, but I can do better,' Gail said proudly. There was nothing to say to this, and if they were feeling anything like I was, Keisha and Bronwen wouldn't want to talk. So I got up and went into my own room, got a lump of clay, and started pounding at it. Owl's wings started flying from my fingers, fluid shapes screaming into life. It's good, really good, my work when it's born of pain.

Even if I am the only person who thinks so.

The next week was bloody horrible. Doing that mindless work, with only Jenny to protect me from Seamus. And the trouble was, how beautiful he looked.

My computer was besieged with his e-mails. Little flowers kept landing on my desk – forget-me-nots, as if! And Seamus kept sending me poems in the internal brown envelopes we use for memos. I ripped them open and ripped open my own scar tissue. 'I have spread my dreams under your feet; tread softly because you tread on my dreams.' I couldn't help it, I kept crying. I had to buy loads of hayfever tablets from Boots and litter them all over my desk to convince Jenny it was really an allergy.

The worst thing about it was that Seamus was so persistent. He was tempting me with something I really wanted to do.

Sometimes I had lucid moments. I stepped outside myself, like I was watching a film. I got detached. I thought, hang on, you didn't even know him for that long. But then the emotions returned and I felt swamped with longing.

Inevitably I gave in. It was less than a full week before I was having dinner with him again: *à deux* in his flat, with pale pink rosebuds in tiny vases by our plates, and something delicious on the table, and Seamus in the kitchen singing 'The Fair Maid of Connemara', even though I've never even been to Dublin.

'Don't I satisfy you?' I asked when he'd collapsed on top of me. No, I didn't bring the subject up over dinner. I didn't want to ruin the mood, see?

'What a question.' He dropped a slow, sexy kiss on my bare shoulder, a gesture that pleased me far more than all his grunting and groaning of a moment ago. 'Didn't I just get satisfied?'

'I don't mean that. I mean, just me.'

'Oh, God.' Seamus rolled away, annoyed. If he'd smoked, I was sure he'd have reached for a fag right now. 'Are we back on this again? I thought I'd finally got through to you.'

'But it's not natural, to want so many people.'

'Sure it's natural. It's the male sex drive. About which you had no complaints a second ago.'

That's what you think, buster.

'Dolores understands my needs.' And you don't, his tone accused. I wondered silently if that was true. What Dolores would say if she knew where he was right now. I hated him mentioning her name in my presence. I thought vicious thoughts about tucking one of his love-notes to me in the pockets of all his suits, of sneaking out and spraying all his shirts with perfume, kissing their collars to leave lipstick marks. But I told myself that was not right. I knew it was screwed up to blame Dolores, to want her to find out. 'Alex, my dove. We have a great time like this, don't we? Enjoying each other, just for pleasure, no strings attached?'

A chill shot across my skin like an arctic blizzard. Oh no, no! He's saying, you're a great fuck, honey, this isn't a love affair! How can men put the most heartrending cruelties into compliments, and expect you to love them?

' "Tread softly because you tread on my dreams," ' I quoted miserably.

Seamus gave a friendly laugh. 'You crack me up, Alex!' He slapped my bare ass. 'This is my dream!'

And then I had to let my dream of a reprieve go. I could twist myself into a rubber to please Seamus, but I couldn't make him love me back. What came next was almost a surprise, I've been such a stranger to self-respect.

I jumped out of the bed and pulled on my dress.

'I don't want to see you ever again,' I wept.

'Ah, honey, come on, now.'

'No. And you better transfer me to another department, Seamus. I want my job and I don't want to be around you.'

'Maybe I can't work without you,' he said slyly. To him we were still flirting, jousting with words.

'Transfer me and it never happened. Otherwise, I swear I will tell

Dolores everything,' I managed, and then I got out of there before he could explode into threats and curses.

Jenny Robins came to see me when she heard of my transfer.

'You're going to work for Gloria Huntington,' she said, sounding anxious on my behalf. Great, Gloria Huntington, known around the firm as Glorious Thunderbum. A strapping, tweedy, horsy dame in charge of Personnel. Since most Hamilton Kane high-fliers are recruited by headhunters, her job consists of firing postboys and buying company cars. She is also known to have a fetish for high-fibre diets and to fart unashamedly all day long, bellowing 'Perfectly natural' in a pukka voice.

This was Seamus's revenge. He wanted to asphyxiate me.

He made the last days in his department sheer hell. Loading me down with work and indifference. It was bad to have him pushing me, but it was worse to have him stop. Why didn't he care? Why wasn't he gutted? Was I so unlovable? I looked at my record and it was so miserable it didn't bear thinking about. Eddie 'the eagle' Edwards was better at ski-jumping than I was at dating.

'Sounds interesting.'

'I knew he'd do it to you too. I tried to stop it,' Jenny said mournfully, unbending to me now it was over.

I stared at her, horrified. 'What do you mean, to me too?'

'Oh. You know. Seduce you, then let you down,' she said primly. 'Alexandra, I thought you'd have more sense. He does it to all the pretty girls. Didn't you know we've had fifteen girls in your job over two years?'

'Was it that obvious?' I said. My guts felt like a racoon was gnawing through them. Fifteen girls? Was he the world record holder? It didn't even register that she called me pretty. Jenny is one of those forgiving older women, who calls you 'the young people', when you're all thirty-eight.

'Please, young lady. I'm not stupid,' Jenny retorted.

I tramped upstairs to the ghetto of Personnel. Touchy-feely, unimportant, forever writing mission statements and digging out token black employees for the company reports, that's Personnel departments. Unimportant to the bottom line. Ever been in trouble with your firm? Ever wondered at the sadistic delight those bitches take when they hector you and hand you your written warning?

You're not paranoid, they do hate you. You have a real job, whatever it is. You work in marketing or sales or finance. They don't. They know everybody looks down on them. Managers ignore their hiring advice: the key players are sought by executive search vultures. They are napkin folders, corporate window-dressers with nothing better to do than organise holiday rotas. That's why there are so many women in Personnel, just like PR. It's a non bottom line thing. And they know it. And they hate you.

And now I was one of them. But hey, my life sucked in every other way, why not go the whole hog?

'Welcome to Human Resources, Alex,' Glorious Thunderbum beamed, and volleyed off the most tremendous fart.

I giggled. She reddened.

'Oh, do grow up, it's perfectly natural. Fibre keeps you regular. Now, today we're looking at costing for the Christmas party. I'd like you to collect last year's receipts . . .'

I started doing as she asked and trying to hold my breath at the same time. Oh man, what had I ever done to deserve this? I wondered. The figures were just rows of blinking green lights to me; all I could truly see was Seamus's face.

'Alexandra, it's your mother on the phone,' Gloria said, screwing up her face as she squeaked out one more tiny fart. For luck, perhaps. 'Do try and tell her we discourage personal calls.'

Oh, so do I, when they're from my mum. 'Mother?'

'Alexandra. Why are you working in this department?' demanded Mum shrilly. I instantly saw her there, at the end of the phone, her puffy face and brittle, neatly coiffed hair. I am terrified I will turn into my mother some time soon, start looking at people's cars to see if their insides are kept neatly, or suddenly feel a great desire to take up golf or stand for the local authority.

'I've always wanted to work with people.' What rubbish, but what else do you say? I've always wanted to work with clockwork sea lions? I so admired Keisha for blowing one job interview. The sanctimonious Personnel woman asked her to describe why she loved working in a team. To which Keisha replied that she hated teams and liked to work on her own.

'You can work with people in Seamus Mahon's office. Darling, he's a frightfully big cheese. I'm sure he knows lots of lovely single men. And Fiona Kane said he might introduce you to Dolores!'

'Even for a treat like that, Mum, I—'

'Honestly, it's like talking to a brick wall. Gail says you mope around the flat and never have any boyfriends. Full many a flower is born to blush unseen . . .'

'And waste its sweetness on the desert air, yes, Mum, I know.' Mum quoted that bloody line to me every time we talked. Sometimes I felt her presence behind me, holding up a clock and wagging a finger. I used to be last in the egg and spoon races, now I was last in the boyfriend races. I felt the tendrils of a migraine start to crunch around my temples.

'Is there anything else, Mum? I'm really busy.'

'Oh yes, you're always too busy for your own mother. If it wasn't for me you'd still be in that filthy squat. Actually, I'm calling to remind you about that wedding invitation.'

A wedding, umm. Just what I was in the mood to go to.

'Don't give me that silent treatment. It's Charles Drummond.'

'Tom Drummond's brother?'

'Of course Tom Drummond's brother. You're due to go down to Gloucestershire next weekend for the house party.'

Over my dead, rotting body, I was about to say, but Ma cut in. 'And don't think of making any excuse. I RSVPed Mrs Drummond last month, and said you couldn't be more delighted.'

Chapter 14

'Charles Drummond's getting *married*?' Gail protested. And not to me? her tone implied.

I sighed. 'Gail, you've met Charlie exactly twice.'

'But we got on so wonderfully. He agreed with everything I said about better to go naked than wear fur,' Gail pouted.

'He's the Master of his local beagles,' I said flatly. Tom's kid brother Charles was one of those faceless, horsy types I thought should be first against the wall, come the revolution, back when I believed in revolution. Now I got furiously incensed when strikes caused my Tube trains to be overcrowded. But I knew I still wouldn't care for Charles Drummond, who called me a 'mongrel' and an 'unbroken filly' when we rowed about Mrs Thatcher. He had none of his brother's sense of humour or natural dominance. He was obsessed with class. He liked to hang out with the younger sons of dukes and Old Etonians, and he had watery eyes and a braying laugh. It was true he hadn't contradicted Gail, but then he hadn't been listening to her. Anything a woman said was just so much woolly bleating, as far as Charlie was concerned. 'I've only been invited because Tom insisted.'

'You mean I'm *not*?' Gail shrieked in outrage.

'You go instead of me. Mrs Drummond won't know the difference.'

'But Tom will,' Keisha pointed out.

This was sadly true, so I rang Tom up at his London flat, desperately scrambling for an excuse to get out of it. Right now, my bruised heart couldn't take a bloody wedding. And anyway, Saturday lunchtimes were Notting Hill brunch times, sacred to me, Keisha and Bronwen: scrambled eggs and fried bread and a big pitcher of Buck's Fizz on some ivy-covered terrace overlooking Ladbroke Grove. We would sit and bitch about other women's dress sense and our jobs and life in general, pig ourselves, go window-shopping and go home. It was great and it took all day.

Now, would I rather do a girly brunch and wallow in grief, or spend a fortune on a suit and hat and have to grin like a skull for two days?

'Tom?'

'Alex!' He was so warm, I instantly flooded with guilt. Not only was I letting him down, Tom had been there for me and I still hadn't made the effort to see him. Not once. 'We're so thrilled you're going to be coming down. Can't wait to catch up.'

'But Tom, I don't think I can.' His hurt silence was dreadful, so I gabbled on. 'My mother accepted for me and I'd already promised my flatmates I'd stay in and hold their hands – they've had sort of heartbreak crises,' I said.

'Alex, you can't. Mother has already worked out the seating plan. And your bedroom, and everything, it took her hours,' Tom insisted. My heart dropped. Oh, God, I'm going to have to go. Tom knew exactly the one thing that would force me into being there. I could muck him about, we both sort of knew, but I couldn't muck his mother about. His mother was a civilian.

In the friendly war of niggles between Tom and me, I sometimes flinched at the idea Tom might still be keen on me. He never said anything of course, but . . . how screamingly embarrassing that would be, oh my God.

'I understand about your friends, though. Bring them too.'

'I don't think it would be their sort of thing.'

To my horror, Keisha was halfway across the room, her slim ebony legs racing like a panther. She grabbed the receiver. 'Tom, hi, this is Keisha Roland. One of Alex's mates . . . oh, she has? Great, well, me and Bronwen would love to come. And so would Gail.'

Gail practically ripped Keisha's wrists off as she snatched the phone. 'Oh, Tom.' Bloody hell, her voice had gone all breathy and little-girl-lost, up two octaves. She ignored my jabbing finger in my mouth and my pretend vomiting. 'How *darling* of you to ask us all, it'll be *such* a thrill, and *so* many congrats to Charlie . . .'

Eventually she permitted me to get the phone back. Thank God he couldn't see me because I was as red as a red pepper in tomato sauce. Those bitches! I was so embarrassed I could hardly speak.

'Everyone seems very enthusiastic,' said Tom, with supreme

unconcern. He didn't even sound like he was taking the piss. 'So you'll be there, that's wonderful news. We should be quite a house party, all sorts of guests, bound to find someone you'll get along with.'

'Looking forward to it,' I muttered.

'Lots of our old crowd from Oxford,' Tom said. Marvellous, and will there be stocks in the garden so they can pillory me properly? That's the cherry on the sodding cake, the idea of all my old college friends, most of whom are probably supermodels or interstellar researchers, gathered together to crown me Biggest Loser of All Time.

I hung up with a knot of anxiety already forming in my guts.

Bronwen sat heavily on the sofa. 'Oh, God, if only I could bring Dick. He's so brilliant at weddings.'

'Bronwen,' Keisha said, 'you need professional help.'

I was inclined to agree. Bronwen had developed selective amnesia. She no longer remembered Dick forcing her to go through the *Penthouse* routine, or telling her she was really just a slag who loved it. The mists of time – about two weeks – had shrouded Dick's faults and now all Bron remembered was the chiselled jaw and snappy dressing. Women are so forgiving, except to themselves.

'Therapy's rubbish. It's for weak-willed Americans. Imagine paying someone to listen to your problems,' I said waspishly.

'I think it'd be great,' said Bron, more honestly than me. I was very hostile to therapy because Oliver, my darling ex, had been such a fan. He'd been in therapy for over ten years. 'Let me ask you something. Are you better?' I used to demand, and he would say shrewishly, 'Oh, you just don't understand.' But I did, I understood that these people have a vested interest in you continuing to think you're screwed up. Though in Oliver's case, of course, he was.

When I got as low as I was now, though, it did sound tempting. Imagine something where the point of the exercise is to talk continuously about yourself. No wonder the New Yorkers are all such addicts.

I once knew a bloke who was married. I was his mistress for three years and he flatly refused to tell his therapist about me, because he said his therapist would kill him. It used to bug me to distraction that this man couldn't see that his whole therapy thing was a total sham, if he couldn't tell his shrink something that major. In the end I broke up with him because of it. Seeing your therapist as a father figure, and quailing at being told off, nice one. The shrink was also his wife's shrink, but shrinks are bound by the laws of doctor–patient confidentiality. It's a death-knell for sexiness when you start seeing your man as a self-deluding coward.

And it only took me three years to get to that point?

'How many shrinks does it take to change a lightbulb? One, but the lightbulb has to really *want* to change!' Keisha laughed delightedly.

'So when are we going up to the country?' Gail butted in, bored with a conversation that didn't centre on her.

I grimaced. 'Next Thursday night.' Friday was a Bank Holiday, and Mrs Drummond obviously wanted all her guests there for a big house party. I'd only been to their creaking pile once before, and imagined Bronwen and Keisha smoking and swearing amongst the topiary mazes and manicured lavender-lined walks. God, what an ugly bloody disaster.

Longing for Seamus suddenly gripped me like a pair of red-hot tongs.

How was I ever going to get through this?

Monday and Tuesday I spent in Personnel, trying not to breathe while Gloria master-blasted her farts all round the office. In the end I went in there with Vick's smeared under my nose. But I hardly noticed after a while, so desperate was I to think up excuses for cancelling on Tom. Maybe my granny could die? Too easily checked. Or I could get laryngitis? Mrs Drummond would put a nurse on tap for me. Or that flesh-eating bug? But then I would have to actually die . . .

There was no fighting this, I was trapped.

And Seamus didn't call. I couldn't believe it. He'd been so persistent before, and now, nothing. It was as though I'd dropped off the face of the planet. Even though I kept making excuses to go down to my old stomping ground, and made sure I was wearing the dress he liked the most, Seamus just looked right through me like I wasn't there.

Even the sight of Rhoda Black's vast bottom spilling out over my tiny corporate chair didn't cheer me up at all.

'I finally got somebody who can just concentrate on work,' Jenny said to me cheerfully. She even gave me a conspiratorial wink. 'Mr Mahon has to admit it's done beautifully.'

'He doesn't make comparisons with me, I hope,' I lied. I wanted to hear Jenny say he was moping pathetically for me day and night.

'He doesn't mention you. Sorry,' said Jenny, not fooled for a second.

I blushed.

'It's better this way, dear. Believe me,' said Jenny in a motherly fashion. 'That way you get over them quicker.'

It wasn't 'better this way', though. It was bloody evil. I felt like someone was eating my heart right out of my chest with a rusty spoon. Like being a junkie trying to get off crack, and the drug is all you can think about every second, it consumes you, that longing, like screw my self-respect, screw health, screw everything, *I want my fix.*

'It's Wednesday tomorrow,' Keisha announced importantly.

'Yeah, Einstein. It generally is after Tuesday,' Bronwen said, throwing her copy of *MixMag* across the room. Bronwen was now reacting to her sorrow by getting furiously irritated by everything. Which was not a good idea when you live in our flat.

Snowy and Gail were lounging across the white leather sofa at the back of the room, Snowy showing off to her admiring audience the latest bauble she'd picked up at Garrard's. God, Snowy annoyed me. She must have inherited a fortune from a long-lost aunt in Bolivia, or something. How could she be so impeccably turned out, day after bloody day, and flooded with men and never introduce any of them?

'I wish I was Snowy and I didn't have to work,' I moped.

Keisha gave me one of her wilting looks. It could kill an erection at eighty paces. 'God, Alex, you are fucking stupid.'

I bridled. 'What do you mean?'

'What are you on about, you snotty bitch?' Bronwen demanded angrily. 'You're sodding rude, Keisha, you know that?'

'Give it a rest,' Keisha said simply. Water off a duck's back to her. 'Now. Tomorrow is Wednesday and we're leaving on Thursday.'

'So what?'

'So, stick your hands up, who has suitable outfits for a wedding.'

Bronwen and I looked at each other and I groaned and dropped my head in my hands. God, not only was this going to be the worst weekend ever, I was going to have to bankrupt myself for it.

We set off for Knightsbridge on Wednesday evening. I had had the day to compose myself, to remind myself that life goes on even when you don't particularly want it to. And that, no matter how heartbroken I was, I didn't want to be seen at this wedding in some pile of old rubbish. My friends from college would be laughing hard enough at me as it was.

Besides, working at Hamilton Kane had changed my attitude to clothes. I used to think grooming was for poodles; now I saw it as armour against the world. I tried not to think about the amount I spend on that vital haircut at Neville Daniels, or that vital colour at Nicky Clarke. In fact, when I was still seeing Seamus, I actually booked myself in for a facial. I used a Kanebo moisturiser from Harvey Nicks that cost forty-five quid a bottle. And even though I hated her, I did use that La Prairie cream Snowy bought me. My heart may have been broken, but my skin was glowing.

It was this jones for beauty that had driven me to make the few demands of my working life. My title, in Glorious Thunderbum's office, was now Human Resource Administrator. Yes, I know it's a fancy term for secretary, but the point is, that word, or 'assistant', was not actually on my card. I was technically on the very bottom rung of the executive ladder. And I had Jenny Robins to thank for it.

'You know, dear, you should take advantage of this,' she lectured me during one of my trips downstairs. 'Get a new title and a raise. I can certainly recommend you for an admin position, you're actually quite organised.'

I stared at her, but then it occurred to me that in my misery, my mind had been very focused when it came to actual work.

'Seamus would need to write me a recommendation,' I muttered. And we'd all be eating green cheese from the moon the day that happened.

'I rather thought you had some pull with Mr Mahon,' Jenny said discreetly. Blackmail him, she was suggesting.

I looked at her and glowed with gratitude; I suddenly realised why young Melissa had told me I was lucky to be working with Jenny.

'There would be many advantages to getting a promotion, and money would certainly be one of them.'

That decided me. Money, I needed. People who say money isn't everything have never been poor.

I saw the coast was clear and marched into Seamus's office.

He lifted his gorgeous head from the glowing screen on his desk and regarded me coldly. 'What would you be wanting, Alex?'

'Just to settle stuff. So we're clear,' I said equally coldly, although my heart was squealing, 'Change your mind, sweetheart, don't be like this.' 'I'm going upstairs to Personnel, and I want to go as Administrator. So you're writing the commendation.'

'Now you want a promotion too, is that it?' Seamus asked nastily. The bastard, my entire new salary was probably less than he paid Dolores's chief maid.

'That's it,' I said.

'Well.' He thought it over for a second, but we both knew he had no choice. Still, what came next was another kick in the shin, just when I was sure it could get no worse. 'You'd best give me back the keys to the flat.'

I fumbled around in my bag, my Adam's apple working furiously as I gulped back the tears. Oh fuck, this was so final. He really wasn't going to change his mind or beg forgiveness. I threw the keys in front of him with an almighty clatter, and in the jangle of metal on mahogany I felt the poems and flowers evaporate into thin air.

So that was how I got my raise and promotion. Not the world's most triumphant victory, but the money landed in the bank just the same.

We descended on Harvey Nicks like Attila the Hun. Keisha went first, taking her Chanel products back to the counter with about an inch of cream left in the pots, then saying that her dermatologist had advised her they were causing a rash and she wanted her money back. Bron, Gail and I died a thousand deaths, but by the time a browbeaten manager had retreated from the fray, Keisha was back, waving her credit slips triumphantly.

'Every penny. What are you looking at me like that for? It's free money, honey,' she crowed, so loudly that I had to drag Gail out of the Shu Umera counter and up the escalator.

Bronwen selected a moss-green dress by Jil Sander at eighty per cent off. It was a bit last season but I suppose the discount was just too tempting. She made up for that by teaming it with a three-quarters, single-button burgundy jacket by Ralph for Ralph Lauren, which was so expensive I nearly fainted when I saw the price. The overall effect was very dandified, but just sober enough for a country wedding.

'You look great,' Gail purred. Keisha nodded and I wished my thighs would fit into that boob-tube of a skirt. Bronwen, like Gail, had the ass of a ten-year-old boy.

Keisha selected a mink silk suit with a silver detail on the cuffs. Anna Sui and very expensive.

'I didn't know they paid that well at the BBC,' marvelled Gail.

'They don't,' said Keisha, who never worried about incurring debt when it came to style. The suit clung to all her curves and looked stunning against her sable skin. I knew she'd be planning to wear it with the string of Mikimoto pearls Lennox had come up with for her birthday. I felt proud: she was going to look like a black swan wearing moonbeams. Say what you like about Keisha, you could take her anywhere. She could even be polite if she was having a really good day.

Gail threw a fit when she saw a rack of furs and made us all schlepp over to Liberty's. Liberty's isn't as good for make-up, but it does have the big advantage of a room full of Ghost. Ghost is a secret uniform for London working women, it's more forgiving than a priest. We had to talk Gail out of a long white coat over a white strappy dress.

'Only the bride wears white. And no black either,' I insisted, when Gail flounced over to the rows of black.

'Oh, nobody pays attention to that old-fashioned crap.'

I started to panic, thinking of Gail inviting herself to Tom's, then showing me up at the wedding.

'Look, pick the mint or the sky-blue, or the grape. You're not bloody coming if you go in white or black.'

'Fuck!' Gail shouted. 'No wonder you're such a miserable failure at everything, Alex. I'm not surprised you can't keep a man. All you can do is whinge and nag at everybody, you think you're such a saint. And you needn't think that Tom will be interested in you any more, either. You're so fat even the extra-large dresses won't fit you.'

Chapter 15

'Shut up, Gail,' Keisha said, looking daggers at her.

'It doesn't bother me,' I lied. It was true: even the large dresses in here hadn't hung very well round my comfortable ass.

Not that I'm fat. I know I'm not. I mean, the average size in Britain for women is a sixteen, you hear that in the magazines all the time. But the trouble is, the average size for *my mates* is a ten.

I'm a ten on my top half, and a twelve on my bottom half, that's if we're talking about a skirt. If it's trousers, then I'm a fourteen. And they're gaping loose at the waist. Why do garment manufacturers do this? Surely I can't be the only woman in England with shotputter thighs, as Mummy has it, and a narrow waist. Why can't they mix and match the stuff, like Salon Selectives shampoo?

Or even better, why can't I be thin like Gail?

She really knew how to hurt me. I stood there blushing like mad. God, how I wished for a boyfriend then, because I had no comeback at all to sniping like that.

'When was the last time you got a promotion?' Bronwen said acidly. 'Or went to Oxford?'

'Yeah, and a fat lot of good it's done her,' Gail sniped.

'At least she doesn't date men for their bank accounts,' Keisha snapped.

'At least *I* don't date men for their column inches,' Gail retorted.

'This is getting us nowhere.' There I went, peacemaker again. 'I think I'll try this on.' It was a discounted Donna Karan dress in soft brushed caramel, with a fitted jacket. I ducked inside the curtains to face the mirrors, only I didn't do that 'til I was dressed. Best trick I ever learned for dealing with changing-room trauma: don't! Why upset yourself for a week? Have a look once you've put the clothes on. If God had meant us to be naked he wouldn't have created fig leaves. Or the naked male body, which is the ultimate proof that God has a sense of humour.

I liked it, I have to say. It draped heavily enough to look good on me, it pulled the eye to the thinness of my waist and opened in a V-cut that sort of looked designery. There was a vogue a couple of years back for stuff that looked natural, but then why spend all the money? You might as well go to Gap.

I stepped outside and marvelled at my own curves, at the rich tones of my excellent skin, at how a woman could be transformed by putting on a bit of fabric.

'Oh, that looks lovely.' A rather brisk assistant, a fifty-something who reminded me of Jenny. 'Are you ladies shopping for a special occasion?'

'A wedding,' Gail said shortly. For someone who's so into nature and animals and stuff, Gail can be pretty rude to people. If they're lower on the social scale than herself, of course.

'Weddings are wonderful. None of you is the bride?' she asked, taking the suit from me as I dived back into my old Warehouse bootleg-cut trousers. The look on Keisha's face had quietly convinced me that I must have that suit, even if I had to pledge my unborn child and half my kingdom. Oh my God, I was turning into a fashion victim. I felt an unmistakable urge to get my hair cut.

'No such luck,' Keisha said smoothly.

'Well.' She took my card and rang up my purchase, wrapping the suit in filmy layers of tissue. 'Which one of you girls is going to get there first, I wonder?'

We all stared at ourselves. Wondering the same thing.

'Gail,' said Bronwen after a pause and Keisha nodded in agreement, while Gail grinned smugly. They had to think about that one for a second, though. The one thing I was certain of was that whoever the runner-up was, it wasn't me.

'If you're going to have your hair cut, go to Joel at John Frieda,' Bronwen said suddenly. We were sharing a cajun chicken and a bottle of chardonnay at a restaurant in Camden Town. Everything had got very merry over the alcohol. We were dishing each others' ex-boyfriends' darkest secrets.

'Lennox used to like to be pinned down on the bed,' Keisha said, squealing at the memory. We all shrieked, because Lennox could have swatted Keisha to one side with half a flex of a single bicep. 'And he liked me to tell him he was a bad boy and not good enough for me.'

'He sounds like Ricky,' Bronwen pointed out. Ricky was the Very Famous Footballer I mentioned to you, and Ricky's pet thing was to be kicked with a pair of stiletto heels and then to kiss Keisha's feet.

'Bigger than Ricky. And *bigger*,' Keisha corrected her, giggling.

'Well, Tony thought he was driving a race car. Right before he came, he would shout, "And it's Meadows, first past the chequered flag," ' Gail admitted.

'Well, Dick would—'

'Yeah, we know about Dick,' Keisha said, stopping her. Dick was sick. We already knew how sick, so Dick's humour potential was sorely lacking. 'And Seamus, tell us about Seamus, Alex.'

I racked my brains. Through the mist of the chardonnay, I reached for funny, ridiculous things that Seamus had done. But none of them seemed funny, they all seemed impossibly romantic.

If I burst into tears right now the girls would never forgive me.

'Well, he asked me to pick up the dry-cleaning and bring it to our first date,' I offered bleakly.

To my surprise they all cackled like witches.

'The bastard!' Gail said.

'He might at least have *pretended* to take you seriously,' Keisha agreed.

''Sss an asshole,' Bronwen decided.

'So who's this hairdresser?' I said, determined that they were not going to get my goat. Oh, lovely Seamus, it was only a bit of dry-cleaning, so what?

'You'll love him. I'll make an appointment for you first thing tomorrow,' Bronwen said, with a kind of crisp authority she has when it comes to serious fashion. I keep forgetting that she's a photographer's assistant, she's worked with all the top photographers and she hears the cool insider gossip. I wondered if I was ready for a sneak appointment with somebody like that. Christ, for ten years I used to dye my own hair with the stuff you get in five-quid boxes.

'Alex has to work tomorrow. And she won't be comfortable with somebody that cutting-edge,' Gail said hastily.

'She'll be fine.' Bronwen gave her a steely look. And now I was determined to do it. Why did Gail want to stop me looking my best?

'I can take a morning off. If you can get me in.'

'It's solid, but he owes me a favour. Let me make a few calls,' Bron said, digging out her battered Orange mobile phone. Keisha gave me a wink and lifted her glass. And Gail smiled too, but she looked tight around the edges.

Bronwen managed to get me in. This meant I had to go. Ordinarily I would have cancelled in the cold light of day, but since she'd pulled strings to get me this slot, I took my heart in my mouth and called the office.

I told them I was going to be late. And to my astonishment, nothing happened. Glorious just said, 'Fine, see you at lunchtime.'

'Destiny,' Keisha said as she dropped me in Aldford St. 'You see, you're meant to look great for this wedding. You'll probably meet the man of your dreams.'

I already have, and he was taken, I didn't say.

'This wedding's going to be full of polo-playing Old Etonians.' I shivered. 'Men with no chins and trust funds. I'd rather date Dick.'

'Don't be stupid. And don't be such an inverted snob,' Keisha said tartly. 'You wear Donna Karan now, you're not subscribing to *Socialist Worker* any more.'

John Frieda's was unmarked outside, which meant it must be really cool. I got through the door and managed not to feel like I was in the wrong place. I was wearing a sloppy sweater from Armani jeans, and a dark Joseph skirt and sassy strap heels, one of my best outfits. Nobody gave me the old arched eyebrow, so that was a start.

Joel came over and was devastatingly handsome, and also witty. He was straight, too. Does it make me homophobic to prefer having straight guys cut my hair? I don't think so, it's just that instinctive faith that they'll cut it in a way that appeals to men, whereas gay guys cut in the height of fashion, not necessarily too feminine. Normally I would be thrilled to get my hair cut by a male model type who's clearly a genius with the scissors, but all I could think about was how Seamus was the only other man I know who was this handsome.

People often say when you're in love, all love songs sound suddenly written just for you. But that's not all, is it? *Everything* seems to conspire to remind you of them. Take Seamus. Whenever I saw *Hello!* or *OK* I thought of Dolores. Whenever I saw a businessman, I thought of his flashy suits. Whenever I heard about the peace process on the six o'clock news I thought of his Irish accent . . . and believe me, nothing is as annoying as having that beardy weirdy Gerry Adams remind you of your man. Those poems on the Tube brought tears to my eyes. Flowers crunched my heart into rubble. You get the idea . . .

But I couldn't mope this morning. Joel was tilting my head this way and that, slicing and shearing me like some mousy sheep, and I was not even stressed about my tresses curling on to the floor, I just knew this was going to be great. And it was a sleek pageboy with a slight asymmetrical tilt, it sort of fascinated me as I turned my head this way and that in the mirror.

'Looks great,' I said, breathlessly.

'Something's missing . . .' He called a girl over and they had a quick conference. And before I knew it I was being tilted back in the washbasin and something was being painted on to my hair with an egg-white brush, or that's what it felt like.

'Trust me,' Joel said, and he was a beauty bigshot whilst I, as you might have gathered, was a bit of a novice. So I did.

There's something so therapeutic about getting your hair cut short. It's a chance to start over, and not just with the split ends. I wanted to do this, to walk in this salon looking like one girl, and walk out looking like another. The kind who's at home in that DKNY job. A – don't laugh – a City professional. It's the 'as if' rule. Act 'as if' until you are – that's another Jenny Robins fortune-cookie special. But she's right. If you dress seriously, they take you seriously.

Hey, there was no future for me in sculpting and no future with Seamus. So I might as well daydream about something.

Glorious Thunderbum made fifty K per annum, did I mention that?

'OK,' Joel said as he attacked me with the hair-dryer. Precision-cut strands blasted about in front of my eyes but when the electric whirr stopped I couldn't believe what I was seeing. My sleek medieval helmet of hair was now glimmering, washed through with rich streaks of copper and rust and mahogany, not enough to make me look tarty or overdone, just enough to make me look glowing. Deep, gleaming low lights of red and brown, and it was perfect with my skin, and my muddy green eyes were suddenly alight and shining. The colour set off the cut, too, forced the eyes down to the razor-sharp lines swinging vibrantly round my chin.

I could hardly bear to get up because I didn't want to get away from my reflection. Which is not something you'll hear me say very often.

'What do you think?' said Joel, and grinned at my stupefied look.

'Oh my God,' Bronwen said, when I got in later that night. Pretty much the reaction I'd got all day; the girl on Reception almost stopped me when I walked in. Glorious Thunderbum refused to notice, but I caught her sneaking glances my way when she thought I wasn't looking. I went downstairs to show it to Jenny, but Seamus was out of the office.

'You look breathtaking, that suit's going to look fabulous.'

'Wow, Al,' Keisha gasped, stopping dead as she walked out of the bathroom. That did make me smile, because Keisha is hard to please when it comes to style. 'Does he do black hair? We have to go shopping again to get you some more stuff.'

'I can't afford it.'

'Well, I might let you borrow some of mine,' Keisha said, like a proud mum rewarding her brat for successful potty training.

Then the door creaked open and it was Gail and Snowy, laden down with Harrods bags and Joseph carriers.

'Well,' Snowy said theatrically. 'Darling, how dramatic, it's almost modern, are you sure it's you? It will look much better when you've dropped a few pounds, that cut is designed to show off cheekbones.'

'Alex has cheekbones, Olivia,' Keisha said in her calm but deadly way. I felt a flood of gratitude, it's so good to have girlfriends in your corner.

'But when she's slim, she'll be so much better suited to it. Men like the girls to be slim and sexy these days, Keisha.'

'Well, you'd know all about that,' Keisha replied softly. And Snowy froze, this look passed between them, I could almost see Snowy quailing.

'I don't know why you bothered,' Gail said petulantly. 'You're going to have to wear a bloody hat anyway. Oh, look what Snowy bought me—' and she pulled out a white round box from Philip Treacy, with the most amazing slant and concoction of feathers on top. It must have been hundreds of pounds. It would turn every head at Charles's wedding. It was the colour of sunlight on elm leaves, and combined with Gail's mint-green Ghost job, she was going to look like one of the bloody Flower Fairies.

Despite my new cut and colour I now felt like a bloated heifer. Cheers.

Thursday evening finally rolled around and I went home to pile into Bronwen's car. Keisha took up most of the boot with her luggage, so it was just as well Gail was coming later. I couldn't bear a few hours' drive with her sniping about my weight, or banging on about organic food and her nature novel and the rest of it. Why, why was I born into my family? They all get on so well with each other, and I'm the cuckoo in the nest. I have furious fantasies about Gail suddenly growing by a foot, horizontally, her tiny waist thickening and her bud breasts drooping and her playing golf with Fiona Kane just like Mum. Whereas I will get a sculpture praised by the Royal Academy and revel in a glorious old age of bad behaviour, being a loony like Vanessa Redgrave or Glenda Jackson.

'Guess who I met down at the studio?' Keisha said suddenly, as we pulled out on to the motorway.

We started guessing. Keisha as a researcher on Saturday morning kids' TV was the best joke ever. She actually had to shepherd the kids in the audience, which she did by threatening to have them all tortured to death unless they did exactly what they're supposed to. Keisha doesn't like children, she doesn't want any and she doesn't want anybody else's. So the kids didn't fuck with her, they did what they were told. Whereas put me in room full of kids and it would be total Bedlam before you knew it.

This made her popular enough to shepherd the guests too. So far we'd had Alan Shearer, Trevor MacDonald, Princess Anne and Harrison Ford. They all loved Keisha because she was not impressed. By anything. Ever. You're talking about a girl who dragged Scary Spice off-camera and told her to sodding well behave herself. If an alien spaceship landed on our roof-terrace while Keisha was sunbathing, she'd tell them to move it because she was trying to get a tan.

Up and Running had been good for her career and bad for her heart. That's how she met the Very Famous Footballer whose mother she failed to impress. It's how she met the TV presenter (not one on her own show, of course not, you think Keisha's that stupid?).

'Rick Astor.'

'Rick Astor in Formula One?' I squealed. Bronwen dissolved into laughter, her shoulders shaking so hard I yelled at her before she lost control of the wheel. Formula One was the appropriate name of the boy band *de jour*, and Rick Astor, all of twenty-four, was the teenage girl's dream boat. Or preteen, I should say. At eight it's *Horse and Pony*, at nine it's *Smash Hits*, and at thirteen they're already dressing in black, smoking and reading *Melody Maker*. And they've grown out of alcopops.

'He's not that young,' Keisha said defensively. She was also giving that secret little smile she had when she'd bagged another scalp, another trophy boyfriend to look good in her boyfriend cabinet. Keisha was twenty-nine years old, how satisfying she must have found it to have these boys whom all the lissome fifteen-year-olds were longing for.

It made me feel good, too, a bit feminist. You always see younger women as the enemy, when they're often not, not really. Patsy's five years older than Liam, look at Ralph Fiennes and Francesca Annis. Princess Di was a lovely woman, but I'm sorry, I was thrilled to bits to find out Charles's heart was stuck on Camilla. None of those rock stars with the endless open limbs of schoolgirls available to them actually bother, do they, unless it's a quick poke on a tour bus?

If it's women versus girls, women win, and we should all stop wetting our pants about it.

However, that said, it's usually women like Snowy and Keisha who win.

'He's a cover star for *Just Seventeen*,' Bronwen scorned.

'Come on, Keisha, don't you think you're repeating a bit of a pattern here? He's famous, he's got nothing in common with you, and you're going to date him for three months and then drop him and then cry.'

Bron looked over at me and laughed, and Keisha stiffened in the front seat. 'I thought you hated therapy. And anyway, you can talk, you're the girl who thought Seamus Mahon was for real.'

I sighed, because I didn't want to start a row. And because it was hours 'til we would get to Tom's place. Oh God, I wondered if this was going to be as deadly as I thought it was.

'You'll love it.' Bronwen's psychic. 'You're going to meet the perfect man of your dreams, it'll be like *Four Weddings and a Funeral*.'

Yeah, I thought, and whose funeral will it be?

Chapter 16

It was dark by the time we pulled up to the house, negotiating the last few winding B-roads in total silence. I had a vicious headache, and I expect the other girls had too. The first half of the journey was OK, slagging each others' bosses and ex-boyfriends, not Seamus, Dick and Lennox, you understand, but ones before that, ones whom it was safe to slag off. Isn't it great when you replace boy A with boy B, and you can finally lay into boy A without feeling any of those secret twinges that say, oh God, I still love him?

Every crack about Seamus was agony to me. I was in a lose-lose situation: I wanted to talk about him all the time, but whenever I heard his name I felt an agonising shot of pain.

Girls who are friends with their exes. They're a complete mystery to me, like crop circles or ley lines. Either they've got new men, or they weren't really in love with their blokes in the first place. And yes, yes, I've done it too, that 'I can't bear not to have you in my life, let's always be friends' spiel, but what it meant – on both sides – was, 'I don't really want this to end, let's pretend to be friends so we have lots of opportunities to sink into each other's arms, saying we just can't help ourselves.'

The only help for me is another guy. I know it's pathetic, I really do. And I can survive on my own without a boyfriend, I've done it lots of times. But for forgetting one man, as such, I need another. I am a one-man woman. I never have that torn feeling Keisha gets. If I'm in love with Seamus, Oliver seems utterly unattractive. If I'm in love with Oliver, Gerald has lost his sparkle.

So we were quite happy, lacing into Oliver. How he used to wash compulsively before and after sex. And liked to wear pink ties. And the Very Famous Footballer, who had to listen to 'Sexual Healing' every single time he had a shag.

'He used to try to time it,' Keisha told us, in fits. 'When it goes, "I want *sex*-ual healing", he used to screw up his eyes and come on the upbeat.'

'He could do that?' Bronwen was impressed.

'He had great rhythm,' Keisha dissolved.

And Bernie, Bronwen's ex. How Bernie used to keep a wardrobe full of Mothercare at his place and make Bronwen change whenever she went over there. I liked listening to Bronwen's stories, it was fascinating, like a car crash. I knew that however bad my love life had been to date, there was at least one person who'd had it worse.

Then we put on the radio and found one of those regional stations – 'Ninety-two point nine, Seashell FM' – that only plays Top Forty from 'eighty-three to 'eighty-seven. We were well away on that one. Bawling out 'I just died in your arms tonight' and 'What a feeling!' and 'Rio', halfway up to Gloucestershire.

We left the motorway and got on to the narrow, twisty roads. It was all ooh-ing and aaah-ing for twenty minutes, then we discovered that Bronwen had the map upside down.

Keisha then had a sense-of-humour failure that lasted an hour and a half.

So after the rows, screaming until we were hoarse, slamming on the brakes and hysterical threats to turn round and go straight home, we were finally there and we were not speaking to each other.

I gasped as I saw Carrefour rising towards me under the red harvest moon. Carrefour, it's been in Tom's family for a few hundred years and it's not exactly a stately home, but it's the next best thing. A huge Elizabethan manor house, ghosting up out of the darkness, its grey stone front dotted with diamond-paned windows, exquisitely lovely. I'd been here before but I'd forgotten how pretty it was. And now I could make out the lavender-lined paths on the lawns behind the house, the old sundial to one side and the tall, moss-covered leaping satyr, that made Keisha scream and pull the wheel sharp right.

Gravel sprayed up round the car and I groaned. First bloody offence: they probably spent ages raking it neatly.

There were several other guests arrived there already. Bentleys, Rollers and Mercedes everywhere. I even spotted a Ferrari.

We parked Keisha's Nova conspicuously in the front. There was nothing else to do.

I jumped out, trying to get the blood back into my legs, smoothing my new hair round my face, and we hefted out our bags and walked up to the front porch. Keisha looked around as though she couldn't quite believe the indignity of having to carry her own cases. Bronwen rummaged around in her handbag like a mad ferret.

'Hey, no drugs,' I hissed.

'What do you mean? I need to relax after that sodding drive,' Bronwen spat back, but fear of Mrs Drummond was stronger than my usual cowardice.

'Not here, or I'm leaving. Truly.'

So by the time I'd pressed the bell, and could hear the ancient clanging through the depths of the house, we were all standing on the steps fuming and glaring at each other, and Gail wasn't even there yet.

After an age the heavy oak door swung open. A heavy woman in a no-nonsense Jaeger tweed suit stood there, her white hair coiffed in a real Tory bouffant do, pearls around her crinkly neck, looking us over very critically.

'Are you from the hunt saboteurs?' she demanded angrily.

I leapt forwards. 'Er, no . . . I'm Alex Wilde, Tom's friend, we're here for the wedding.'

'Supper finished over two hours ago,' said the lady, not mollified, 'do you *realise* what time it is?'

Keisha opened her mouth and I had to jab her very hard in the ribs. 'We got lost, I'm so sorry.'

'Louise, are you scaring these poor people?' said a familiar voice, and Tilly Drummond, Tom's mother, appeared behind the Gorgon Medusa, smiling graciously, like the Queen Mum. Tilly was also grey haired, but softly elegant in moss-green cashmere and a skirt that skimmed her narrow frame to just below the knees. I could see Bronwen and Keisha nodding approval. We all want to be old like that. When the time comes.

How on earth did such a bird-like woman produce a great hulk of lard like Tom, I wondered silently.

'Alex, how lovely to see you again! And your friends – Keisha, Bronwen, how do you do.' Mrs Drummond sounded just like Penelope Keith in *To the Manor Born*, but nobody made a sarky remark under their breath. You just wouldn't dare. I felt instantly overwhelmed by the flagstone floors and grandfather clock that probably cost half of our flat. From the living room – I suppose they'd say drawing room – came the sound of drunken, braying laughter and

Mozart, and the warm glow of candles. 'You've met my sister, Louise
. . . was it a *nightmare* journey?'

I let myself be steered towards the throng, muttering things like, 'So
kind of you,' and 'Terribly sorry about the time,' in my best imitation
of upper-class manners. My ego was shrinking like Alice in
Wonderland after eating the mushroom, or drinking the potion,
whatever it was. I was so glad my mother wasn't there, my mother
who right now would be putting on an obviously fake voice and
saying 'Pardon' and crooking her little finger whilst drinking coffee,
and all the other things she fondly imagines are posh.

It was one of my secret shames at Oxford. I was meant to be this
big revolutionary, but I was fascinated by Tom's manners. By the way
he did everything without thinking about it. His class was just bred in
the bone. And although I didn't mind working-class guys at all, I
developed a repugnance for the straining, striving middle class I was
born into, with its obsessions as to how to hold the forks and what
table you sat at in restaurants.

Tom never gave a bugger about stuff like that. He was secure in his
position, I guess.

'We've put you in the green and red bedrooms upstairs. Come and
have a drink before you turn in.'

I reached for my case, but Tilly waved it away. 'One of the boys
will do that for you, we have so many on tap – Jack, come here,' she
said, grabbing some hapless reveller as he staggered out of the kitchen.
'Take these up to the empty bedrooms on the second floor, could you
dear? Thanks.'

There was nothing for it but to acquiesce, so I smile weakly and
followed a furious Keisha and Bronwen, not to mention Aunt Louise,
into the drawing room.

The party was in full swing. We'd dressed nicely enough for
travelling, but everybody here was in evening dress: slinky silk things
and dinner jackets and the older women in ghastly Laura Ashley frocks
in purple and orange and eggshell blue. Clearly they hadn't stinted on
the port.

Horsy laughter stopped mid-whinny. Insistent voices shut up.
Everyone stared at us, it was like a spaceship with three aliens had just
landed in the middle of their creaking old pile. Instinctively, I moved
closer to Keisha. You'd think they'd never seen a black person before.
Christ, didn't these people know it's rude to stare?

I scanned the room desperately looking for Tom, but I couldn't see him. Anybody would be good news right now, anyone at all . . . even some of his lame friends from Oxford.

'Everybody, this is Tom's friend Alex, and Keesha and Branwen,' Mrs Drummond said loudly.

'Bronwen,' said Bronwen.

'Keisha,' said Keisha.

'That's right, Brunwane and Kraysha. Come in and meet some of the crowd,' but she was spared from making any formal introductions by a vast apparition in crushed claret velvet and a face to match, a frightful old boot whom my mind scrambled to get a lock on.

I don't know, is it possible to be born with selective amnesia? My memory for telephone numbers is spot on, despite all the 'e's in the disused quarries, but my memory for names is worse than a sieve with three-foot holes. I get so bloody embarrassed with people, I remember their football team and whether they read their star sign, but ask me their name and I'm a total blank. And they never understand, they always get so annoyed. They all say, 'Oooh, I'm just the same, I'm terrible,' but their mouths make those little cat's arses of annoyance and you have to scramble to get back the lost ground.

Tom, actually, taught me the only technique that works here. He was so famous at Oxford everyone knew him, and forgot that he didn't know them back. So Tom said, 'Say, "How *nice* to see you again. How have you been?" and later, say, "I'm so sorry, I've forgotten your name," and when they go "Mary," you say, "I know *Mary*, of course, I was thinking of your surname," or the other way round.'

'How *nice* to see you again. How have you been?' I stammered.

She gave me a crocodile smile with a strange edge to it. 'I've been fine, Alex, why haven't you kept in touch? Ellen asks about you all the time.'

And then it hit me in the head like the tennis balls I kept missing at school, and I couldn't stop myself gasping, 'Ellen *Jones*?'

'Not for long,' said the creature, who was of course Mrs Jones. With a sinking feeling I recalled that Mrs Jones never liked me. Ellen was the fat girl at school I used to hang out with, remember I was telling you about her before? We were two weirdos together. Maybe Mrs Jones resented that Ellen couldn't do any better than me. Or that when Ellen and I sat together in the cafeteria, I only needed one space on the bench.

We didn't keep in touch after school. We didn't have much in common, really, except misery. It's like being stranded with someone in a plane crash – you hold on tight to each other during the ordeal, but afterwards, you probably don't go to the same dinner parties.

'Not for long,' she repeated triumphantly. 'It'll be Ellen *Drummond* on Sunday afternoon.' There you go, missy, stick that in your pipe and smoke it, said her look.

I grabbed on to a foaming glass of champagne proffered by an elderly butler and glugged it down in one second flat.

Ellen! Ellen was marrying Charles! Oh my God, fat, ugly Ellen Jones, the only girl at school more unpopular than me, was about to get married! And I didn't even have a boyfriend to my twenty-seven-year-old name.

'I know, isn't it wonderful?' Keisha butted in, with that sixth sense of hers coming in to the rescue. She could see me floundering. Doing my 'goldfish on the floor' impression.

'And how do you know Tom?' Mrs Jones demanded.

'Keisha's a friend of mine,' I explained.

'Well,' Mrs Jones said smugly. 'I see you're not married yourself, Alex. It's nice for spinsters to have lots of friends. I expect you keep a cat, do you?'

I wanted to say, 'I expect you keep a vibrator, do you?' but I just smiled weakly instead.

Oh God.

'It has been a long time! Tom's been telling me all about your goings on. Oxford, how impressive, you little bluestocking.' I got the impression that wasn't a compliment. 'Ellen will be *thrilled* you're here and so will Charles. He's a City trader, you know, makes three hundred thousand a year.'

'How marvellous,' I said dully.

I hoped Charles was fatter than Roseanne Barr and had ginger pubes. Then I felt hatefully guilty: poor Ellen, it was hardly her fault. Just because I was a dumped, bitter, shrivelled-up old maid!

The conversation started to flow again, in low, subdued tones that gave me the impression everybody was talking about us. Mrs Drummond left me to it, and went to introduce 'Kreena and

Bronwine' to a fusty group of Young Tories behind me. And I was left to Lady Macbeth.

'Is Tom about?'

'No, he's out in Gloucester with Charles. Supervising the stag night, though I must say, I don't think it'll be too riotous. Charles is so considerate of Ellen's feelings. Tom waited to welcome you in for absolutely ages, they were late getting off,' Mrs Jones disapproved.

'And Ellen?' I was damned if I was going to start apologising to this old bag.

'Ellen's upstairs asleep. You musn't disturb her, she needs her beauty sleep.'

She certainly does, I thought unkindly. Oh, I know, but I was tired and stressed.

'Sounds like a fabulous idea. I'd love to turn in as well, I've had a shattering day.'

'Alex!' I spun round to see Sue Cooper standing at my left elbow, flicking her hair in what we used to call the 'St Mary's flick'. It was annoying then, and it was annoying now. Sue went on from school to Oxford, only not like me, doing a real academic subject, French at St Hugh's. 'What *have* you been doing with yourself? Are your sculptures selling?'

'Not so far.'

'Never mind – I expect you have some frightfully well-paid job and are dating Brad Pitt,' Sue said, in a voice which suggested she thought the exact opposite. 'I'm in the Civil Service and I married Dan, do you remember him, he's a lawyer now. And I've got little Tommy, aged two, staying with his granny.'

'I'm an administrator in Human Resources for Hamilton Kane.' I hoped fervently that this sounded more impressive to her than to me.

'Oh?' Sue arched her perfect eyebrow. 'How refreshing, downsizing your life, very post-modern. I heard you were dating Oliver Call?'

'Not any more. We broke up,' I muttered. Georgia Jones was listening to this with triumph.

'Did one of your ex-boyfriends *really* wind up in prison? It's too exciting, all our lives are so boring, good job, getting married,' said Sue, who didn't sound bored in the least. Now I knew how one of those butterflies feel when boys stick pins through their tummies to watch them wriggle.

'I'm so tired, I'm going to have to go to bed.' It sounded firm to the point of rudeness, but it was better than starting to cry in front of this shower. 'Excuse me.'

Mrs Drummond was very sweet and steered me off up the wide stone staircase. I couldn't see Keisha and Bronwen making any move to join me, but then they probably found these guys fascinating, whereas I'd been trying to escape this sort of scene all my life. Plus, Keisha and Bronwen had fantastic jobs, whilst I basically organised holidays for a woman who farted like a carthorse.

'Do get tons of rest. There are so many parties and terrific things to do tomorrow, and I know you'll want to catch up with Ellen and the boys,' Mrs Drummond said briskly.

I sank down wearily on to a queen-size bed with stout oak legs, covered in a stiff white linen cloth that felt a hundred years old. The red flannel on the sink, the dusty books piled thoughtfully on the bedside table, the soft green lampshade with little tassels, it was so country, so relaxing, I almost envied Ellen. Outside my windows drifted the scent of freshly cut grass, delicious in the warm night air. I remembered what the landscape was like round here, the hedges thick with cow parsley and dandelions, and dry-stone walls bisecting the hills.

Ellen wouldn't be queening it over Carrefour, though: Tom's father died when Tom was seventeen, so Tom's been the owner of this ever since. He's the elder brother, they do it like that in families like this. Last time I was here his mother controlled the trust fund, but Tom's all grown up now.

I suppose I was looking forward to seeing him, but to be honest, this all seemed like a waste of time.

I wondered what Seamus was doing right now.

Chapter 17

I woke up to a sound so strange my sleeping brain couldn't compute. Then I realised what it was: quiet. And birdsong.

I got up and padded across the wooden floor to the window, throwing it open. The air outside was chill but so fresh I could have breathed it for ever. I vaguely remembered when I was a child, first going up to London from Surrey, how it was so filthy I thought I could taste the dirt every time I inhaled, but you get used to anything after a while.

The faint tang of grass clippings was still there. Somebody had actually laid out croquet hoops on the lawn. There was a hoary old orchard weighted down with apples behind that, small misshapen ones grown without pesticides, I bet they tasted fantastic. And the meadows rolled up past the grounds, peppered with black and white cows lazily whisking their tails about, their breath rising like plumes of smoke in the cold. The sky was clear blue, it would be a blazing day later on.

I was staring at the lavender beds and the kingcups lining a tiny stream to my right when the door creaked and Keisha walked in, swathed in a huge ancient bathrobe. 'God, I slept like a log.'

I realised I had too. Whether it was the drive or the country air, I must have been asleep almost before my head touched my pillow.

'You'd better grab a bath before all the hot water runs out.'

'Who says it's going to?'

'Well, think about it, Alex, how many people are there in this house?' Keisha pointed out, so we legged it into my bathroom, which was small, whitewashed and decorated with dead starfish and ships' timbers. The bath was a big old iron thing standing on dolphin legs, and the water clattered into it. 'I *love* it,' Keisha said, enchanted, while I stripped off and jumped in, pulling the Pantene 2 in 1 out of my nylon bath-bag.

'Do you really? Aren't you . . .' I tailed off.

'What, 'cause I'm black?'

'They are a bit stuffy, Little Englandy,' I said.

'Al, I'm telling you. At least five guys older than my dad were practically falling down the front of my dress,' Keisha said smugly. 'And three of the girls were desperate for tips on how to get into TV.'

Relief flooded over me like the lovely hot water. God, it was such bliss to sink your head in it and scrub in the shampoo, and grab that Victorian shower attachment which probably *was* Victorian. I never feel good anywhere unless I've washed my hair. It's even more necessary than the first cup of coffee.

'How's Bronwen doing?'

'Lost to the world. She got bogged down with this bunch of Tories who wanted to talk about Welsh devolution,' Keisha laughed.

I grinned, because Bronwen and politics was like William Hague and modelling. An ugly thought.

'They should be just Bronwen's type. Staid and boring and probably deep into sexual perversions, with oranges and polythene bags.'

'What about just your type?' Keisha demanded. Ignoring my protests, she brought out a white-tipped Marlboro from her fluffy pocket and struck up. 'There's a whole bunch of gorgeous young men here. Or so I got told yesterday.'

'I didn't see any,' I sulked.

'That's because they were all out at the stag party. There's even Lord Henry Molyneux.' She made an airy gesture with her hand. 'Younger son of some Irish geezer. Maybe you could bag him.'

'Vom,' I made a sick noise. 'Harry has thick glasses and he's going bald.'

'You're so superficial. I could overlook it,' Keisha giggled, 'Lady Keisha, wouldn't they all drop dead of shock?'

'If you're into stag-hunting and freezing old Irish castles—' and I stopped dead, because that reminded me of Seamus.

'What about Tom? I know you like him.'

'Of course I do, but –' I stepped out on to the mat and grabbed a towel big enough to cover Kansas, reached for the Aussie Hair Insurance and drenched my split ends, a sort of advance apology for the hair-dryer. My hair takes so much punishment it's amazing it hasn't all dropped out. Lucky Keisha only has to get hers washed once a week, it's not fair.

There was a photo of the Drummonds on the shelf and I showed her what I meant.

'That's Charles.'

'Uuurgh. And that's – oh my God, is that one person?'

'Exactly,' I said, smiling fondly at Tom. Then it hit me, perhaps I had better not be so picky. Perhaps Tom the Goodyear Blimp was the best I could hope for in life. After all, so far I was Oh for Five, as the Americans would say. Ellen's getting married had hit me pretty hard, I know it must make me seem like a complete bitch, but it seemed that everyone in the world was paired off except me. And Bronwen, but Bronwen is built like Gail, that sort of wispy fairy elf vibe, the type whom men fall over themselves to get close to. Once she was over Dick, there was long line of eligible blokes who would crack open the champers at the very thought of her.

Why had my life gone so wrong?

'There's bound to be someone here. You're just closed to anyone who not perfect. The trouble with you, Alex,' said Keisha, and now I was gonna get a lecture from a girl who only dated blokes on the covers of magazines, 'is that you're a hopeless romantic.'

'Girls are supposed to be romantic.'

'But they're not supposed to be hopeless. You meet a man and you're head over heels in love with him in five seconds. You never take the time to check him out. And if he *doesn't* appeal immediately, you dismiss him.'

'Don't you believe in love at first sight?'

'No,' Keisha shouted calmly over the whirr of the dryer. 'Lust at first sight. You've got them mixed up.'

'It was love with Seamus.'

'How could it be love? You didn't know anything about him. But you latched on to him, and then you couldn't see any of his faults, because you wanted it to be right so badly. You're so desperate to get paired off you're just sabotaging your chances of anything real.'

'Well, thank you, Dr Keisha.' I was so annoyed, I flung the hair-dryer down and struggled into a Nicole Farhi knit suit without even looking at her. Because maybe something she was saying had triggered something I was not ready to face yet.

Memories of the first time I saw Oliver. I was still in my squat then, dragging my sculptures round to galleries and getting the door slammed in my face. It was after another rejection that I bumped into him, literally. I was rounding the corner in a blur of tears and barrelled into a thin, rangy bohemian type who was pointing a camera at a very beautiful girl. Only now he was pointing at a Westminster Council dustbin instead.

'Cut! Jesus, why the bloody hell don't you look where you're going!' he shrieked, so loudly I dropped one of my carrier bags, and a statue of a twisting otter smashed into a million pieces.

My inhuman wail worried Oliver so much he handed his camera to an assistant and dragged me into the nearest pub.

'Get the lady a brandy,' he barked, and even while the tears were streaming down my cheeks I remember thinking how cute his sloppy blond fringe was. I might honestly be in the depths of misery, but one part of me is always open to the possibility of a gorgeous male. 'What was it? My God, I'm so sorry.'

'My sc-sculpture,' I sobbed, downing the brandy and sputtering, because it seared my throat like paint stripper.

'Shit. Look, how much was it worth? Of course you must let me pay for it.'

'It was worth bugger all,' I said, commencing a fresh round of sobbing. Oliver had actually called a halt to filming and taken me back to his hotel, let me use the bathroom, which was rapture, and heard my whole sorry story. And he didn't even try to get me into bed, not that time, anyway. I could dimly make out the flood of feeling I had that afternoon – that Oliver was a white knight and he was here to save me.

Pretty much the same feeling I'd had with Seamus.

And then there was Gerald. How passionately he'd wooed me when I was first down from Oxford, the flowers he used to buy and rip to shreds in front of me, throwing the petals on the road: 'You should have blossom strewn under your feet.' Gerald had taken me to the opera, to the ballet, to just about every cultural thing going. 'You'll love Strauss – Der Rosenkavalier is perfect for you.' And he was enchanted by my sculpting, so much so he wanted me to come to the British Museum, to the Ashmolean, everywhere we could stand and look at male nudes. Gerald shivered with delight. 'The curve of his buttocks . . . oh, look at the muscles sliding under the skin, Alex darling.' I took his refusal to have sex as a sign of his sensitive soul. I didn't realise that Gerald's enthusiasm for romance was frantic fire-fighting of his gayness. Gerald didn't want to be gay. But he was, as I found out when I lost weight and chopped off all my hair, looking as gamine as I was ever going to, and Gerald still didn't want me. We had our first and last row, in which he declared his undying passion for Hillary St John, the scoutmaster of my parents' village.

I suppose, deep inside, I had known something was wrong. Men always want to have sex with you. They might not want to marry you or talk to you or even date you, but they do always want to shag you. That is one of life's eternal truths.

What if Keisha was right, what if I was such a believer, it was always going to turn around and kick me in the face?

Lust at first sight, hmm. I wonder. I mean, I do long for men when I first see them, but it's not in that overblown, squirmy, panty way you read about. It's a sort of longing that they be the one. That they like me. That they notice me.

'See you at breakfast,' said Keisha, walking out and heading downstairs.

I frantically slapped on my protective covering of make-up. Mouth open as I daubed the eyeshadow on with my Shu Umera brush that cost forty-five quid. Forty-five quid for an eyeshadow brush, I must be going bonkers. But the effect was pleasing, even in the harsh daylight and this tilting dressing-table mirror, brown-spotted with age.

I had to be prepared to face Ellen Jones. And her mother.

Maybe I shouldn't be too hard on Kevin Harvey the postboy. I mean, let's face it. Kevin was straight. Single. Between puberty and death. And up for it. What more could a girl want?

The big kitchen had copper pans and dried hops hanging from the ceiling, and bacon and mushrooms sizzled invitingly on a huge green Aga as we wandered in. Keisha's heels click-clicked on the sandstone floor as she breathed in the scent. There was warm baked bread on the oak table, and a pot of fresh coffee, and some fishy thing – kippers? – and pots of marmalade and Marmite and home-made honeycomb in a jar. Sue Cooper was cracking the top off a brown speckled egg, wearing jodhpurs and a neat cashmere jumper. Her long, smooth hair looked as glossy as a Red Setter's coat, and she had the sleek look of a pedigree greyhound. Various Sloany boys were making eyes at her as they stood around draining coffee and wolfing slabs of toast and honey.

'I'm starving,' Keisha announced.

'Well, do help yourself.' Sue's effortless superiority really put my back up. 'Everyone's just piling in. And Alex, try anything, Mrs Drummond wants us all fattened up. Oh. Crispin, you know how we girls *always* worry about our weight –' this to one of the young bucks drooling at her across the pepperpots – 'but Alex is so *lucky*, she simply doesn't mind. She eats anything.'

I wanted to have just a cup of English Breakfast, but unfortunately I was too hungry. Keisha pile toast and mushrooms and crispy bacon on both our plates. I knew I was going to eat every scrap of it, so I tried to copy Keisha and pretended I didn't care.

'Oh.' A rangy whippet of a girl stretched herself like a Siamese, and half the boys' eyes slid off Sue and on to her. 'I've strained myself *so* badly in the Harbour Club, I can feel muscles I didn't know I had.'

'Can *I* feel them, Melissa?' asked one of the lads, to roars of laughter.

'God, I love Charlie for asking me over,' said another. 'He really does have the most distracting friends.'

They all introduced themselves. Danny Boyle, film producer. John Crates and Bill Radcliffe, City types. Ted Loman was training for Formula One, Lionel was an MP's researcher and Karl Arthurs was a solicitor. And Whippet Girl Melissa was a kindergarten teacher, one with blue eyes, blonde hair, a slender frame and the clear desire to marry somebody with money. Penny, Bill's wife, was doing a catering course, Gillian was married to Ted – which, judging from her tone of voice, was career as well as a description. All of them were the kind of women who would stay home looking after the children, but with a nanny or two to do the dirty work for them, and then frown on girls like me who wanted to do something with our lives, other than be a postscript to a man.

The men were successful and the girls were decorative. Isn't life grand?

I was trying to gulp down a forkful of bacon without being noticed when all the heads turned, and the girls were instantly on their feet, scraping their chairs back on the flagstones.

My fork stopped in mid-air. My God, it was Ellen.

And she hadn't slimmed down to nothing or had radical plastic surgery. She was not quite the heifer she was, but she was still Fergie rather than Di, and she still had that brush of freckles right across her nose. Her ample bottom was snug in a pair of faded Levis and she'd thrown a comfy suede shirt over her straining bosom, and her red hair was dyed a nice coppery mahogany, and she looked great.

Happy and great. Glowing with it.

My emotions were thrown for yet another loop. 'Ellen.' I got up shyly, and she did a classic double, triple-take, she was staring at me as though she could hardly believe it. Blimey, did I really look that bad?

'Xandra! Oh, Xandra!' Ellen squealed like a mad piglet, and hurled herself across the room at me. 'Oh wow. Mummy told me you were here but I didn't really believe it. How *are* you, it's so great to have you here! Now everything *will* be perfect!'

I introduced Keisha and Bronwen, who'd slumped her way downstairs when nobody was looking. Ellen was bouncing around like Tigger, she was so bloody happy. Ellen is the only person I've ever met who went for Xandra rather than Alex. She just got everything wrong, that girl. But she was the one who was getting married.

A shadow fell in the doorway and I lifted my head from Ellen's bear-like hug to see Charles Drummond, smiling away as though he only drank Perrier on his stag night, which, let's face it, he probably did. Charles looked much the same as usual, except he'd toughened up and he appeared to be completely bald. Actually this suited him. Better than being a ginge, anyway. He looked like Patrick Stewart off *Star Trek* and now he was coming up behind Ellen and smothering the back of her neck in kisses. Everybody went 'Aaah,' dutifully.

'Xandy, it's terrific to see you. Tom will be so thrilled, and your friends, yes,' Charles said, shaking hands warmly.

'It's Alex these days.'

'Oh, Xandy, always so contrary,' Charles laughed annoyingly. Who are you calling Sandy, slap-head? I thought but didn't say. 'Have you got a fella yet? Oh no, Tom told me you were on the shelf. Better make a move on some chap smartish, eh, before the dust settles!' He roared with laughter.

Bronwen jumped in to defend me but Sue got there first, teasing Ellen loudly about babies. 'Charles will want his own cricket team. You'll be *so* snowed under.'

'What about you and Dan?' asked Gillian, flashing her own wedding ring smugly. 'You see, Alex? The married life really has so much to recommend it.'

'Not according to all the husbands who ask me for a quick poke,' said Keisha suavely.

A dead silence fell, as though someone had just flung a dead racoon on to the honeypots. Bronwen couldn't help it, she was going to giggle. And she had a mouthful of coffee. She whipped around just in time to spray it over the sink.

'Well, really,' Melissa sniffed.

I was biting my cheeks trying not to laugh.

'No, honestly, you wouldn't believe it,' Keisha continued, not batting an eyelid. 'Six of them last night. It was disgraceful. With their wives in the same room.'

'Which ones?' asked Danny curiously.

'Don't know. And wouldn't say if I did,' Keisha told him smoothly.

And then everyone started talking very fast.

I got to eat precisely four mouthfuls of bacon before the next bomb dropped.

'Alex, we have a couple of friends of yours over. They deal with John and Bill sometimes, as well as my coochie-pie,' Ellen said warmly.

'Great, who's that?' I asked with total disinterest.

'Oh, it's your old boss,' Ellen squealed, 'Seamus Mahon, and his wife Dolores, I know you'll be dying to catch up.'

Chapter 18

I took a determined swig of coffee. It was hot and it blistered the inside of my mouth but I hardly noticed. The room was suddenly hatefully bright, like it becomes when you've got flu.

'How lovely,' I managed.

Oh God, I had to get out of there. But did I? I was pierced by an absolute longing to see Seamus again, up here where he couldn't hide behind an office wall. And where he'd get to see my new cut and colour, my new suit, where he'd realise that I had friends and connections too. I had been invited here and it was nothing to do with him.

I wanted to sit firmly on Renewed Hope, to drag it back into the cage of Realistic Despair where I'd locked it up for the last week. But it was a slippery little bastard. It kept undoing its chains with its teeth.

Seamus here! That *had* to mean something, didn't it? I wanted to dive on the *Daily Mail* and check Jonathan Cainer's horoscope, he's always very positive. Amazing how all girls think the star sign thing is crap, I mean I know I do, but whenever I get a good one I'm always hopeful just the same. If it's bad I say it's a load of cobblers. There's a great story about the *Daily News* tabloid in New York that hired this columnist who was always writing things like, 'Today your wife will sleep with your brother and your dog will get cancer of the liver.' So many readers complained, that the proprietor wrote her a note: 'Dear Madam Zaza, As you will have foreseen, we will not be renewing your contract . . .'

It looked like destiny when Seamus first spoke to me, but now . . . and I'd changed, I had truly. I was a sophisticated working woman, I wore designer stuff and I had a flash hairdresser. I was not even a secretary any more. He had to respect that, right? He had to see I was not that coffee-spilling klutz any more.

'I hear Dolores has bought a *stunning* Versace electric-blue dress suit,' purred Melissa.

Keisha looked at me and lifted one eyebrow just a touch. Yes, that 'I hate you, you rich cow' jealous thing was squirming in my tummy like a polecat in a sack, but I was also curious. To get another look at the creature who had that ring on her finger. At a woman who allowed Seamus to carry on the way he did. I wanted to see how she reacted to me. She must know *something*, surely? Could she be that stupid? And though I longed for Seamus, would I want to be the wife, if the wife had no career and was constantly cheated on?

And all these thoughts took under a second to process. God, if only our office computers were that good. I had spun the whole thing out before that gulp of coffee had hit the back of my throat.

'Darling, do go and hurry Tom up,' Ellen said to Charles. She reached across the table for the Alpen and winked at me. 'He'll be *so* thrilled finally to see you again. He was up for *hours* last night, talking about you to Seamus, when all the other boys were watching that awful stripper.'

'Boys will be boys, darling,' Charles said, handing her the cream and sugar. Ellen still had her appetite, I saw, but I couldn't concentrate on how much cream she was drowning her cereal in. What had Tom and Seamus been saying about me? What a facer for him when Tom had mentioned I would be here!

I beamed, I had glorious visions of Seamus in his cups, unbending to Tom that he missed me and couldn't live without me. *In vino veritas* and all that.

'Tom did most of the talking, Seamus just let him prattle on,' Charles said, 'but then Seamus has always been a great listener, don't you think, Alex?'

I could feel Keisha and Bronwen's eyes boring into the back of my shiny layered crop.

'We didn't socialise,' I replied.

Keisha moved in and swooped like an angel of mercy to save me. 'Done, Al?' She bustled about, grabbing my plate and cup, giving me a breather to recover my poise. I was buggered if I was going to let all this turmoil bubble over in front of the perfect wives here. Darling little Melissa and marvellously married Sue were having too good of a time laughing at me as it was.

'Wonderful, are you all eating properly?' It was Mrs Drummond, looking fresh as the Morning Glory trumpets outside the kitchen window. She was wearing a moss-green trouser suit, very elegant, with calfskin boots. She was just a million miles away from Mum and her relentlessly colour-co-ordinated 'brights' (crimson skirts and jackets, blue shirts and matching shoes). 'We're going riding in Bridlington woods today, for anybody who can manage it.'

'Oooh, terrific, I love your wonderful ponies,' purred Gillian.

'Well, Hector's been pining away since you were here last,' said a warm voice I recognised.

My God, it was Tom! I knew I was being rude, but I had to check him out twice to see if it truly was him.

He smiled across at me. His grin was so open: none of Seamus's mystic seductiveness about it at all. Tom Drummond would never make you think of soft babbling brooks and plucking harp-strings. He's the kind of geezer who thinks plucking harp-strings is for poofs. As for poetry, well, Tom once called rugby 'poetic'. It was as lyrical as he ever got about anything.

'Hullo, Alex,' he said. Cheerfully.

I'd have jumped up and given him a hug, but the room was too crowded for anything that spontaneous. 'Tom, where's the rest of you?'

I'd love to be able to tell you that Tom Drummond was now as svelte and gorgeous as Tom Cruise, but it wouldn't be true. He must have dropped about a quarter of his body weight, though. He was tall and stocky instead of fat. The rolls of flab that used to settle comfortably round his belly had been exorcised and replaced by taut muscle. Now you could see ox-like shoulders and a ridiculously square chest where all that lard had been. He could play rugby himself now.

'Army,' Tom said succinctly. 'Don't like chaps carrying around too many extra pounds.'

I was painfully aware of Keisha and Bronwen staring at him like he was Mel Gibson or something. How ridiculous, and Tom would tease me about it for ever. He was just a walking mass of testosterone when we were at college – even in his Giant Haystacks days some idiot females would flirt with him. I kicked Keisha's ankle and that snapped them out of it.

'Your hair's different.'

'You're observant.' I grinned back. Really, it was like all those years had sloughed away: we were teasing each other the way we always had. I was utterly pleased to see Tom, at last an ally up here.

What could he and Seamus have been discussing? I couldn't wait to probe him. What had he said? And what did Seamus think?

'Tom, the house looks so incredible,' breathed Penny, the catering student.

'Mmm, the gardens are heaven,' said Sue, and now they were all over him, this bunch of *House Beautiful* harpies, flirting away in their mumsy cardigans and cable-knit sweaters. And their husbands didn't seem to mind, either. God, it's pathetic how people suck up to people with money.

'Alex, introduce me to your friends,' said Tom, after a few murmured 'So kind's and 'Glad you think so's.

'Hi, I'm Bronwen and I work in fashion,' Bronwen said, fluttering her eyelashes to deadly effect.

'I'm Keisha, I'm researching on *Up and Running*,' Keisha purred, doing a sort of husky thing with her voice.

'Wonderful,' Tom said enthusiastically, 'that blonde presenter looks tons of fun.'

Keisha thought she was an egotistical junkie bitch, but she just smiled and nodded.

'And you'd have to work in fashion with that marvellous dress, it's the most stylish thing I've seen anyone in all year,' Tom beamed at Bronwen, making her open up like a water lily, and all the other girls started pouting. I exchanged the briefest glance with Mrs Drummond, who looked amused. I guess she was used to Tom having this effect on stray females.

'You girls still tucking in? Try some of the devilled mushrooms, they're great,' Tom urged, and Bronwen actually reached across to the Aga to get some. Bronwen, who thinks she's being a pig if she splurges on an extra olive in her G&T. 'Would you mind if I borrowed Alex for a while? We've got such a lot to catch up on.'

'Mmm,' Ellen said, as I gratefully sprang to my feet. 'Don't keep her too long, Tom. We used to be best friends at school, you know. I'm going to want to know *everything* about the men in her life. I was always sure you'd wind up the most romantic of us all.'

Tom led me out through a boot room thick with coats and wellies and a metal thing to scrape the mud off.

'Maybe you'd better pull on a pair of wellies.'

'Oh, these'll be OK.' I glanced down at my Pied à Terre loafers.

'Nonsense.' He had a quick rummage and yanked out a green pair. I slipped into them perfectly. 'You remembered my size.'

'I remember everything, Alex, you know me,' Tom said companionably. He led me out into a small walled kitchen garden, thick with the smell of herbs: sage and basil and parsley were everywhere; runner beans trained against the wall; ripening tomatoes and empty raspberry bushes. He offered me a tiny blood-red tomato, and it was a revelation when I bit into it, nutty and sweet.

'They don't taste like these when you get them at Safeway.'

'What about this? Ma's thrilled with them this year,' Tom said, pulling a spotty apple off a tree. It looked grim but it tasted incredible, all smoky.

'God, that's good. How awful if Gail's actually right about organic food.'

'Gail's coming tomorrow, yes? So glad you could come. With all Charles's awful friends descending on me like a plague of frogs,' Tom snorted.

We wandered through one section of his gardens into another. Past the crumbly golden kitchen walls, the herbs gave way to neat flowerbeds, lavender paths and rosebushes. The flowers were glorious, everything from hollyhocks to azaleas, and there were rambling dog roses in the hedges.

'I don't know how you can bear to be away from here.' It was true: I could almost feel the tension unknotting in my back.

'I'm only in town twice a week. The rest of the time I manage to run things from here. Got an office upstairs: ISDN line, local secretary . . . seems to work.'

I was remembering my reading now. Tom ran the Carrefour Trust, and he'd made another fortune on top of the one he inherited, by picking great stocks. Boring way to do things: he'd never run any flash deals like Seamus, but it didn't surprise me Tom went for the 'get rich slow' approach. Or slowish. He was still pretty young, I supposed. He had been a doctoral student when I was up, so he must have been, what, thirty-five? I was pleased for him, I was truly.

'Mmm. You've done wonders.'

'And you're climbing the greasy pole, too, so I hear. Seamus Mahon was telling me you're an Administration Executive now.'

'Oh?'

If it had been anyone other than Tom, at this point I would have pressed urgently for details, but something stopped me. I could be too rude, we hadn't seen each other for ages.

'It feels strange, doesn't it?' Tom said. His walk was so fast I found it hard to keep up. He didn't look at me when he talked, either. Maybe that would be too emotional for him. 'This, I mean. Because we've been talking to each other.'

'I know what you mean.'

'Are you still sculpting? I hope you haven't given up just because of a few Philistines in London.'

'I throw a few pieces together now and then.' Normally I would just deny it, I hate discussing my art, but Tom made me comfortable. He was so interested in me, even though he was such a big shot himself. I didn't quite feel the failing worm I should have been feeling right now.

'You must keep it up. It's who you are,' he said simply. Then his face clouded. 'So are you still seeing that Oliver chap?'

I smiled, because Tom disapproved violently of Oliver. But then he disapproved violently of everybody I dated. He played the parental role: my own father didn't give a stuff, as long as his bridge and tennis were unaffected, and my mother absolutely salivated over anyone at all I dated. She called Peter the thug 'delightful', Gerald the homosexual 'very manly' and Oliver 'sensitive and charming'. She was always so amazed someone would even date her loser daughter, she was more desperate for things to work out than I am. Mum had never got over Justin jilting me, and having to tell all her friends in the Lady Taverners. Her attitude was a real vote of bloody confidence.

''Fraid not. His secretary dumped me from the set of his new film in LA.'

'My God, what a bastard,' Tom said, sounding like he wanted to rip Oliver apart with his bare hands. Then he paused, and added, 'What a *stupid* bastard.'

'What about you?' Before, I wouldn't have asked, I mean, looking like that whale that was beached on the Severn Estuary, who would have dated him? Apart from the obvious gold-diggers that Tom wanted nothing to do with. It was always a laugh at Oxford, the mad American women who would fling themselves at Tom, and him struggling to extricate himself with frantic murmurs of 'how kind'.

'I saw Linda Severn for a while,' he said diffidently.

I bristled. I remembered Linda Severn, uptight daughter of some Tory industrialist who'd got elevated to the Lords by flinging John Major's war chest a few mil. Linda was like the other girls back in the kitchen: soft as thistledown, never raised her voice or swore in the presence of a man. I thought she was as fake as Barbara Cartland's eyelashes. But she was pretty and upper class.

'Linda was as boring as natural yoghourt,' I spat.

'I'm afraid she left me a year ago,' Tom muttered, but his eyes were sliding off mine. This meant that Tom dumped her. In the nicest possible way. But he's too much of a gentleman to suggest it was that way round.

I was pleased by that. It just bugged me to think of a bloody boring heifer like Linda in charge of this heavenly garden. That's all.

'Anyone else?'

'There's the City and the Army. Neither one very conducive to romance. As you know.'

Did I? I steered him gently back in the direction of the house: it would be too awful to find Seamus had left to go riding by the time we walked back.

We discussed our lives in a soothing, not-too-revealing manner. Tom snorted with triumph when he heard about my politics changing. 'Although it's too bad to have that bunch of rabid commies in charge.'

'Tony Blair, the rabid commie.' I smirked. 'He's mates with Maggie Thatcher, how can he be?'

'Ah, they'll reveal their true colours in time,' Tom said distrustfully. Now if this were Seamus, we'd be on to wine and lovers' compliments by now. Seamus had never asked my opinion on anything political in his life.

'You must be thrilled at the wedding, anyway.'

How odd, we'd spent half an hour talking just about ourselves. Tom recognised this because he brightened. 'Mmm. Terrific stuff. I was so pleased when he went for Ellen. Charlie always used to go for looks, just looks, and he was never happy. I told him he'd picked the right mount this time.'

'The right *mount*? God, still the old male chauvinist pig. And why shouldn't Charles go for pretty girls? I think you've both improved with age.'

'Many thanks for your kind observation,' Tom said dryly, 'but Charles needs to realise that physical passion isn't everything in a relationship.'

'I think it is,' I said firmly.

Tom picked the yellow flowers off a deadnettle and threw them at me. 'It's part of it, you goose. But it's only wrapping paper.'

'I never met a shiny present I didn't like,' I told him flippantly.

'Indeed. And are you happy?' He must have relented on seeing the storm clouds that crossed my face, because his shoulders slumped a little. 'Look, one needs the outside to be attractive. But the inside has to match up.'

'Maybe you can get the inside to change.'

'I think that's the flaw.' Tom was now half talking to himself. 'The inside almost never changes.'

'Good job the outside does,' I yelled, running ahead of him, 'or your floorboards would have given out long ago. Come on, I'll race you back,' and he careered after me, with a speed that belied his weight, and bloody hell, he got across the lawn faster than I did and we were yelling insults at each other, and my face was all red and my neat bob all windswept. I'd forgotten I was supposed to be elegant, and suddenly we crashed into another couple who were walking out to take the air.

The woman was wearing tight cream jodhpurs and a fitted jacket straight out of Ralph Lauren. She looked stunning. And the man, who had his arm linked through hers, was in chinos and an Arran knit sweater. He looked at me like I was a half-dead pigeon some cat had dropped at his feet.

'Would you ever be *careful?*' she said coldly to me.

'Hello, Tom, how's yourself? Hello, Alex,' muttered Seamus.

Chapter 19

I frantically smoothed back my hair. God, Dolores looked fantastic. Her long flaxen hair hung down her back like a glossy waterfall. It was in incredible condition. Her skin was smooth and tanned. Her nails were shimmering with pink. The jodhpurs fitted her ass like it was a twelve-year-old boy's.

'Hello, Alex, I didn't see it was you. You're the girl who used to be Seamus's secretary, aren't you?'

Her teeth were so white. It couldn't be natural to have teeth that white. She must get them bleached in Harley St.

'Alex wasn't with me for long,' Seamus said.

'I'm awfully sorry. Very careless,' I told Dolores. I was going as red as Tom's tomatoes. 'Did – did you have a good drive up?'

'It was fine.'

I watched Seamus. He was shifting from foot to foot.

'Do you need the loo?' said Tom. 'First on the left.'

Seamus looked so surprised, that I burst out laughing. And then instantly wished I hadn't, because his face darkened with thunderous disapproval.

'We were just grabbing some air. Let's all go back inside and sit down,' Dolores suggested. To my horror, she slipped her arm into mine. 'I want to hear all about you, Alex. You can give me the story on Seamus at work. Is he a monster?'

In the drawing room, everyone was sprawling around reading the morning papers. Bill and Penny loudly suggested expeditions to see the local churches. 'Oh *do* come, Danny, wouldn't they make wonderful locations?'

'Not if your movie is set in Las Vegas,' Danny said smoothly.

Keisha and Bronwen had vanished. Mrs Drummond breezed in to tell me they'd gone shopping in Gloucester with Gillian Loman. Bitches, how could they abandon me, just to shop with some Formula

One wife? Or maybe they were trying to thin the party so I could be alone with Seamus.

I felt Dolores's hand on my arm like a blazing poker. Burning me.

'I'm game,' Charlie Drummond bellowed across the room. 'Fancy a bit of a spin, darling? Come on, Tom, let's show the troops around.'

Tom looked reluctantly at me but had to get his coat. Seamus was right behind him. I got up but Ellen stopped me, waddling over and plumping herself down on the sofa between us.

'Alex isn't going anywhere. We've got too much to catch up on. Don't look at me like that, darling, I'm the bride and I get to do what I want.'

'Right,' cried Charles and kissed her on the cheek. And before I could say or do a bloody thing, the room was emptying, they were all piling out to the gravel. I could hear the men teasing Ted Loman about the speed limit. I could see Seamus getting into his cherry-red Ferrari.

And I was right here between Ellen and Dolores.

Oh God, I know it was only ten but I needed a bloody drink.

Ellen got me off the hook for the first ten minutes by talking about Charlie incessantly. 'He's so sexy, I can't think what he sees in me.'

'Blimey, I wouldn't go that far,' I said before I could stop myself. Ellen's pudgy face crumpled. 'Er . . . only joking, he's very dashing. I'm sure you're going to be very happy.'

'I know I'm not much of an oil painting,' sighed Ellen, and the flesh round her upper thighs wobbled when she did it, 'but he says he really loves me, you know. It must be so strange for you, Alex.' She beamed as she turned to Dolores. 'Alex never had any boyfriends at school either.'

Thanks! I gritted my teeth.

'But I was always sure she was going to be married *ages* before me. Being so thin and pretty.'

Did Dolores smirk at hearing me described that way? I thought I was going to be sick. Boy, I had been right the first time. I could never have competed with a girl who makes *Vogue*'s 'Best Dressed' list every year.

'Charlie always used to go for pretty girlies. But we have such a laugh together,' said Ellen earnestly.

'Seamus is exactly the same. Always running around after any fancy woman he sees. Can't keep it in his pants,' said Dolores bluntly.

'Don't you mean *was?*' asked Ellen tremulously.

'No. But you've got to tell yourself it doesn't harm the marriage.'

'It would harm mine,' Ellen protested.

'Well, I'm sure Charlie'll be different. They're not all as bad as Seamus. Jaysus, show him a girl not famed for the strength of her knicker elastic and he's off. Of course he only ever picks no-account whores.'

She pronounced it 'hoors'.

'He takes precautions, and he's never seen in a good part of town with them. So it doesn't embarrass me too much.'

'How can you stand it?' asked Ellen in horror.

Dolores lifted her hands to show her huge sapphire. 'First the engagement ring. Then the wedding ring. And then the suffering,' she said. 'Men are dogs.'

I could only say, 'Mmm.'

'His girlfriends are two a penny, none of them means a damn thing. Seamus would never divorce me. And they know it, the little tramps.'

'Maybe you should divorce *him*,' Ellen said, going puce at such a feminist thought.

Dolores gave a little bark. 'Maybe I should. Or maybe I should take some brave lover boy and give your man a taste of his own medicine.'

I know you're going to think this is supremely weird, but a part of me wanted to get up and cheer at that.

'So tell us all about your lovelife, Alex. It must be so exciting, it's so cool to be single these days. Us old married women are going to rely on you to supply all the passion in our lives,' Ellen gushed.

I shrugged. 'There's nothing to tell. I'm still looking for the perfect man to sweep me off my feet.'

'And has nobody done it for you yet?' Dolores asked me. Keenly. Was I being paranoid, or did she know? Was this whole thing warning me off?

'No. They all wanted to sweep me under the carpet instead.'

'You are *awful*, Alex,' Ellen tittered.

I couldn't take it any longer. I got up from the sofa pressing my hands to my skull. 'Look, I'm sorry, but I've got a crushing migraine. Can I leave you two to it?'

144

★

I was so thankful when my bedroom door closed behind me. I felt like a medieval Catholic seeking sanctuary in a church. Oh hell, the whole thing made me want to die. All the golden yuppie couples, and fat Ellen with her millionaire. And now Dolores. Whether she was warning me off deliberately or no, she'd done a bloody good job.

Seamus screwed around. I couldn't hide from the truth any more; not with Jenny and Dolores saying the same thing. I was just a passing bit of skirt. Most likely he went through the same routine with all of them.

I wished I could cry. That seemed the normal – the romantic – thing to do. But if I was honest, I'd done my crying on this one. The feeling was worse than that. It was just flat. Empty. Like love and passion had let me down once too bloody often. I sat here, and I wasn't really thinking about Seamus, I was thinking, what if I never find anyone to work me up the way Charles works up Ellen?

I didn't *want* to be alone. Christ, I had a bloody horror of it, of winding up a lifestyle piece in the *Evening Standard* – 'Unattached and Flirty at Forty.' But that was what was going to happen to me if I kept waiting for true love.

Maybe it didn't exist. Or worse, it *did* exist, just not for me.

I was limp. Absolutely whacked out with disappointment. Everything seemed monochrome, like all the colours had been sucked out of the sky.

I thought about Seamus some more. And in this disillusioned mode, my memories came back with a new twist on them. It *was* a bit sad, agreeing to pick up his dry-cleaning on our first date. And those suits – I thought of what Tom was wearing, and I wondered if those funny colours were flash? Weren't they actually a bit dandified? God, they *were*. I sat there and saw my face flush in the speckled antique mirror. Seamus's physique. I'd been telling myself it was poetic and slim, but didn't those descriptions go better with girls? And how he'd talk about himself all the time . . .

I sat very still, the rose colour draining out of my romance spectacles. Wasn't Seamus Mahon a bit *corny*, with those electric poems and flowers? Hitting on his secretary? Getting annoyed when he was interrupted?

Wasn't he actually a dandy? And a bit of a wimp?

This was something of a revelation. It hit me pretty hard. For a second, all I could do was gaze stupidly back at myself.

If you put *Seamus* through an Army assault course, he'd last about five minutes, I thought. Now God knows why that came into my head. But it did. I was blushing, actually blushing, because Dolores had made me see how silly I'd been. And guilty: she was hurting too, probably more. Seamus had told me his marriage was over, but I'd been bloody quick to accept that, hadn't I? Wives and mistresses, we believe what we want to believe. I couldn't just see Dolores as a *Tatler* photo any more. She got period pains, just like the rest of us. She was flesh and blood. And she was stuck with Seamus.

Imagine being stuck with Seamus.

I got up and crossed to the window. The cows were chewing buttercups and daisies most contentedly. Time rolled around and it didn't give a bugger about our broken hearts.

Maybe I should flirt with everybody, love nobody and marry the first single man who asked me. Keisha says a lot of women do that when they get to twenty-nine.

Gail rang to say she would arrive this afternoon, and Snowy was coming with her. We were discussing how much the Wildes should spend on our joint wedding present when all the cars rattled back into the drive. Ellen pounded past me like a mad thing. It was so soppy, she was like a puppy who couldn't wait to see her master again.

'Go for a silver teapot.'

'How about some crystal glasses? Harrods has some lovely Waterford.'

'Fine, whatever.' I really couldn't get too excited about the present. I guess it had to be something smart.

There was a tug on my elbow. I spun round to see Seamus, staring down at me urgently.

'I'll call you back,' I said to Gail, and hung up.

We stared at each other for a second. Then I backed off, but his grip tightened on me. His face was wary, but contorted with lust.

'Let me go.' I shook my arm free.

'You look amazing,' Seamus breathed. 'That haircut, I love it. And that suit. Whenever did you get so flash, Alex Wilde? You're killing me.'

'You've changed your tune. You looked pig sick to see me, before.'

'With herself standing right there?'

'Look.' I took a breath. 'You needn't worry, Seamus. I'm not going to chase you, I'm not bothered about it any more. We won't see each other in the office. If I'd known you were such a mate of Charlie's, I'd have got out of this.'

'Uh-huh.' He gave a nasty little laugh. 'Playing hard to get, is it?'

'Not playing at all. For God's sake, anybody could come along—'

'They're all busy,' Seamus said. The glint in his eye was pretty determined. 'I know how badly you've wanted this, Alex, so don't try and kid yourself. I hate it when the girls get coy.'

'I'm not interested.'

'The old "no means no" nonsense? I'm not the kind of fool who buys that,' Seamus said, and then he pounced on me and started to kiss me. I squirmed against him in fury, but his arms round my waist were locked tight. Thin little wimp he might have been, but it's a rare man who's not stronger than a woman. (Xena Warrior Princess obviously excepted.)

I would have yelled get off, but his mouth was clamped on mine. And he was pushing his tongue at me. Man, I'd longed for this, but now it was so repulsive, like some wretched little chihuahua licking at me. Seamus was reaching down a hand to fondle my ass now. I squirmed even harder, but we were in the west wing here, everybody else was at the front of the house – and *shit*, now he was getting an erection, shoving it crudely up against me—

'What the bloody hell do you two think you're playing at?'

A great paw clamped itself on Seamus's shoulder and ripped him off me like a child ripping off a plaster. Tom Drummond, standing there solid as a Stonehenge boulder and just as forbidding. He looked absolutely enraged.

'Jesus. Spoil somebody else's party,' said Seamus sulkily.

'This is my bloody house,' Tom snarled, 'and you'll behave in it or you can get out. My mother is coming up the garden with your wife.'

Seamus glanced out of the lead-paned windows with a stricken-rabbit expression. He bolted up the stairs before I could say a single word.

I glowed at Tom. I'd never been so glad to see anyone in my entire life. 'God, Tom, I—'

He held up one hand. He was still glowering. I could hardly believe he was the same comfy old Tom I'd been chatting to this morning, he was incandescent with rage. I wouldn't have liked to be the enemy when Tom was a soldier.

'You needn't try to excuse yourself. I saw you wriggling away.'

'What?' I gasped.

'If a bitch of mine acts like that, we have to tie her up, before all the dogs in the neighbourhood come running. Christ, Alex, he's married.'

'Who the bloody hell are you to judge me?' I snapped, tears prickling my eyes.

'I don't know how you can be so shameless.'

I was seeing red now. I was buggered if I was going to explain myself to him. 'Hey Tom, nobody died and made you God. Don't sit in your fancy house and give me lectures.'

'You act like a bloody alley cat!' Tom snarled. 'I suppose if I hadn't walked past you'd have been screwing right on the stairs?'

I reached forwards and slapped him round the face. Hard as I damn well could. He didn't even flinch, and it must have hurt, because I could see my palm print white on his face.

'You and Dolores were alone earlier. I suppose you chatted about all the things you had in common,' he said softly. 'Or did you tell her about climbing the ladder – how much easier it is to do it horizontally?'

'Fuck you!' I spat.

'I'd rather not. I don't know where you've been,' Tom said contemptuously. 'I think you'd better make some excuse and leave. Dolores Mahon is a friend of Charles's.' Then he turned on his heel and walked off.

I felt like someone had hit me in the solar plexus. Tom Drummond had never, ever treated me like that in his life before. I knew he was old fashioned, but – I wanted to start sobbing. The self-righteous bastard!

I didn't get the chance, because an ancient door creaked open and there was Mrs Drummond, with Ellen and Dolores in tow. Oh Christ, I thought miserably, I hope she can't smell her prick of a husband on me.

'Alex, are you all right?' Ellen said nervously. 'You look like you've seen a ghost.'

Seen a guest, you mean, I thought but didn't say. I was frantically searching for an excuse to leave this house but my traitor imagination had packed up on me. 'Come on upstairs and have a look at the bridesmaids' dresses,' Ellen burbled. 'God, I'm *so* glad we've been reunited for this. It must be fate. I'd die if you couldn't stay.'

I managed to calm down. Admiring Ellen's taste with a straight face took all my energy. Ellen had gone for the Flower Fairy look in a big way. Nobody's seen that many ruffles and bows since Princess Diana in 1981. Her red, puffy face beamed as she displayed the pink skirts for me.

'Stunning. So . . . striking,' I told her, but I was off in a world of my own. Feeling damn angry, if you want the truth. I always knew Tom was a male chauvinist pig. Looking like some Victorian prizefighter. Laying down the law like some bishop. Smug, priggish, arrogant bastard! I would be damned if he was going to run me out of this house.

I didn't want to stay – but now *nothing* would make me leave.

I pressed my lips together. Ellen was the bride, and *she* wanted me around. That was more important than being invited by the groom's brother.

'Do you know,' Ellen said slowly, like she'd just had one of those cartoon lightbulbs pop on over her head, 'I've only got my cousins as bridesmaids, and they're five – they're twins. They're bound to muck up the flower throwing. It would be *wonderful* if I had a matron of honour to keep them in line. I don't suppose you would, would you?'

Ten hours ago, no way José. But I thought of Tom when he got that news.

'I'd love to.'

Chapter 20

I spent the rest of the morning with Ellen. Quietly fuming while we played with all her bridal toys.

Brides have a whole bunch of toys. I suppose you never find this out until you're actually married. There was the dress. The slippers – extra-wide toes for Ellen, the Ugly Sisters would have got into these things fine. The ring – her engagement rock from Charles was a huge ruby on an antique silver band, and her wedding ring was plain white gold. She kept opening and shutting the box. She showed me the flowers, took me down to the pantry to see the cake – six tiers, white and yellow. 'Champagne sponge,' Ellen gushed. 'We wanted everything to be special. Oh gosh, Alex, did I show you the booze?'

I stared out at rows of Krug Premier Grand Cru. I knew Ellen's dad, Tyler, was dead – and these things cost major money. And this was just the drink.

'Who's paying for all this?'

'Tom,' Ellen glowed. 'He's been so generous, you can't imagine. As soon as Charlie told him he just took over. Charlie said *he* should do it, but Tom – well, he can be quite forceful.' She laughed. 'It's so wonderful, being a bride.'

I'll bet it is. Somebody should pass a law forbidding brides to go on and bloody on about their happiness and their nuptials in front of single women.

It's like eating a Big Mac in front of an Ethiopian. It's cruel and unusual punishment.

I'll tell you something pitiful. I have, on occasion, bought a copy of *Brides* at the newsagent, to read on the Tube. Just to live the dream for a tiny bit. To dither over simple shifts versus pretty embroidery. Pure white or cream? Heart neckline or scallop? To read articles about calming down the bridesmaids when the redhead won't wear pink. Do you go for the country bower, the beach at dawn or the smart

London church? Do you ask the Pope to book the Vatican, or elope to Vegas in jeans and a T-shirt? Veiled or bare headed? Wreath or tiara? Train or—

OK, OK, you get my drift.

The girls' magazines often run articles about how stressful a wedding is. And I clutch them to my chest and think, oh Lord, it wouldn't be stressful for me, I swear I would never think one irritated thought. I would *love* every bloody second of it. Picking the forks would be heaven. Posting the invitations would be utter bliss. It would be so joyous, even the mix-ups would be joyous.

But my abortive engagement to Justin was as close as I ever got. His ring was an emerald, a tiny green chip surrounded by seed pearls. I gave it back to him. I once saw a picture of Hannah in *Country Life* and her engagement ring was a socking great diamond. I suppose he felt her rolling acres deserved more in the way of ostentation. Sometimes I wonder what happened to that cheap little bauble he got me, think how I should have guessed the depths of his commitment when I saw it. But I can say honestly enough that getting that ring – at the bottom of a glass of wine, how clichéd – was one of the happiest moments of my whole life.

I know I wouldn't have been happy with Justin. Right now, he's campaigning to reinstate chains on women prisoners giving birth. 'Let's not forget these people are felons,' he was quoted in the *Telegraph*. 'If you can't do the time, don't do the crime.'

But still. Back to the *Brides* thing. The other part of it was that when you had one of those magazines – on the train, the Tube, anywhere really – other women noticed. The whole world noticed. Girls smile wistfully and wish they were you. Fat housewives give you motherly grins. Old men wink. Young guys say, 'You're better off wi' me, luv.'

And now I was in the middle of a walking, talking *Brides* feature, except Tom would never be so tacky as to let a magazine take photos of his brother's wedding. Ellen was going where Sue and Melissa and Gillian and Penny have been. Where Bronwen and Keisha and Gail could have been several times. Where the whole world, except me, seemed to go. She had got it all. The flowers, the cake, the rock on her finger.

And she'd got me.

'We've got *no* time to run up a matching outfit.' Thank God, because the twins' floral print was better suited to curtains. Or a Holiday Inn bedspread. 'What do you think of magenta? Mrs Drummond has a lovely Laura Ashl—'

'Er, I think I'll pop into Gloucester,' I interrupted hastily. 'Grab something simple.'

Ellen's pudgy face fell. 'Magenta would be smashing with the bouquet.'

Bloody hell, woman, I'm not going to look like an over-boiled Frankfurter just to coordinate with your flowers! 'But it's horrible with copper hair. I'll pick something that goes, I promise.'

Outside the ancient windows I could see a squirrel hanging on the branch of a yew tree. He stared at me despisingly before throwing a nut in my direction. I couldn't even get rodents to give me any respect.

'Please, Ellen.' I was desperate to get out of the house. But then I remembered I didn't have a car: Keisha and Bron had nicked our wheels.

'OK.' She looked crestfallen, but she didn't want a row. That was the Ellen I remembered: she'd always give in to me. 'If you're sure.'

'Double sure with a cherry on top. Oh look.' I pointed out the window as a Bentley screeched to a halt outside the front door. 'That must be Gail.'

Gail flung her arms round me in a pretty display of sisterly delight. Pukesville, she was usually as glad to see me as the gas bill. She was wearing a peach silk suit and she must have spent the whole of yesterday in a tanning salon. Her tiny legs were nutmeg brown, her blonde hair was blowing about her face.

'Wow, those look like Manolos,' I said, looking at the strappy, sexy bits of nothing on her feet.

'Mmm. Snowy got them for me. Snowy, darling, could you grab the luggage?'

Snowy stepped out of the driver's side. She was willowy and elegant in a white cotton pant suit, with a chic little hat and huge dark glasses. Her long hair was braided down her back. She walked around to the car boot swaying like a greyhound and lifted out two Louis Vuitton cases.

'Gosh, let me get those for you.' Charlie rushed forward, practically ripped them out of her hands. He was flushed, his mouth slightly open. His gaze travelled all over Snowy's gorgeous lean silhouette. His tongue was practically on the gravel. It's sick-making, the effect that girl had on men.

Snowy favoured him with a smile and whipped off her glasses, to reveal blue eyes silvered and turquoised into smoky beauty. Her perfectly neat plucked brow arched just a touch.

Instinctively I pressed finger to my own Noel Gallagher specials.

'Gail, how sweet of you to come,' Mrs Drummond said, and there was a hasty round of introductions. 'I don't think I know your friend.'

'This is Olivia White. She's our schoolfriend and she ferried me down,' said Gail artlessly, 'hope you don't mind.'

'The more the merrier,' said poor Mrs Drummond.

Ellen came across to hug Gail and Snowy. Next to them she looked like a pregnant elephant. Charlie muttered nice things but he could hardly take his eyes off Snowy's ass in that tight suit. There was no VPL whatsoever. My God, I wondered if she was wearing underwear? Most of the guys were back from scouting the churches. Danny and Ted were watching my sister and Snowy and talking intently to each other. Karl and Bill were laughing loudly and grinning like Cheshire Cats. I felt a sick little thud of jealousy. Wouldn't it be great if guys looked at *me* like that everywhere I went?

'Alex, you never told me your sister was so ravishing,' Danny Boyle said loudly. 'And with such edible friends. Any time you want me to babysit . . .'

I smiled weakly and fled into the house.

Ellen grabbed me before I could make a dash for it upstairs. 'Are you going to borrow your sister's car for Gloucester?'

I'd rather not. It was Snowy's, and I didn't want to owe that bitch any favours.

'I think she might be needing it,' I lied.

'Then Tom will take you. Tom!' Ellen padded across and pulled Tom out of the kitchen. His face tightened when he saw me; a little muscle was going in his cheek. 'Would you run Alex into Gloucester? She's going to be my maid of honour. And she needs a dress.'

'Didn't you want to use Mummy's pink Laura Ash?' said Tom.

'I don't think it'll suit me,' I said levelly.

'I'm sure Ellen will love it,' Tom said.

'Maybe.' I took a breath. 'But it won't suit *me*.'

Ellen was a little worried now, her huge cheeks were reddening.

Tom glanced at her. "Course I'll take her, Ellen. Come on, Alex, we'll go now.'

Outside I could hardly look at him as we headed into the maze of cars.

'Which one's yours?'

'The Rolls over there.' He pointed to a stunning, low-slung Silver Phantom. 'It's not locked.'

The old Tom would never have let me get into a car myself. I wrenched open the door and slid inside, frowning. Tom got in without a word, buckled up and eased us out on to the drive. We slipped noiselessly through his grounds: the trees half-golden, half-green; chestnuts scattered across the path and all the lawns perfectly cut.

'You know, the wedding day is about the bride,' he said stiffly, once we were out on the open road.

'What?'

'It's not about the dress suiting *you*, it's about what Ellen wants.'

'Well. I'm stepping in at the last minute and I'm not going to look like a Christmas decoration,' I snarled.

Tom laughed. 'Don't worry, Alex. Nobody could mistake you for an angel.'

'You've got no idea what it's like in the real world,' I spat. 'Dating Miss Perfect Linda and all those other nice girls. Life's not that neat for the rest of us.'

'You prefer a using bastard, a shabby little playboy like Seamus Mahon,' Tom said blandly.

'Seamus and I have nothing to do with you.'

'You do while you're under my roof. And Dolores is also my guest.'

'Wrong again. Ellen wants me to be her bridesmaid. Would you like to explain to her why you've chucked me out?' Tom was silent. 'See, your hands are tied, so you can shove it with the lectures, OK?'

'So you will not give him up? You don't care if people see you together?'

It was not like that any more. It never had been. Part of me wanted to explain, what Seamus told me, how I broke it off. But screw him!

'My life's my business.'

'Seamus Mahon.' Tom sounded almost bitter. 'Well.' He paused for thought, his knuckles white on the wheel. 'Maybe I owe you an apology. It's your life, why should I care?'

'Why indeed?'

'He's your speed. I – I once thought I was your speed.'

Oh right, and now you know I'm a scarlet woman, now you know better. 'Well, Tom, don't trouble yourself with those thoughts any more. I could never go for a man like you.'

'Oh?' he asked softly.

'No.' I wished I smoked, I would have struck up a fag right then. 'Insufferably arrogant, Tory, moneyed idiot. Think you're better and cleverer than the whole world. And you're so damn pious, they should build a church to you. "Saint Thomas the Slimmer." It's a good job you're not Catholic, Tom, you'd bore the priest to death in the confessional, wouldn't you? Being so much purer than everyone else. But it's pretty easy to be pure when nobody wants to tempt you.'

Tom was quiet for a moment. 'I had no idea you thought of me that way.'

'And I had no idea you would sit in judgment on me.'

'Was I wrong? Was it not how it looked? Maybe he did just pounce on you.'

'He did.'

'So you weren't having an affair with him?'

My turn to be silent. Tom looked away from me and put his foot down. We were going at a raging speed.

'I'm not scaring you, am I?' he asked.

My fists were clenched but I wouldn't give him the satisfaction. 'Not a bit.'

'Great,' Tom said, and pushed his foot to the floor.

In Gloucester Tom parked outside a big shopping centre.

'This isn't much good to me,' I told him. 'W.H. Smith's and Debenhams. Do you expect me to get something decent in Marks & Sparks?'

I was so frazzled now you could have fried an egg on me. It was an unseasonably hot autumn day, I was sweating madly in my smart knits and Tom had made me furious. What with Ellen and Seamus, I was feeling pretty wretched, if you want the truth. What were we doing in this provincial hellhole? I doubted there was a Prada boutique in the whole county. God, he probably expected me to go shopping in

C&A. He was trying to blackmail me into wearing the magenta thing with the huge bow.

'It'll have to do.' Tom leant back lazily against his car and looked me up and down. Damn it, I didn't like the way he did that. It used to be OK, but then Tom used to be as big as a house. Now he was still big, but he was stocky. Muscular. He looked like a real male.

I found it disturbing.

'There must be some designer shops round here. Gloucestershire's full of rich women.'

'But I'm not a woman,' Tom said flatly. 'Why the hell should I know where they are?'

I stomped off towards the shopping centre to find Tom following right behind me.

'What the hell do you think you're doing?'

'Coming with you,' he said simply.

'I don't need some hulking brute following me into womenswear.'

'You prefer pansies like Mahon who can be taken for women?'

'He's not a *pansy*. And what kind of a word is that?'

'I don't go for political correctness, Alex. The man's a pansy. Coloured suits and long hair and couldn't lift a can of baked beans without help.'

'He's got short hair.'

'It's coming over his collar. And you're going to get me, I'm afraid. I can't afford to have you getting lost and then delaying me getting home.'

'Go *away*.'

'What are you going to do?' asked Tom, smiling sunnily. 'Call a policeman and tell him I'm stalking you?'

I was spitting mad. 'Maybe.'

'Well.' He grinned infuriatingly. 'There's one, over there. Be my guest.'

A WPC with a face like a horse's butt was striding across the square right in front of us. She looked very important and busy.

I clenched my teeth and hit him. 'Bastard!' My fist connected into solid muscle, it actually stung my fingers.

'Now, now, violence never solves anything,' Tom said.

Had he always been like this? Overbearing, insistent on his own way? I suppose he had, but Tom and I had seen eye to eye at Oxford. He'd never approved of Justin, but he'd never given me any lectures either. Although Justin was single. And when I wanted to quit at Hamilton Kane, he'd laid down the law then too, but I hadn't minded, because I'd truly wanted to stay.

I minded now. I rejected everything in M&S in a second flat. Debenhams was better. Before you start laughing, they had a Pierce II Fionda exclusive design, a long, scoop-necked silky thing in dark iris. I tried it on, deliberately taking ages.

'Oh, it does suit you, modom,' the assistant told me, peering in through the curtain.

I stepped out to show Tom. He could eat his heart out. The long sweep of the material forgave a lot of sins. It showed my height and my smallish waist, it gave me a decent cleavage, and the colour was amazing with my hair and eyes.

I twirled, letting it catch the light. I knew I looked like a deep-blue tiger lily.

'You're not wearing that,' Tom said flatly.

I bridled. 'This is perfectly decent.'

'You're not wearing that. You're not going to upstage the bride,' Tom said, adding firmly to the saleswoman that we didn't want it, thank you.

'I bloody do want it,' I snarled.

'Then you can get yourself back to Carrefour. I suppose you could take a taxi, but you don't know the way, do you, sweetheart? You'd have to ring Ma for directions. And tell her why I left you here.'

'You're insufferable,' I gasped as I peeled the gown off. It was even worse because the assistant forgot who was in what cubicle and whisked back my curtain, flashing me in the full glory of my grimy M&S knicks to Tom. She screamed, I screamed, she yanked back the curtain.

'Don't bloody gawp at me, you peeping Tom!'

'Appropriate, huh?' I could hear the smile in his voice. 'Don't worry, Alex, there's nothing there to interest me.'

Chapter 21

'We could try BHS,' Tom suggested, when I finally made it out, dishevelled and red faced. 'There's one downstairs. Or a Next across the street.'

'You must be out of your bloody mind. Do you think I'm going to be a maid of honour in something from *Next*?'

Tom shrugged. The thick set of his shoulders had all the little shopgirls making eyes at him over their tills.

'What are you frowning at?'

'Those girls are staring at you.'

Tom grinned as I followed him out of the door. 'Are you jealous, Alex?'

'I don't happen to go for brutes and bullies,' I said, stomping off to River Island. 'I like my men poetic and sensitive.'

'Mmm. Like the pop star who looks like a stick insect.'

'Do you mean Jarvis Cocker? Pulp are brilliant, actually.'

'Pulp, what an appropriate name. I don't see why you can't grow up and listen to some Mozart occasionally.'

'Maybe because I wasn't born two hundred years old,' I howled, frantically flipping through the racks in search of something suitable. Nothing was demure enough, dressy enough, or pretty enough (without being *too* pretty). Time and again I would sigh and pick up something soft, and Tom would say, 'That's upstaging.'

'Goddamn it. I would upstage Ellen wearing a paper bag!' I fumed.

Tom gave me a considered look at that. 'You really can be a spoilt brat, Alex. She's supposed to be your friend. You've got no idea how much you wallow in self-pity.'

'That's it.' I hung the silver shift thingy back on the wall peg. 'You win. Take me home, I'd rather wear that fucking magenta horror than spend another second in your company.'

'Marvellous, we finally agree on something.' He shifted his great rangy bulk out of the tiny Hennes chair. 'You put all that stuff back and I'll meet you at the car.'

Insufferable! I seethed quietly as I traipsed round hanging the damn dresses back up. I was so angry I kept knocking other dresses off their hangers, and they'd all slither to a pile on the floor, and the assistants would give me the old look of death as they dived on top of them. But I couldn't give a bugger about the assistants, I'd had enough aggro for this incarnation already.

It was by the exits that inspiration struck. There was a wall-mounted telephone. And I had a credit card and stacks of ten pences.

'Hello, is that Debenhams? I was in there earlier trying on the Pierce II Fionda dress? Why don't I give you my Visa, and I'd like to pay extra for express delivery. I'll ring you with the address in about half an hour, is that OK?'

They couldn't have been more helpful. Ha ha ha, I thought with triumph, I am woman, hear me roar.

We drove back ludicrously fast. But I smile lightly like it didn't scare me at all.

'Don't worry,' Tom said maddeningly.

'I'm not worried. Do I look worried?'

'I took advanced driving in the Army. Off-road too. And flew a chopper, so I know how to handle this.'

'I'm not interested in your exploits in the military regime. That *Boys' Own* stuff doesn't impress me.'

'Ah. Still a bit of a leftie, are we? Somebody's got to man the watchtowers, Alex, so you can buy your designer frocks in peace.'

I ask you, what kind of a man says frocks?

'We'll put the wireless on. Listen to a bit of the Grand Prix. Do you like Formula One?'

'Not in the slightest.'

'Oh dear,' Tom said unrepentantly, and twisted the dial to Murray Walker.

'Your sister's blossomed,' Tom said when we got nearer the house.

'I suppose so.' I thought of Gail, her birdlike prettiness, her waify, elfin quality that she plays up all the time. Tough as old boots, but who cares? Fragile girlies like that are what all the boys go for. She makes them feel like big, strong men – not that Tom needed any help.

'All the chaps looked mad keen. And who's her friend?'

'That's Olivia White. She was at school with us, and now she's a neighbour.'

Tom didn't say a word. I worried that Gail shouldn't have brought an extra guest, it would throw Mrs Drummond's seating plans out, but even though we were fighting, he was too polite to mention it.

'Your sister works for a health food magazine, doesn't she? What does Olivia do?'

'I don't know. She sort of shops and parties. A bit like Linda Severn, I suppose.' I flung in a dig at his ex.

'She's nothing like Linda,' said Tom, so darkly that I shut up for the rest of the drive.

The house was in chaos by the time we got back. Everybody was picnicking on the upper lawn, there were huge, old-fashioned wicker baskets everywhere and rugs and paper plates scattered across the grass. The men had all had a boozy lunch, I could hear raucous male laughter coming from the drawing room. They were all probably watching the stupid racing and kissing up to Ted Loman, who might be on the circuit next year.

The Drummond friends were fairly flash, if you like that obvious sort of thing. I saw Gillian Loman, Keisha and Bronwen finishing off a quiche to my right. Gillian was sprawled out on the tartan throw. She was wearing a Chanel suit, pink with white piping. She looked stunning, just right in the sunshine.

'Did you find anything?' Ellen asked, waddling up to me.

'She's going to stick with the magenta,' Tom said.

In your dreams, mate, I thought, but I just smiled blandly at Ellen.

'Oh, right. Well, come and have lunch, Alex, you must be starving.'

Actually I was. I followed her across to Gillian's patch. Ellen rummaged around in the delicious-looking hamper and pulled out a champagne flute. 'Most of it's gone, but we'll rustle something up — how about a salmon torte, and have a Scotch egg, and some *foie gras*, here's some crusty bread . . .'

'This is masses.' I helped myself to a little parma ham, a roll and a white peach. Keisha filled up my champagne flute with Perrier Jouet.

'Aren't these hampers wonderful?'

'They certainly are. Mrs Drummond has really pushed the boat out,' I agreed.

'Oh no.' Ellen's florid face was beaming up at me as she started tucking into everything I just refused. 'Tom got these in for us, he ordered them from Harrods. Oh, I know I shouldn't,' she added as she sliced up the Scotch egg, 'but it's so heavenly, don't you think?'

She was getting married in a couple of days. How could she stuff her face like that? What was her ribbed bodice made of, steel girders?

I ate my food sulkily. It certainly was delicious. 'Where's Snowy?'

'Charles and Karl are helping her unpack,' Bronwen said.

I looked round, and saw Tom had finally wandered off. He was being fawned on by Penny and Melissa, and was telling them some very amusing story. I wondered angrily if it was about me.

'Who's coming for a ride?' Elspeth Drummond asked us after lunch.

Carrefour has a riding stables attached to it at the back. They lease their facilities to a local riding school, but for the wedding weekend, they'd made sure there were twelve available horses.

'Oooh me, I love animals,' Gail cried.

'And me. Bags I ride Hector,' said Gillian.

Keisha said she thought she'd pass, Bronwen wanted to sit and read.

'I've got tons of things to do,' Ellen declined, and most of the boys made their excuses. Perfect. A chance for some fresh air.

'I'd like to go. If it's not too strenuous.'

'You'll love it, Alex, a lovely gentle ride,' Mrs Drummond said. That old bag Georgia Jones was up for it too, worse luck. Then Seamus Mahon, with a furtive look at me, said he'd love to try it.

'Really? And maybe it'd do me a power of good,' Dolores said sweetly.

'And me. Nothing better for clearing the head,' Tom said firmly.

Bloody wonderful.

Then there was a rustle at the top of the stairs and all heads turned to see Snowy, her perfect thighs wrapped in jodhpurs, her perfect boobs snug in a soft tweed jacket, walking slowly down the stairs in chestnut leather riding boots.

'I wonder if you could spare a mount for me,' she said. 'I love a good ride.'

'I bet you do, darling,' said Ted Loman under his breath.

'I'd oblige her,' whispered Bill Radcliffe to his mates. I flashed him a dirty look but he didn't notice: all the boys' stares were glued to the panty less V of Snowy's crotch.

'Of course,' said Mrs Drummond obliviously. 'Do you prefer your mounts fast or slow?'

'It depends on my mood,' said Snowy softly. I could see Charlie Drummond, hanging in the door behind us. Both Charlie and Tom were spellbound; Tom couldn't take his eyes off her. 'Anything's fine.'

'I might tag along. Make sure they don't run off with you, 'Livia,' muttered Charlie. She flashed him a thousand-watt smile – maybe I should have passed out the sunglasses. 'Oh Charlie, how sweet of you to look after me.'

'Darling, you promised to run through rehearsals with me,' Ellen objected, but Charlie was hardly listening.

'Can't we do that on the day? "I do" is quite a short line – I'm not likely to forget it,' joked the blushing groom.

Mrs Jones gave Olivia the look my mother reserves for other people's dogs when they scent-mark our sofa.

The stables were ready when we arrived, the horses assembled in the yard. Most of the party had smart riding kit on, including Gail; I was still in Tom's spare Wellingtons and some baggy jeans. Charlie Drummond faffed around, helping Snowy on to the smartest horse, a grey mare.

'She's as pure bred as you are,' I heard him whisper.

Snowy flicked her long golden locks behind her helmet. 'What makes you think I'm so pure? I can be a very bad girl, you know.'

I was sure it couldn't be necessary for his hands to dwell quite so much on her bottom as he helped her up. I expect he was just enjoying a rear that didn't swallow his hand when he pressed against it.

'Maybe we could ride together. You can tell me all about Alex and Gail,' said Charlie, who hardly knew me from Adam.

Snowy seemed to swallow it, and she nodded and whispered, 'Mmm, up close and personal.'

Tom came charging up to me, astride a socking great Cleveland Bay, a gelding. It looked a vicious brute, but Tom ignored the whisking head.

'I mustn't let Charlie monopolise Olivia, must I, Alex?'

'Certainly not.' This was Gail, trotting over on a small Palomino.

She smiled winsomely up at Tom. 'You'll make sure everybody mingles, Tom.'

'I do my best. God's teeth, Gail, how pretty you've got.'

Gail blushed and batted her eyelashes. 'Thanks. And you're so slim.'

'I certainly hope not. I may not be a hopeless bucket of lard any more, but,' he flexed his muscles under that lumberjack shirt, '*slim* I'm going to have to leave to the ladies. Such as yourself.'

'I'm as heavy as a house,' said Gail.

Tom shook his head admiringly. 'As a dolls' house. Why don't you ride with me? We can catch up. I suppose you must be knee-deep in admirers.'

Gail's eyes lit up. 'Not really. Nobody I truly fancy.'

'There is a God,' Tom laughed, and the two of them clip-clopped a little way from me, which suited me fine, I can tell you.

'So we meet again, Alex Wilde,' said a quiet voice behind me.

It was Seamus. He pulled up beside me, in what I guess he thought was a subtle move. Like maybe if he looked over at his wife while he was talking to me, nobody would notice.

'Seamus, I've said everything I'm going to say,' I told him heavily.

Will somebody please explain why I couldn't get this man to acknowledge I existed last week, and yet now he was all over me?

'Don't let one quarrel come between us, darlin'.'

'There is no *us*. Honestly, Seamus, I'm not attracted to you.'

'You didn't say that in the flat last month,' he whispered meanly. 'Think about it, Alex. I could make things very difficult for you.'

'For God's sake, what about Dolores?' I hissed. Dolores turned her head, just at that moment, and the look on her face – oh Christ, she was so hurt, and then this second look came across her and she was all composed again.

'You didn't think about her before either.'

'Yeah, well, you lied to me, you little toe-rag. Sod off.'

'There's nothing worse than a filthy mouth, Alex.'

'Except a filthy mind. Seamus, I wouldn't touch you with somebody else's.' That's a phrase of Keisha's, but I relished having to trot it out now. I could see him stiffen beside me. 'I'd rather sleep with a leper. OK?'

Seamus forgot to look at his wife. His head whipped straight around to me. 'You'd better learn to play nice, Alex. If I want you, you'd better be ready to go. And don't be giving me any lip, either.'

'Oh yeah?' I turned my head too. I could see people were watching us, but I didn't care. 'What, you've got mates in the IRA and they're going to put me in a concrete overcoat at the bottom of the Thames?'

'Nothing so dramatic. I'll just see to it you get fired. And put it about the City that you're a sex-mad little tramp.'

I swear that's what he said. I was looking at him with my mouth hanging open when a shadow fell across us, and Seamus glanced up like a toad to see Tom Drummond looming over him like the wrath of God. Tom was Dolores's placid mount by the bridle.

'Your beautiful wife's getting lonely over there, Mahon. You'd better watch out, or somebody's going to swoop on her.'

'Ah, darlin', you know I'm always after talking shop,' Seamus said gently. He smiled at poor Dolores with the full wattage of his charm. I was still breathing heavily, trying to collect myself. Her beautiful face was tight with humiliation, and she gave me a look that said, 'How could you, you Judas?'

First I wanted to tell her it was not like that, but then it hits me: what could I say? 'It's OK, I *was* sleeping with him but I'm not any more?'

Seamus and Dolores looked like they were still having a furious row when Mrs Drummond mercifully struck off over a field.

Ah, the country. How restful. How peaceful.

I hate bloody horses. I hate them. Bastards. All they do is whisk their stupid tails and eat grass and fart, and then stop to take a massive crap while everybody else is miles ahead of you.

My ass was numb, my thighs felt like I'd used a thighmaster and it had got locked at the widest point. My hands were white with straining on the reins. And I was also spattered with mud and I was sore and tired.

We'd gone up hill and down dale. Even though the woods were tinder-dry, we still managed to hit the only filthy patch in Gloucestershire by riding along 'the banks of the stream', as Mrs D kept enthusing. I was last in file, because Coach – obviously short for Slowcoach – refused anything faster than an amble and kept stopping to feed. And she was not a fussy eater. She had a go at twigs and branches and bushes. Whatever. She was Ellen's spiritual horse. Being last meant everybody else's animal had churned up the ground to liquid shit, and then their nasty little hooves kicked the mud up at me.

And everyone kept yelling, 'Buck up, Alex!'

Of course, the rest of the Sloane Rangers were having the most *wonderful* time. Dolores was riding up front with Seamus and Mrs D; at least I didn't have to worry about him right now. Although what he said did make me queasy. It wasn't easy getting the lousy job I had. Could he truly get me fired? With a dreadful reference, who'd take me on?

Chapter 22

Snowy and Charlie were locked in it. Flirting away like mad. Every time Snowy pulled ahead, she rose and fell in the saddle like real riders do. I was convinced it was just to give Charlie a better look at her butt.

'Look at Dolores and Seamus. Isn't it sweet?' she said.

Charlie nodded. 'So marvellous, a good marriage.'

'Mmm, you're lucky. To be so sure, I mean. How awful, if you picked the wrong person! You'd be stuck with them for the rest of your days.'

I couldn't hear Charlie's reply, but he looked thoughtful.

Gail was trotting along with Tom. My God, she had him spellbound.

I yanked Coach's reins a bit harder, trying to pull her on to the bridleway. It was overgrown with bracken and thorns and there were midges everywhere.

'Look at the marvellous blackberry flowers,' said Mrs Jones loudly.

Charlie whipped his head round to encounter the freezing gaze of his mother-in-law. 'I ought to ride with Dolores Mahon,' he muttered reluctantly.

'Do whatever you like,' Snowy whispered back, 'but faint heart never won fair lady.'

'You're right. By God,' Charlie said, and pulled his horse a little closer to Snowy's. Maybe they didn't realise how their words were carrying. I prayed that Coach wouldn't decide to go for a late burst of speed, and drag me right into the middle of it. I supposed I should have been more shocked, but I was beginning to think I'd been a bloody fool. Maybe all men were like this. Maybe none of them knew how to keep it in their pants.

When a man tells you it's Tuesday, you should check the calendar, right?

'You ought to have a little fun while you still can,' Snowy said, her voice risen by a good octave, and she was breathing hard like she'd just finished a marathon. Her tits were swelling like a summer sea.

'What d'you mean?'

'Well. After the wedding, you won't be able to. Freedom will be a thing of the past.' Charlie looked bit green. 'But think of all the advantages,' Snowy went on, 'your own wife to make love to every night.'

'It's not like that. Our – er – relationship, it's not that physical,' Charlie mumbled.

'Mmm. How disappointing. If you were my husband, I'd insist on my conjugal rights.'

'You would?' Charlie stammers. His jodhpurs were beginning to strain with the most enormous erection. God, I couldn't tell you how huge it was. You couldn't exactly miss it, against the tight beige fabric. For a stupid second, I wondered if Tom was equally well endowed.

Oh well. What was I supposed to do about it? Fortunately Mrs Jones was riding slightly ahead, pointing out the lovely squirrels and the lovely butterflies, and Seamus and Dolores were still fighting, and Tom was dancing attendance on Gail. Coach decided she wanted some mouthfuls of bracken, which gave me a second.

Hmm. Seemed Ellen's perfect wedding wasn't so perfect after all, I thought triumphantly. Why should I be the only one whose lovelife was a crashing failure? Why should Ellen and her dragon of a mother and her coven of married harpies triumph over me and—

Suddenly I felt a little thrill of fear pass right through me. The bloody horse was speeding up. She paid no attention to my tugs on her bridle, in fact she started trotting, faster and faster. Oh shit.

Then suddenly she neighed loudly, ducked her head between her knees and gave a huge, plunging buck, making me grab tight to the pommel of her saddle.

'Bugger it, careful,' shrieked Gillian Loman.

'Alex! What the hell are you doing?' squealed Gail, taking the opportunity to cling passively to Tom like a damsel in distress.

I would have said I was sorry, but I couldn't speak in case all that comes out of my mouth was a terrified moan. I squeezed my knees harder and harder round her podgy little stomach, but the nasty brute wouldn't pay any attention, and turned the trot into a canter.

I couldn't ride. I hated this. Shit! My breath was coming in Snowy-like gasps and I wanted to puke up. Slow down slow down oh God can everyone see me panicking?

Isn't it amazing how you always fantasise yourself as calm and resolute in moments of terror, when what you actually are is a gibbering mass of cowardice?

I always have morbid deathbed fantasies. One of my favourites is being seated on a jumbo jet when both engines cut out, and as the plane goes down, and everybody's screaming, I turn to my neighbour with a rueful smile and engage him in a passionate, defiant kiss.

Of course, my neighbour is always a handsome, single man. Not like in real life, where he is a fat bastard with bad breath or a spotty teenage mother clutching a puking baby. Also, in real life, I find I get reduced to tearful jelly at the slightest bit of turbulence ('I don't know why you're gripping your arm-rests and pulling that rictus face,' Gail sniped the last time, calmly reading her *Vogue* while our plastic spoons were jittering off the edge of the tray. 'It's not going to keep the plane up').

So there I was, wishing the hateful horse was dead and thinking about Christopher Reeve, and trying to cling on, and not look down – when the galloping (OK, cantering, but it felt like galloping) shuddered to a crashing halt. I screamed as I was jolted forward, but a solid bulk blocked me, holding me still.

I squealed. Maybe I was a bit hysterical.

'Easy! Easy,' said a deep voice, and I glanced up and it was Tom. He had my mount's reins twisted in one hand, and was steadying me with the other. 'It's OK, Alex, you're all right now.'

'What do you mean, *all right*? Your fucking horse nearly killed me!'

'I doubt you were in any danger,' Tom soothed me, with an annoying grin.

'She wouldn't slow down,' I said tearfully, 'I was squeezing and squeezing, she was going to bolt any minute, she's a psycho.'

Tom tried to bite back a smile. 'I thought you loved all those Jilly Cooper books.'

'I do. In Jilly Cooper the ponies are all sweet. Not psychos like this thing.'

'Uh, Alex – when you squeeze a horse's tummy with your legs,' Tom said gently, 'you're telling him to go faster. If you want him to slow down, you have to sort of lean back in the saddle and stick your legs out either side.'

He shows me this ridiculous 'Farmer Giles of Ham'-type pose.

'So I was making it go faster? It would have bolted off?' I asked urgently, because the others were catching up now.

'Maybe. She thought you wanted a gallop,' Tom said gravely, 'but don't worry, I knew you weren't in control.'

'How?' I snarled.

'Because I know you,' Tom said, looking right at me.

To tell the truth, my emotions were seething. I was so relieved I could have cried, but I'd be damned if I came over all girly in front of Tom. I was grateful but resentful. Who would want to feel thankful to him?

I looked around me. We were in the middle of nowhere. Just a few feet ahead of me, the ground cut away. It was an old quarry. The Cotswold stone sides plunged a hundred feet straight down, but the horse probably wouldn't have noticed that 'til we were over the edge.

Tom saw my stricken face.

'You weren't going over that, Wilde.'

'Tell that to Coach.' A cold sweat had doused my body. 'You saved me rushing into that.'

That sentence caused me such a fever of embarrassment I could scarcely look at him. It came out pretty begrudging, but so what?

It could have been worse. I could have betrayed the sudden, utterly ridiculous sensation rocking through me. Desire. Primal desire, actually, naked lust like I hadn't felt in a long time. Not the mist-shrouded, gift-wrapped mooning I had for Seamus, but something so dark it surprised me. Amazed me. A vivid picture of Tom Drummond, naked and solid, nothing romantic in his build, just a strong male animal with too much testosterone. Arrogant, yes, chauvinist, sure, but kind of sexy all the same. Like Mr Darcy in those britches, or Sean Bean in *Sharpe*.

A type of bloke I'd always despised. And I wasn't interested in Tom, I knew I wasn't. This was just that feeling I'd read about, the life-urge, or something. You know, whenever you have a near-death encounter, you're supposed to want to have sex immediately afterwards just to affirm you're still alive.

That's what this was. Hormones.

'Hey.' Tom looked down on me. His horse was taller than mine (and I'd have liked to make mine smaller still, about the size of some cans of Winalot), and he was rangy himself. Tom's dark eyes were locked on to me with a curious light in them. 'I couldn't do without the maid of honour.'

'Yeah, whatever.'

'And I'd have hated to upset the beautiful Gail.'

Gail, of course. How silly of me to think he didn't used to fancy her, when we were at Oxford. Obviously he was just being polite. Why wouldn't he fancy Gail? She weighs the same as a thistledown and she's as delicate as a cobweb. Pure sexist gits like Tom are made for Gail. She would quit her job in a nanosecond and settle down to wearing Chanel and Philip Treacy hats, and having the odd baby for a nanny to look after.

'Maybe she wouldn't have been too upset. Black's a great colour for Gail,' I said bitterly.

'A little sisterly disapproval?'

'None of your business. I think we should be getting back,' I told him, looking away. Yes, I definitely fancied him. I must have been going mad from the country air. Maybe it was the pesticides on the fields, because if I had been in my right mind I wouldn't have given a damn about him hankering after Gail.

'Let me check you first,' he said, and before I could stop him he was running his hands across my body. Very sharp and professional, like he was still a soldier and he was looking for a concealed gun. His fingers were dry, precise. They didn't pat, they didn't stray, more's the pity – now where did that come from? I didn't truly want this rich egotist pawing me, did I?

Tom lifted his stubby fingers and tilted my face towards his. Oh man. The dry stroking, and now this. Thank God my jean jacket was more roomy than Charlie's jodhpurs, because my nipples had stiffened despite myself, and it was too balmy out here to pretend it was the wind.

He stared at me. Minutely. It was crying out for a kiss, this was, and for a second I thought he was going to do it, to tilt that square jaw down to me, but then he pulled back suddenly, like he was afraid of giving me the wrong impression.

'You don't look bruised.'

'Not on the outside,' I muttered.

'What?'

'Nothing. Look, we have to get back, they'll be worried. If you can tow this damned pig of a horse.'

'Not much of a reader of *Horse and Pony*, I take it?' Tom released Coach's reins and moved round behind her. 'Let's have a look at her rump.'

I was paralysed with mortification at the thought of him having a look at mine while he was at it. Not that I *cared*, exactly, but let's face it, my bottom is so big it's twinned with a small village in France. It was probably spilling out over the saddle in a squishy and disgusting manner right then.

'That's one hell of an ass,' Tom chuckled.

I pulled myself up to my full height, as far as it went. 'You can talk, mate! You're no Adonis yourself, you know. Besides, if I want personal comments I'll ring my mother. Thank you very much.'

There was a stupefied pause. 'Not you, you nitwit, the horse! Its backside is covered in scratches. No wonder she bucked, she must have torn it on some brambles.'

'Oh,' I replied lamely. Gail would have passed it off with casual insouciance, I'm sure, but I couldn't be that cool.

'Easy, girl, easy,' Tom murmured, and pulled around to caress the horse's ears. She snorted excitedly, the kiss-ass. If she thought I'd forgiven her for bolting just because of a few pesky stings, she was mistaken. That was how our cavalry troops beat the Cossacks, or whoever it was, was it?

I wouldn't be coming round to her stall with a handful of Polos, I can tell you.

'We'd better get her back and call the vet. He can give her a shot for the pain,' Tom told me.

'Well. *I* need a shot for the shock.'

'What of?' Tom asked blankly.

'Brandy or whisky,' I grinned, but Mr We Are Not Amused failed to crack a smile.

'I hope you're not going to get drunk and fling yourself at Seamus Mahon.'

'Going to threaten to chuck me out again, are you?' I asked nastily. 'I thought we'd gone over this, Tom. I don't need your lectures.'

'Christ, will you listen to me for once?' Tom ran a big paw through his thick dark hair. 'I saw you earlier, locked in it with Seamus. And I'm not the only one, Alex. Everybody else saw you too – including Dolores. Do you really want to make an exhibition of yourself?'

'No, of course not. I was trying to—'

I was about to launch into a detailed explanation, but the contemptuous look on that chiselled face suddenly shut me up. 'I'm not seeking to talk to him, OK? That's all you need to know.'

'You're not. Well, I'm sure that'll be a great comfort to his wife.'

'Oh congratulations, Tom,' I snarled. 'You didn't tell me the Queen made you Archbishop of Canterbury. And here I am thinking you were just a mate of mine, when you're actually responsible for the nation's morality. Seamus has other women, you know. Lots of them – it's not like Dolores doesn't know it, she told me herself. She should divorce him if that's how she feels.'

'I can't believe you,' Tom said softly. Somehow that tone of voice hurt me more than when he flew into a furious rage. 'Lots of other women. So that makes it all right? You don't mind being part of his harem?'

I took a deep breath. 'There's nothing between Seamus and me, Tom. And I don't owe you any explanations.'

'Fine.' He stiffened in the saddle and tugged on Coach's reins. Amazingly, she responded instantly, walking obediently alongside Tom's gelding.

I wanted to have a screaming fight with him about this, but I bit my tongue. What could you do, when the annoying bastard had just saved your bacon?

We were in sight of the others when Tom deigned to speak to me again.

'We're going to have to have a little talk.'

'I don't think so. I've had enough of your little talks to last me for a bit, thanks.'

'It's about Olivia.'

'What about her?' Now he'd got my dander up. He was deliberately trying to make me feel one foot high. Everything I did was wrong: even if it was actually Gail who had brought her along, yours truly was the one who was going to get the lecture. 'If you objected to another guest, you could have said so when she arrived. It's going to look a bit weird if I have to tell her to leave now.'

'I hadn't—' Tom broke off, looking awkward. As well he might, the rude fucker. What kind of a host was he being? 'I hadn't thought it through then.'

'I see. And now you have, and my friends aren't good enough for you.'

'I didn't say that.'

'You might as well have, though. If you want her to leave, you'd better speak to her yourself. I'm not your social secretary.'

'Actually . . . I did have a word with her last night,' Tom muttered. He couldn't even look me in the face. Now I was shocked, even more shocked than I was angry. Had Tom Drummond really changed that much? He had always been the perfect gentleman, back in the days when he was fat and I didn't fancy him. Now he was uninviting my friends from his house. Not that Snowy was *my* friend, but he didn't know that.

Is it a life rule? All attractive men are bastards? Tom had got attractive, so he had to turn into a bastard too?

Chapter 23

'She refused to leave,' Tom said.

I spurred Coach pretty hard, sending her trotting towards the others. The late afternoon had turned a rosy gold, the sun over the hills washing banners of scarlet behind the forest.

'Then you've got a problem, I don't see what I'm supposed to do. I can't force her to go. Don't you think it'll look a bit odd, when she's been here for a day already?'

Tom looked crossly at me. 'Well then, get her to keep herself to herself. The way she's flirting with my brother is appalling.'

'It takes two to tango, mate. Charlie's the one who's promising to forsake all others, not Olivia.'

'Don't you give a damn about the sanctity of marriage?'

'I'm not *getting* married. I don't see your brother politely excusing himself.'

'I see I can have no effect on you,' Tom said stiffly. 'Maybe I'll have more success with your little sister. She seems willing to listen, at least.'

I was sure Tom would have every success with Gail. She must have been thrilled, I thought bitterly, she had always set her cap at him, how triumphant for her that it was all coming right.

But the cheek of him! Like his brother couldn't take any decisions on his own. Men like to excuse themselves – oh, she made me do it, I couldn't resist her. It's a Galactic cop-out, if you ask me. Tom could do his Sex Police thing on his own. I mean, sure, Snowy shouldn't have been flirting with the groom, but Snowy flirted with every man. Charlie was the one in the 'committed' relationship. For most men, a 'committed' relationship means they'll be staying for breakfast, and you'll be cooking it.

Coach finally ambled on to the bridlepath again, and I told the gawking guests what had happened and listened to Gillian and Gail coo over Tom's heroism.

'Buck up, Alex. You look so grumpy,' Snowy giggled.

I glanced at Charlie but his hard-on had mercifully disappeared.

'I'm going back, if that's OK. I need a bath,' I mumbled.

'I'll come with you,' Seamus said right away.

Tom stared at me with all the warmth of an arctic iceberg.

'No thanks, I want to be on my own. Feeling a bit shook up,' I told him firmly.

'Maybe later,' Seamus said.

'I'll go with her,' Mrs Jones said generously, shifting her vast bum in the saddle. 'I'm sure too much exercise is no good for me. One has to pace oneself.'

The bathroom had been tidied up in my absence. Someone had laid out gallons of Floris bath essence and fresh fluffy white towels. As I scrubbed my scalp, I stared out at the rows of lavender, washed rose in the approaching sunset, and tried not to be too miserable.

Seamus Mahon was a problem I would just have to put off. I couldn't think about work right now.

I wondered how Tom Drummond could be having this effect on me. He was so priggish and aggravating. And of course anybody was vulnerable when somebody had just stopped them from charging over a cliff.

But he was not interested in me. He'd made that very clear. First he thought I was the Whore of Babylon because I'd had an affair with Seamus. Then he told me I was selfish about Ellen – me! – and finally he let me know that my friends weren't good enough and I should uninvite them from his house. That's what he was really saying, after all. Snowy and I went to the same school, we were not upper class like him, our parents were relentlessly suburban. He was saying Snowy should go, and what he meant was, I should go.

Perhaps he had been different at Oxford because he had had higher hopes of me then. Maybe he thought it would be smart to have a little commie, a leftie artist, in his circle. But now I was not a commie or even an artist. Now I was just failed old Alex. He probably invited me down just so he could confirm to himself what a tragic disappointment I really was.

It was too morbid to be thinking like this. I decided to try and think about something else.

I came down from my room two hours later in my Donna Karan silk suit, with my hair blow-dried and gleaming, and my best make-up on.

Tom Drummond was offering pre-dinner glasses of sherry to everybody in the drawing room. He didn't give me so much as a second glance.

Ellen and Charlie were sitting together perched on a corner of the sofa. So were Seamus and Dolores, both of them sending me hostile glances. Snowy was lounging about with Gail, Keisha and Bronwen, wearing a backless satin cocktail dress that drew the eyes of the men like a homing beacon.

'So Dolores, what's the secret of a happy marriage?' Ellen beamed plumply. 'Good cooking, I expect,' and she squealed with laughter.

'I'd say it's not to expect too much out of life,' Dolores said bleakly.

'But friendship is so much more important than sex, isn't it?' Ellen said earnestly. 'I mean, that's what you've got left when you're eighty.'

Snowy got up and crossed the room. The whisky decanter was right in front of Charlie, and she bent over to freshen her crystal tumbler, giving him the full Grand Canyon view. Scarlet satin slithered around the lean contours of her body like a snakeskin. 'The trouble is, there's a few years to go before you reach eighty,' she said smoothly.

'But passion's so overrated,' Ellen said nervously. Her eyes were fixed on Snowy like a mouse on a cat.

'Do you think so?' Snowy asked sweetly, before going to sit by Danny Boyle. Danny was a single man, of course. I shot a meaningful look at Tom as Danny put a tanned hand on her upper arm and started to stroke it.

Charlie Drummond looked like he wanted to strangle Danny, but that was hardly Snowy's fault, was it?

'I find it's vital,' she went on. 'I can't live without it.'

Suddenly every man in the room started to cough and take large swigs of their own drinks.

'What do you say about passion, Alex Wilde?' Seamus Mahon suddenly asked loudly, causing his wife to shoot him a look of pure hatred. I blushed fire-engine red to the roots of my hair, making me look guiltier than ever. Oh God, what had I done?

'It's never been anything to write home about for me,' I said firmly. 'I agree with Ellen.'

Seamus bridled. 'I'm sure some of your ex-boyfriends would tell a different tale, now.'

'How on earth would you know about my ex-boyfriends?' I demanded craftily. 'And anyway, you ever seen *When Harry Met Sally*? That's all men understand.'

Keisha laughed out loud and started clapping. Seamus shut up in discomfiture, and Dolores Mahon gave me a small – a very small – smile. I'd almost say it was fellow feeling.

I took a slug of sherry and went on. OK, I know I'm no Snowy or Gail, and all the women here were thinner and prettier than me, but my new suit was making me feel at least presentable.

'And good divorce lawyers. Men have to be careful, these days. A prominent wife can walk off with fifty per cent, you know. Like Terence Conran's. He said she'd only cooked a few meals, but the judge gave her ten million quid.'

Now Seamus had gone a bit green about the gills. All the wives were staring at me like I'd sworn in church – talking about divorce law at a time like this. The expression on Tom's face was unfathomable, but I didn't care. That felt good, it truly did. And Dolores Mahon just winked at me.

I suppose faking orgasms doesn't fit Tom's 'social topics for discussion list'.

'We've only got tomorrow to do the rehearsal. I'm sure you'll be fine, Alex,' Ellen said reassuringly – patronisingly, I thought.

'I'm sure the magenta Laura Ash will look *fabulous*,' Mrs Drummond said warmly. As a matter of fact, it made me look like a stick of salami – the big fat ones, not the Pepperami bite-size ones, and it clashed with my hair. I was sitting here with massive red streaks round my temples and they didn't seem to have noticed. It reminded me of what Ellen and I used to sing at school whenever we saw one of the mistresses walk past in a brown skirt and orange jumper, to the tune of Queen's *Flash Gordon* – '*Clash!* Aaah! Saviour of the Universe!' I expected the Lower Fifth to pop up and yell that at me as I tripped down the aisle in a flounce of cod-Elizabethan ruffles.

I knew this because Mum had the exact same Laura Ash at home, and forced me to wear it to a Rotary Club dinner dance one night.

'It goes so well with my dark pink roses,' Ellen gushed.

Snowy looked like she wanted to puke, and she was not the only one.

'We'll see,' I told them.

I thought smugly of my long, iris gown arriving tomorrow. Ho ho. Cinderella, you shall go to the ball.

When I woke up there was a light drizzle of rain falling over the fields outside. It softened the scent of the grass, it just hit you when you opened the window. What an amazing house. I could almost be sorry that tonight was my last night here.

There was a heavy rap on my door.

'Come,' I said. I do that because it reminds me of Captain Picard in *Star Trek*. I've always had a big crush on Captain Picard, bald head and everything, and make a new resolution only to moon after Captain Picard. After all, he never gets it together with Dr Beverly Crusher, not properly, so he is available, and he has the advantage of being a fictional character who will therefore never be able to break my heart.

This is a strangely cheering thought. I can add Han Solo and Indiana Jones (quite similar when you think about it) and James Bond and Robin Hood to the list. Or I could just go for dead people, like smart Mrs Drummond, who has photos of John Wayne everywhere in her kitchen. I could fall for Sir Francis Drake and Richard the Lionheart.

But wait a second, he was gay, wasn't he?

See? Even my dead boyfriends let me down.

You think that's weird, you should have seen me when I was a kid. I had a crush on Hercules, and he was a cartoon character.

Ellen bounced in. Ripples of flesh shuddered around her generous thighs.

'Come! Gosh, Alex, you should be more careful. People might mistake your meaning, ha, ha, ha! Come on, we've got to get you dressed and down for breakfast. Full dress rehearsal at ten o'clock.'

'Right.' I staggered out of bed and headed for a shower. 'Where's Gail?'

'She's gone off with Tom to pick out a wedding present. So sweet,'

Ellen said, 'and isn't she looking pretty? Tom can't stay away from her.'

'Mmm, so I noticed.'

'Charlie is going through the speeches with Keisha, Bronwen and Olivia.' Ellen's face fell a bit. 'She's awfully pretty, isn't she? Charlie seems very taken with her.'

'Well, you're the one he's marrying,' I said lightly. Still, thank God Keisha was with them. I wasn't going to say word one to Snowy, I had decided, but how much better if they weren't on their own.

Why did Ellen put up with it? I thought with a flash of irritation. Why didn't she just take Charlie aside and bollock him?

'She's so slim and pretty. I mean, I could never look like that.'

Not when you have three helpings of potatoes and two of pudding every night, no.

'I don't know what he sees in me,' Ellen sighed, 'I don't really.'

Oh, spare me. I wanted to start playing an invisible violin. The bloody man had proposed, hadn't he, and the fact was, Ellen, the unmarriageable lump who was as dull as ditch water, was about to marry a millionaire, and my list of exes would have been enough to fill two full *Oprah* shows. Ellen was going to be a society wife and gracing the pages of *Tatler* next to Dolores Mahon and the rest of them downstairs.

'I expect he likes your sense of humour,' I lied.

'Oh, do you think so?' Ellen asked, pathetically eagerly.

I told her yes with the same fervour I used to tell her that puppy-fat was a stage she'd grow out of. 'You two have probably had some brilliant laughs,' I said insincerely. Like maybe you both looked in the mirror.

She brightened. 'We have. We have excellent talks.'

'And you probably have great plans for your future careers, that sort of thing,' I shouted over the hiss of the shower attachment. To my dismay, Ellen followed me into the bathroom and lowered the loo seat to sit on while I got under the water.

'*His* future career. Obviously *I'm* not going to have one,' she beamed. 'I'm going to stay home and have lots of wonderful babies.'

Well hey, at least nobody'll notice you're pregnant, I thought, maddened. She had just said the single thing most likely to send me nuts. Obviously? *Obviously?* Was Ellen part of a giant set-up by my mother, to make me feel utterly inadequate as a female? Mother thinks

that despite all equal-rights legislation – which she and Dad still call
'Women's Lib' – girls who 'have to work' are missing out on their
oestrogen destiny.

'You're so lucky, not having a boyfriend. You can still sow your
"wild oats".' Ellen laughed at that idea.

'What does Charlie think of you giving up work?'

'He's all for it, of course. And so's Tom.'

'Is he indeed,' I said tightly, scrubbing Pantene into my locks.

'He says he thinks babies and looking after Charlie will be a fulltime
job, and he thinks I'll be totally fulfilled.'

I might have known. Tom was such a sexist pig, listen to that. Oh
man, he and Gail would get on beautifully, all she would want to do
would be to take his credit card and start shopping. She would never
try and make it as an artist. Or bother about having an independent
job of her own. No, girls like Linda and Gail were perfect for Tom.
Looking back, I must have misinterpreted it. Why would a guy like
him ever ask out a girl like me?

Chapter 24

I towelled myself off as fast as I could. Anything to get away from Ellen and her constant bleating. Charlie, babies, home decoration . . . some people apparently find carpets and curtains utterly fascinating.

'I was asking Tom, should we go for a Regency stripe on the sofas, or French chintz, or should we pick one of the William Morris prints? And do you know what he said?'

' "That's something for you girls to choose"?'

'Exactly!' Ellen beamed. 'How did you know?'

'A wild guess. Look, Ellen, I'll be down in ten minutes, OK?'

'Sure. You're such a brick, Alex,' Ellen said, clumping mercifully out of the door.

I pulled on my 501s and a tiny Joseph sweater and padded along the corridor to Gail's room. The door was shut so I pushed it wide open.

Gail was standing at the window, her mouth tilted open, looking up doe-eyed at Tom Drummond, who had both hands on her shoulders.

I froze. I couldn't believe it. I know I'd been going on about it, but seeing him and her like this – it was a shock, and it felt all wrong, and I suddenly realised wretchedly that a wave of jealousy was crashing through my stomach. Jealousy of my own sister.

'Excuse me,' I gasped.

Tom slowly lifted his hands away from Gail. 'Wait, Alex, we need to talk.'

I wanted to come back with some dry, but not bitter, response – a sort of witty Stephen Fry thing – but all that came out of my mouth was 'Oh – um, really busy – er . . .'

I shut the door on them like I was clashing shut the gates of hell. Oh man, if Tom was going to start kissing Gail, I'm sorry but I didn't want to be around to see it.

★

Downstairs Ellen was tucking into a huge plate of bacon and eggs, with fried toast on the side. I wondered if I could get a photo of her somewhere to stick on my fridge as a deterrent?

'Eat up, darling, you'll need all your strength,' Mrs Jones advised. Like mother, like daughter, she was racing through the Cumberland sausages herself. 'Oh, good morning, Alex. Ready to be the maid of honour? I expect you've been a bridesmaid lots of times before.'

'At least three times,' I said, thinking of various childhood disasters.

'Oooh *dear*,' pursed Mrs Drummond with her cat's-arse mouth, 'then you shouldn't really do Ellen: you know it's four times a bridesmaid, never a bride. Although I gather you're not very likely to be a bride any time soon, are you?'

'Huh,' I grunted. Who did she gather that from? Did she have a hotline to my mother? Or had Tom just been shooting his mouth off?

'You were engaged to Justin Webb, weren't you? But then Tom told me you dumped him, almost at the altar.'

I looked down at my cornflakes. I didn't want to feel grateful to Tom, thank you very much. Justin had dumped me fifty foot underground like I was nuclear waste, but I had to thank God the Merciless Marrieds didn't know about it.

'You have to be careful, Alexandra,' cried Mrs Jones gaily. 'Only the really *sparkling* beauties get several proposals. The rest of you girls just wind up gathering dust.'

'I'm gathering paycheques at the moment,' I said firmly.

Gillian Loman sniggered. 'As an Administrative Resource.'

'Human Resources Administrator. It's a start, it means I'm independent. I'd hate to have to rely on a man to pick up my bills,' I told the Merciless Marrieds.

'Not to worry,' said Melissa snidely.

'You should take a tip from Gail. She wants to get married as soon as possible. After all, I never heard a résumé read out at a funeral,' Mrs Jones lectured me.

'Yes, I mean, what do you see on gravestones? Wife of such-and-such, daughter of so-and-so, mum of . . .' Penny Radcliffe bored on, as her husband grinned approvingly.

'I get the idea,' I said quickly.

Oh my God, I was under siege from the Stepford Wives. I thought of Wonder Woman, taking off her glasses and twirling around and then deflecting bullets with her funky bracelets. I wanted to be

Wonder Woman. It would also give me the advantage of being unrecognisable, even though I would look exactly the same, except wearing a swimsuit.

And I could fly out of there.

'What I mean is, it's marriage that matters. Marriage and family,' said Penny in saintly Women's Institute way.

'I don't know,' I protested, 'William Shakespeare isn't best remembered as the father of Judith.'

'Yes, well,' Seamus chimed in, with a scornful look, 'you're not exactly William Shakespeare, are you?'

Mrs Drummond, wearing a royal blue cashmere jumper and small tartan skirt, appeared at the doorway, her tiny frame weighed down by a sea of magenta.

'Alex! Come and try on your gown!' she said.

'It's very different,' Mrs Jones said enthusiastically.

'It's certainly striking,' Mrs Drummond agreed.

'Bright colours are the in thing this autumn,' Dolores Mahon told me sympathetically. I think Dolores had worked out that I hated Seamus almost as much as she did, with the added bonus that, unlike her, I didn't sort of love him while I was at it.

Anyway, if she was minded to have her revenge, God was smiling on her now. The dress was worse even than I remembered it. The violent magenta would give an acid house fan a migraine, and there were enough ruffles for a whole series of *Blackadder*. Not to mention the enormous velvet bow, so kindly drawing attention to my arse. And lest we forget, could my clashing hair colour take a bow, and my skin that looked pasty against this neon horror, and my plump shoulders with little bits of flesh gathering at the armpit because the bodice didn't fit, and my tits looking as flat as Ellen's feet.

Maybe I could keep it. I could go as an Ugly Sister to the next fancy dress ball. Or use it as my Halloween costume. Or audition for the Rocky Horror Show. Or—

'Nobody's going to miss you in that, Alexandra,' said Melissa sweetly, but I could tell she was just dying to get away with the other girls and shriek with laughter.

My reflection stared back at me. I looked like an erect penis. With ruffles.

Seamus Mahon popped his head around the door.

'Very enticing,' he mocked, making faces like he wanted to puke up. 'Perhaps there'll be photos in a magazine.'

'Oh yes, we've asked tons of press,' Mrs Jones said smugly. 'But off you go, Seamus, no men are allowed to see the bride.'

'Seamus should be fine, then,' I insisted, and gave me a look of pure loathing. Man, I had trouble when we went back to work. But sufficient unto the day is the evil thereof, as Dad would tell us on Sunday after a few glasses of vintage port.

Melissa shut the door, trilling and cooing as Ellen opened her door and emerged.

She was wearing the most incredible dress. White silk and lace, tinted by age to the mellowest gold, with stiff brocade sleeves that hid the plumpness of her arms. The bodice must have been Victorian; it was a corset, a proper, old-fashioned corset that had laced tightly at the back. It didn't transform Ellen into Amber Valetta, but it hid her fatness and made her simply statuesque. The most glorious bosom spilled out, creamy and inviting, from the top of her heart-shaped neckline. A tiny white rose in the centre only drew the eye to the chasm in between Twin Peaks there. Her generous bottom and thighs were nowhere to be seen under the billowing crinoline-style skirt, decorated with stitching so delicate it looked like the mice from *The Tailor of Gloucester* had done it.

'Amazing, darling,' sighed Mrs Jones and Mrs Drummond together.

Ellen blushed a pretty pink and attempted a heavy twirl in the mirror. She still had the grace of a drunk hippo, but she certainly did look good.

'And Tom's got people coming over to do my face and hair,' she said. 'Oh Alex, how pretty you look, just like a flower.'

'The lesser-spotted stinkwort,' Gillian said in a loud whisper, at which the coven giggled.

Ellen and I regarded our reflections. Ellen looked like Juno, a huge Roman goddess, a Titian beauty. And I looked like neon frilly puke. Ellen's waist now looked defined and imposing. Mine looked non-existent – everything was huge. Ellen's ass had disappeared under clever hoops of bone. Mine had a huge bow advertising its presence.

There was no denying it. I actually looked worse than Ellen Jones. Much worse.

'Can I borrow the bridesmaid for a minute?' Gail twittered, bouncing into the room like Bambi, in one of her horrible natural knits. 'Great breakfast, Mrs D, thanks, I loved the organic unsweetened museli. So much better than that nasty commercial poison my flatmates eat.'

I would have made a loud slurping noise here, but I supposed that was too immature.

'What museli's that, dear?' Mrs Drummond asked blankly. 'We have Alpen in the pantry.'

'No,' Gail looked horrified at the thought of refined sugar, 'I meant the marvellous, *natural* brand in the grey stone jar.'

Gillian Loman gave a nasty cackle.

'Oh dear,' Mrs Drummond said faintly, 'you haven't eaten the goats' feed, have you?'

Gail looked like she wanted to heave. Normally this would be grand news but I saw Melissa and co. starting to snigger, so I bundled her out of the room. I mean, only I am allowed to laugh at Gail's pretentious diet. They just want to have a go at the common Wilde girls, and I'm not having that, even if Gail does bore me to tears about essential oil aromatherapy burners for the loo every month.

'Goats' feed?' Gail sputtered.

'Never mind about that, what is it?' I demanded. Keep her talking. Anything to take the focus off the Frill of a Lifetime here.

'I think – oh, Alex, I think we should tell Snowy to go home,' Gail started whining.

'You've been talking to Tom.'

'Yes, and he seems very insistent,' Gail said smugly. She couldn't help but relish Tom hitting on her. It was what she had always wanted.

'Gail! No way. How can you say that? She's your friend. Tom is just being a crashing snob.'

'Well, it is his house,' said Gail virtuously, 'and I think we should do as he asks.'

'I'm not going to help Tom Drummond sling Snowy out,' I told her, digging my heels in. The irony being that I couldn't stand the bitch. But just to spite Tom, I would insist she stayed. 'Did he give you a decent reason?'

'Well. He said he had a very good reason indeed,' Gail said importantly.

'And what was it?'

'He said he couldn't tell me. But that she was a dangerous person to have around the house.'

'If Charlie Drummond has romantic amnesia, that's his problem,' I snapped.

'I think we should listen to Tom.'

'Just because you fancy him,' I said bitterly.

'And what's wrong with that? He's quite dreamy actually. So charming. Such a gentleman,' Gail blithered.

'So rich.'

'What? You know I don't care about material things. Anyway, Tommy says Snowy isn't a fit person for us to have as a friend and we should drop her immediately.'

'Oh?' My voice was dangerously cold coming out of the hot-pink nightmare. 'And why is that? Because his brother can't keep his hands off her? Because she's a bit of a flirt? Sure, women are damned to hell for that sort of thing in Tom Drummond's book. Now he actually thinks he can tell me who to have as a friend?'

'Well.' Gail folded her stick-insect arms petulantly. 'I'm going to take his advice. You'll have to take me back in your car. I'm going to tell Snowy I don't want to see her any more.'

I gaped at her. Even for Gail, this took the biscuit. It had been Snowy this, Snowy that, when the cow moved in: Snowy was bribing my friends away from me with her make-up and her tickets, and Gail was doing all the cheerleading. Gail was first in line to go to the celebrity parties with Snowy. Snowy was supposed to be Gail's new best mate and she was going to drop her just because some geezer told her to?

'Gail, you can't. He hasn't even given you a reason.'

'Tommy –' Tommy? What is he, a rock opera? 'Tommy says he does have one, but it wouldn't be the right thing to tell us. He just wants her out of the house and thinks we should drop her. Tommy says to trust him, OK? And I do trust him, I think he's just wonderful,' Gail finished defiantly.

'It wouldn't be the right thing to tell us. My, how convenient.'

The door creaked open again; Ellen was beckoning me back in. And I could see Tom heading up the stairs towards us.

'Excuse me, OK? I have to go.'

And I bolted inside, so Ellen could give me lessons on how to hold a small posy and walk behind her up the aisle.

If I were to wear this dress, I'd be completely coordinated. My face would be a perfect match.

'Stand back from Ellen, dear. A good three paces,' Mrs Jones insisted. 'The bridesmaid's place is always *behind* the bride. You mustn't detract from her.'

'Not to worry,' said Melissa again, sniggering meanly.

I took a step backwards and scowled at everybody. Ellen tried to give me a sort of placatory look, but I ignored her.

'It does truly look lovely with the flowers,' Ellen twittered. 'And we'll get my make-up girl to give you a bluey sort of eyeshadow, then it'll be marvellous on you.'

'Yeah, well. We'll see,' I told them mutinously.

Keisha, Bronwen, rescue me! They won't let me take the Magenta Monster off until we've done the 'walk through' on the croquet lawn. Bloody hell, what was that fat eejit's problem? I thought murderously. I mean, they gave you your lines to repeat, she didn't even have to ask for the ring. Then we had to walk down the aisle, Ellen on Tom's arm because her father was pushing up the daisies. It was like the supermodels. What's so damn super about looking anorexic and walking? Walking's pretty easy, you know. Even Kevin the postboy can manage it. I mean, I could be a supermodel, if I had heroin for breakfast, cocaine for lunch and 'e' for dinner. And facial plastic surgery of course. Well, look what they did for 'in no sense a sell-out, money-hungry professional widow' Courtney Love! Two stone overweight and face like a horse's bum and now she's on the cover of *Harper's* with Madonna's nose.

Don't you hate it when fashion editors do photos of the waifs eating hamburgers? Yeah right – and now show me the shot of her puking it up in the loos five minutes later. Hey, I'm six foot and weigh eight stone three – and of course I eat normally!

Sorry. Got carried away there for a second.

Anyway, I'd had as much of Gail bleating at me as I could take. She was the poster girl for the new men's movements, she thought anything a potential husband said was binding as the laws of the Medes and the Persians. Tommy this and Tommy that, and did she mention Tommy's marvellous pesticide-free orchards and organically reared cows. Snowy may have been her mate but Snowy stood as much chance now as an electric toothbrush in a nunnery.

I couldn't believe Tom Drummond's arrogance. He thought he was going to make us all knuckle under to his social order. But I was afraid he was going to have a surprise or two on the way.

Chapter 25

Keisha came striding across the lawn to meet me.

First I thought she was having a fit, then I realised it was just her natural reaction to my lovely dress.

'Pretty,' she smirked.

'Oh, sod off, you bitch. Where's Charlie and Snowy?'

'Practising his speeches,' Keisha said, lifting one eyebrow.

'She's behaving herself, is she?'

'Well, they're not having hot monkey sex in the library,' Keisha said.

'Then there's nothing to worry about.' If they weren't actually doing the nasty, it was none of my business, I thought smugly. Ellen was a big girl. She'd have to take care of herself.

Everybody assembled in the dining room for lunch. I sat next to Bronwen and watched Tom carve the joint, his thick stubby fingers so deft on the handle of the knife. Charlie poured the wine, lingering by Snowy's glass. Ellen had a look of panic on her face as she saw the glance that passed between them.

Honestly, if some people can't cope with a little flirtation . . .

After tomorrow Charlie would be hers. They'd be off on honeymoon: 'St Lucia. So wonderful at this time of year.' In a *very* expensive hotel, miles away from Olivia White.

The other guests started talking. The local hunt, the Paris fashion shows, the crisis at the Royal Opera House. Nothing the London hicks could talk about.

Gail didn't care. She was gazing adoringly at Tom, her big blue eyes locked on him like a newborn calf. Her plunging neckline revealed her smooth skin, as white as meadowsweet, her manicured nails freshly painted a light shell-pink. Her hair was as glossy as one of Tom's horses.

'The beef's safe, isn't it, Tommy? He only uses grass-fed cattle.'

'That's right.'

'Alex probably won't touch it, then. She likes her food with chemical garnishes,' Gail giggled.

'Oh, Alex never likes anything I do,' Tom said coolly, looking at me.

'She'd have been glad of this when you were poor students together,' Gail probed. She glanced at me jealously.

'At Oxford, I wasn't poor,' Tom replied, still gazing at me. I withered under his stare, it was so clinical. 'And she wouldn't have touched this then. She used to be a vegan. She wore a T-shirt saying "Meat is Murder".'

'How silly!' Gail breathed.

'That was a Smiths album,' I muttered. 'Anyway, I was different then.'

'I suppose you can afford a bad diet when you're at college,' said Gillian nastily, 'and you're young and fresh like Gail. It's when the bloom has gone that it starts to show. Old women like us have got to watch it, Alex.'

Tom bit back a smile, and I looked at my plate.

'I don't have a bloom,' Gail said, fishing madly.

'You most certainly do,' Tom replied instantly.

Keisha made an exaggerated fishing rod motion, but Gail ignored her, triumphantly. She looked over at me. 'Honestly, Alex, I can't think how you let a catch like Tom go,' she said loudly.

There was a crashing silence. Mortified, I flushed purple.

'Alex never "let me go". She never had me,' Tom said. 'We were only friends. We never dated seriously.'

'I can't imagine why not,' Gail breathed, sounding like she'd just won the lottery.

'I'm not romantic,' Tom said quietly, looking into my sister's eggshell-blue eyes. 'But maybe I was waiting for the right girl to come along.'

'Oh, Tom and I were never even a starter,' I said fiercely. 'I really couldn't be more different from anyone.'

At that moment the dogs set up a mad barking, rushing towards the hall from their begging positions under the table. Snowy's white wine was knocked over as they jolted her chair.

'Oh dear,' she said, dabbing at it with her napkin.

'Let me help you,' Charlie begged, leaping up from his chair as though he had a firework in his pants. He was round at her side, mopping up the spill solicitously, gently wiping her tanned forearm. Tom gave me a pleading look which I completely ignored. They could all take care of their own problems.

'It's a delivery man,' Mrs Drummond said loudly. 'I wonder what that can be? We have all the wedding goods arriving tomorrow!'

She opened the door and took a small box from him.

'Goodness, Alexandra, it's for you,' Mrs Drummond announced. 'From Gloucester.'

'Is it our wedding present?' Ellen asked miserably. Charlie shot her a furtive glance and stopped drying Snowy's upper chest.

'Not exactly. It's a new bridesmaid's dress,' I was forced to admit. 'Much better than the Laura Ashley, truly.'

'Oh,' said Ellen uncertainly.

Tom stared at me in complete disgust.

I marched upstairs. Ellen was struggling into her corset again for the rehearsal, while I slipped seamlessly into the violet dress. Out of the harsh shop lights it looked even better. I admired myself sorrowfully in the age-spotted mirror above my dresser. I was a wash of iris against the soft greens of the clipped lawns outside; tall and pretty as a delphinium. With no ruffles to obscure it, my long neck looked almost swan-like. The clever reds in my hair took on depth and movement.

I may not have been Gail, but I was very pretty.

I was turning to the right and left when Tom walked in to the room. He stopped dead when he saw what I was wearing. He breathed in hard, then sort of shook himself and fixed glittering eyes on me.

'Don't you ever knock? And don't even *start* with me,' I flounced. 'This is a beautiful dress. I'm not going to look like a trussed turkey, and that's it.'

'I'm not going to,' Tom said coldly. 'You're clearly determined to have your own way.'

I sat down on the bed, making sure he caught my skirts in all their silky, swishy glory. 'So what do you want?'

Tom started walking backwards and forwards across my bedroom.

Very disconcerting. He was striding, like a soldier. It made me want to snap to attention.

'Olivia White has been flirting with my brother all afternoon.'

'Yes, Gail told me you had spoken to her,' I said icily. 'Why don't you talk to Charles? Or give Olivia one of your marvellous lectures. Maybe she'll come to heel a bit better than I do.'

'Will you grow up?' he shouted angrily. 'It's not about you and me. It's about this – this *woman* trying to get her claws into my brother. You don't know Charles, he can be foolishly impulsive.'

'For the last time, it's not my problem,' I snapped.

'She is not a fit person for you to be friends with. OK? Can't you just trust me, Alex? For the sake of the friendship we used to have?'

Used to have. So that's it, I thought. He wasn't interested in me any more.

'Nobody tells me who my friends are going to be.'

Tom stopped walking and pointed at me. 'Very well. You leave me no choice. That woman is out of my house as of this afternoon. I am going to throw her out. You may as well pack up her suitcases. She's gone, Alex, with or without your help. I had hoped to avoid these dramatics.'

'Are you finished?' I asked languidly. 'I have to touch up my make-up.'

I turned to my mirror, ignoring the burning sensation of his eyes on my back. It was the most infuriating gesture I could manage. In a few moments, he clomped heavily out of the room, not bothering to close the door.

'Come on, Alex,' Gail called, 'you're wanted on the south lawn.'

The south lawn? Boy, was she familiar with the layout of Carrefour. She had probably earmarked all the loo roll for replacing with the scratchy recycled crap we refused to use in the flat.

'OK.' I dashed out and put on a pair of walking boots. They looked a bit Mel B under the formal gown, but I wasn't ruining my little silk heels on Tom's croquet lawn, however dry the ground.

'Wow,' said Gail, annoyed. 'That dress makes you look like you dropped ten pounds. Did Tom see you in it?'

'He hates it.'

'Really?' beamed Gail. 'What a pity. Anyway, he's going to tell Snowy to leave.'

'So he said.' I shook my head as I opened the garden gate. Clouds of late butterflies, red-brown and white, tumbled up from the buddleia bush. Thick wallflowers were a blaze of copper against the hedge. 'I'm going to warn her.'

'Alex! You can't do that!' Gail protested. 'Tom would go—'

'I don't give a bugger what Tom would do,' I said furiously, 'I'm going to warn her, he can't just treat one of us like that.'

'But you can't stand Snowy.'

'That,' I told her firmly, 'has nothing to do with it.'

'And that dress!' Gail whined, trotting up behind me. 'Don't you think you should wear the one they want you to? Don't you think you should do what Ellen wants?'

I clapped my hands over my ears. 'No. I don't care. I've had enough of everybody. I'm going to please myself from now on and you can all bloody well watch out.'

When I arrived running onto the croquet lawn all the hoops had been cleared away. Ellen was standing next to Tom in her wedding gown. Snowy was watching from a wicker chair, sipping a gin and tonic, and the coven were milling around talking.

They took in the new dress with looks of amazement and envy. Very gratifying. I heard some of their husbands saying things in the low tone of voice they use about Snowy, and that suited me fine.

I flashed Tom Drummond a look of triumph.

'Where's Charlie?' I asked.

As I got closer, Ellen turned to face me. She took in the long, luscious sweep of my new dress, with its wasp waist and cloud of perfect colour. Now I no longer looked like Coco the clown. Ellen's antique concoction looked fine, but there was no longer an ugly froth behind it to make it look delicate.

Now she did not look the better of the two of us. I had clawed back my place.

I made a point of walking past Snowy's chair. 'Could you help me with my zip, sweetie?' I asked loudly. Tom Drummond could huff and puff all he liked.

Snowy stood up to tinker with it, stretching her long, rangy legs. 'Wonderful dress. Did Gail pick it?'

No she didn't, you snotty cow, I thought, but what I said was, 'Snowy, you'd better watch out. Tom Drummond is going to throw you out. He's dead serious, I think he might call the police or something.'

'God! Did he say why?' Snowy murmured carefully. She didn't seem that surprised.

'He wouldn't say, but, you know,' I giggled, 'he thinks your flirting with Charlie is serious. As if! Anyway, if I were you I'd grab your stuff and check into a hotel. I mean, he can only ban you from his house, can't he? He can't stop you coming if you're a friend of the groom's. Get Charlie to give you your invitation,' I suggested warmly.

'Mmm,' Snowy whispered, 'maybe I will.'

I said, 'Thanks, that's better,' and walked over to Ellen.

'Charlie's not here,' she said in a small voice, 'he can't rehearse with me, because he can't see the dress, and I thought it might be bad luck, anyway. If he walks me down the aisle once it's a miracle. Twice would be pushing it,' but she didn't smile.

She was looking miserably at my dress.

'Who's that pretty lady?' asked one of the flower-carrying brats behind me.

'That's cousin Ellen, darling,' said her mother proudly.

'No, not fat Ellen,' said the brat loudly, 'the pretty one, the one in the blue.'

Everybody talked very fast while Ellen went very red. I should have felt a fist of victory form over my heart, but to tell you the truth, I didn't.

Maybe it was Ellen's beaten-dog look. Or worse – though I didn't want to admit it – maybe it was Tom Drummond's glance of absolute, profound contempt.

'It is – it is a *much* nicer dress,' Ellen struggled gamely. 'Gosh, it makes me look like an elephant. A white elephant, huh huh.'

I was conscious of the approving grins from the men in the party, and Snowy White giving me an extravagant, rather cruel wink. She got up from her chair and walked back towards the house, but not before she'd given Ellen a despising once-over. And she was smiling at me like I was thinking the same thing.

An unpleasant feeling started to gather in the pit of my stomach. Guilt. And unease. I didn't care for that knowing expression on Snowy's face.

'Actually. Ellen, do you know what,' I started to say, 'I, uh – I don't think this dress is right after all. I was only trying it out.'

'But it makes you look so pretty, Alex,' Ellen said bravely, 'of course you must wear it.'

'No, really. It's not weddingy enough. And, uh, it does clash with your flowers.'

'You haven't seen the flowers.'

'You've told me what colour they are, and I know I'm going to clash. I'd much rather the other dress, honestly,' I told her fervently. But I saw to my horror that Ellen had tears prickling the corners of her big eyes. She kept glancing at her little bridesmaid – that's the bugger about kids, they tend to speak the truth – and I suddenly sensed the awful, dreadful humiliation of what had just happened to her.

It wasn't a game any more. This was her wedding – and I was ruining it.

'Nothing you wear is going to make me less of a fat lump,' Ellen said, striving to be wry, but just ending up with a big tear trickling down her plump cheek.

'Don't be silly. Pre-ceremony jitters,' said Tom comfortably, getting out a crisp linen handkerchief and dabbing at her. He was smiling warmly, but disgust for me showed in his rigid back, the way he couldn't even look at me.

In desperation I picked up my heavy boots and clamped them down on the hem. Then I toppled myself forwards, 'til I could hear the fabric tear. I put out a hand to steady myself against Tom, but he shrugged away, like the contact would sting him.

'Shit!' I cried. 'I've ripped the damn thing, I'm going to go in and change.'

'I'll come with you,' Ellen said. 'The dratted pollen, it's making my eyes water.'

I daren't look at Tom as I clumped back with her to the house.

'Why don't we both get changed? And you can go and get Charlie,' I suggested desperately. 'Do the practice in something else. No need to ruin that lovely dress.'

However, now we were safely inside, Ellen's thin control had ripped apart like my dress. She was properly crying now. It made me frantic with worry, like when I was a teenage babysitter and my charge was screaming itself blue.

'Why – why would I go and see Charlie? He's probably flirting with your friend,' Ellen sobbed. 'I knew it was too good to be real. Why would he want a fat lump like me?'

'You're not fat. You're voluptuous,' I lied. I tore my dress off my skin like it was napalm, reached frantically for the magenta horror. Oh God, I would have added neon stripes to it if it would have made Ellen feel better. 'He loves you, Ellen, nobody forced him to ask you.'

'Then why is he hanging around with Olivia?' Ellen asked, her face crumpling. 'If only she'd listened to you. Tom told me you were going to ask her to leave.'

I flopped down on the bed, ruffles and all, vowing to not wash my hair tomorrow, and to do it without make-up, even concealer.

'I . . . yes,' I stuttered, panicking. I didn't know what to say to her. I felt like the smallest worm in the whole of creation.

'You've always been such a good friend to me,' Ellen sobbed, 'you always stood up for me when nobody else would.'

'Tom will sort it all out, don't worry,' I said. I clung rather pathetically to that. I thought it was true. Tom would know what to do, how to make her feel better. I would speak to Snowy tonight, drive her out of here myself!

You silly little cow, said the voice in my head, *look what you've done because you were feeling sorry for yourself.*

I tried to give Ellen a hug, as far round her as my arms would go. I was seeing myself as Tom had been seeing me, I realised, and I hated my reflection.

His heavy footsteps were padding down the corridor.

'Quick, put something on,' I said, flinging my dressing gown at her. 'Tom will get rid of her. Tom! Tom! Come in here!'

The door burst open. But it wasn't Tom, it was Charlie. And he was dragged into my room by Snowy, who bad one arm through his elbow, and who was grinning from ear to ear.

'Oh Alex, thanks so much for warning me! I had to persuade Charlie in time . . . oh,' she said, flushing just a little at the sight of Ellen's bulk, wrapped in a dirty towelling gown.

Ellen's mouth was a round O of amazement. Charlie wouldn't look at her, at first, but then he raised his head and set his mouth sullenly.

'You'd better tell her, darling,' Snowy said softly.

Ellen gave me a quick look. There was such a world of betrayal in her eyes I couldn't bear it. 'You were helping her,' she said.

'Come *on*, darling, best get it over with,' Snowy insisted.

Charlie cleared his throat in a fury of embarrassment and shame, but he knew he was cornered.

'Sorry, Ellen,' he muttered. 'The wedding – uh – we've got to call it off.'

Chapter 26

Merry hell broke loose. Ellen burst into tears and tried to flee past the door, but she tripped in the corridor, and had to scramble to her knees, her large back wobbling as it shook with her sobs. Snowy leant back against the wall with a smug grin, and Charlie passed a worried hand through his hair.

'Better that she find out now,' Snowy said smoothly.

'But not like that. Bloody hell,' Charlie cursed.

'Come on, sweetheart. Let's get out of here,' Snowy pressed him, leaning her slim frame in towards him and licking her lips. 'It's going to blow up now. We shouldn't be here. I can grab the car and we'll shoot off to London.'

'I'm not going to run away,' Charlie said flatly.

'It's not running away, it's for Ellen – she's not going to want to see you and me in the house,' said Snowy, angelic as you like.

'Fucking hell! Why don't you just go to Gretna Green?' I snarled.

'Good idea,' Snowy agreed. She gazed at me with complete indifference. I had never seen anyone look so calculating, not even my old cat Luther when faced with a nest full of chicks. 'We can't stick around here, love – think of Ellen.'

'Oh hell,' Charlie said again. He looked mesmerised by Snowy, his eyes were simply glazed over with lust. I could see the idea of doing a runner was highly attractive to him.

From the garden below came the sound of people running up to the house, attracted by Ellen's wailing, which was drifting over the house like an air raid siren.

'Charlie, you know you love Ellen,' I pleaded, 'don't do this to her. And Snowy – Jesus, he's getting married tomorrow!'

'Shut up, Alex, you ghastly hag,' Snowy spat. She was beautiful when she was angry, as they say. Spitting and fiery like a puma. 'It was love at first sight. You can't expect him to spend his whole life with a pig like her!'

'Better a pig than a vicious bitch,' I gasped.

'And anyway, you're in no position to lecture me on married men, you little tramp.'

She flounced out of the room, pulling Charlie obediently behind her.

I admit, I did nothing for the first thirty seconds. Well, would you? I sat on the bed in all my ruffly glory and started to cry.

I'd done bloody marvellously. I'd managed to make an enemy of my boss, ruin an old friend's life, and utterly alienate the man I'd fallen for as heavily as Robbie Coltrane doing a high dive.

I collected myself as soon as I could and rushed down the corridors, looking for Ellen. My eyes were red and and my nose was streaming, or was it the other way round? A sweat of sheer panic made my skin damp and clammy.

I crashed straight into Tom, who appeared bounding up the top of some stairs.

'Oh, it's you,' he said flatly. 'Where are you going? Not caused enough misery for one visit yet?'

'I was going to find Ellen,' I said, fresh tears running down the bridge of my nose.

'Well, don't bother. She doesn't want to see you. The best thing you can do is to pack up and get out. Your sister and your other friends are already loading their car, but I did apologise to them – this mess isn't their fault.'

'Tom,' I sobbed, 'I swear I didn't—'

'I'm not interested in your excuses, Alex, OK? Amazing though it may sound to you, you are not the first person on my mind at the moment.'

It hurt like a punch in the stomach. His face was set against me like flint.

'I'll go,' I whispered. 'Right away.'

'Good.' Tom's dark eyes were almost curious as they bore down on to mine. 'To think I once fell in love with you! You have no idea how you've changed. You used to be such a beauty in your cheap jeans and T-shirts and messy hair. And now you've got designer clothes and style and you're just wallowing in selfishness. I've never seen anybody more sorry for themselves.'

'What?' I stammered.

'Oh, you heard me. You think that being a stunning beauty entitles you to everything. But you do nothing for me. I need a girl who loves something in this world more than her mirror,' he barked, and strode off towards Ellen's bedroom before I could say another word.

Keisha had the car engine running when I staggered out of the front door, laden with open cases. I hadn't even bothered to pack. I couldn't take it, the funereal groups of people gathered at the foot of the stairs, the way they shut up when I approached.

I could hardly see the car door for my floods of tears. I dropped one bag on the gravel, and all my knickers spread out over the drive.

'Oh, for Christ's sake,' Gail said, jumping out of the car to pick them up, 'this is all your fault, Alex! Maybe you could embarrass us some more? Why don't you strip and do a can-can?'

'Shut the fuck up, Gail, and get in the car,' Bronwen said calmly.

Finally we had all my underwear and stuffed it in the boot, and Keisha tore off, spraying gravel like she was Damon Hill. Say what you like about that girl, but she sure can drive fast. Actually she has her own chapter in the road rage book of all-time greats – 'Get out of my way, you fucking walking corpse!' as she shrieked at some old-aged pensioner who took a left a bit too slowly – but that's another story.

'I don't know why you didn't listen to Tom,' Gail sniped all the way home. Eventually I told her Tom was a snob and a self-righteous bastard.

'*I* think he's lovely,' Gail said, 'and you needn't expect me to drop him just because you've had a fight with him.'

'What do you mean, drop him?' I was aflame with jealousy. 'You never even had his phone number.'

'Well, I've got it now,' Gail triumphed, 'and we got on wonderfully. I can't think why you were so horrid to him. Still dying for Seamus, I suppose.'

Seamus! My crush on him seemed about as relevant as my schoolgirl crush on Paul Weller.

'That's over.'

'You could have fooled Dolores, she was highly upset by all your little chats. I don't know why you had to be so obvious. Anyway, Tom told me I had flowered. He's going to give me a call some time.'

I said nothing. I watched Gail toss her golden hair in the back seat.

'He makes over a million a year,' she said proudly.

'Bully for him,' I sulked.

'He *said* Snowy wasn't a fit person to be our friend,' Gail insisted. 'You ought to have paid more attention.'

'I don't see how he could jump to that conclusion. He didn't know she was going to run off with Charlie. He's not a mindreader.'

Keisha turned towards me and smiled. 'Oh man, you two really didn't twig, did you?'

'Twig what? Tom said it wouldn't be right to tell me why she wasn't suitable.'

'How old fashioned,' Keisha grinned. 'I could almost fancy that gentleman act myself. Do you think a guy like him would like a bit of black?'

Ridiculous, now I wanted to warn *Keisha* off, and she was my best friend.

'Why is it old fashioned?'

'He's trying to spare her reputation. You blind idiots, don't they have any call-girls in Surrey?'

'Any what?' I gasped.

'Not-so-Snowy is on the game,' Keisha laughed. 'No wonder he wanted to get her away from his brother.'

We got back in to the flat to find it reeking of dead fish. Bronwen forgot to empty the bin again. So before I could collapse into bed, we had a half-hearted onslaught on the mess. Our sofa was thick with enough dust to blanket the moon and our fridge had sufficient wildlife in it for a preservation order. I reckon we had a reverse case of the elves and the shoemaker. At night they came with their magic wands and turned our dwelling place into a dumping ground.

'I've found it,' Keisha said to me.

'What?'

'Your bedroom carpet. It took a while, but now I've found it.' She threw some of my dirty laundry into the laundry basket.

'Yeah, well, at least my relationships aren't a case of "'Til Dawn do us Part,"' I cracked back feebly.

"'Til Dolores do us part,' Gail sniggered. 'No, no wine for me, Bronwen. I want to lose a few pounds in case Tom gets in touch.'

'Are you sure Snowy was on the game? Why didn't you say anything?'

'None of my business, honey,' Keisha said, striking up another fag and offering them around. 'Cancer, anyone?'

'Cheers,' said Bronwen, grabbing one.

'She may not be. Now, I mean. But she still has a lot of "friends" round, doesn't she? And all blokes.'

'Maybe she's a man's woman,' I suggested.

'Oh, get real, Al. She's any man's woman for five hundred quid. You told me her folks had no cash, so what's she doing with a better flat than us, a wardrobe full of Prada, a flash car and no job? She knows every rich Arab in London – the sleazy ones, that is. Remember those charmers who took us to the party? Please.'

I was silent. I felt like a total mug.

'Tom probably knew someone who had had her. Or something. But if she gave up the life, perhaps he didn't want to wreck it for her by telling everybody. At least, that's my guess.'

'He's so honourable,' Gail breathed. 'Wow. How . . . gallant.'

I thought so too. 'How could she have got Charlie, then?'

'Charlie didn't know what Tom knew. Face it, Ellen was no oil painting. Some of those upper-class boys have never had a decent sniff of pussy in their lives,' Keisha said, leaning back on the couch and taking a long draw on her white-tipped fag. 'She gave him the fuck of for ever and managed to talk like a lady. Probably the education she got at your convent school, girls. Before she started selling her booty for a living,' she cracked up.

I drank four big glasses of red and crawled into bed. I didn't even cry. There was no point.

When the alarm fired it was a big shock to the system. You wake up to the sound of birdsong and lowing cows, and suddenly it's back to London and the pollution and dirt. And the workweek.

My mouth felt like Swampy had been squatting in it, and my head was crunching and I was as dry as the Gobi. God! I staggered into the loo, gulped some water and realised I'd fallen asleep in my make-up. Sticky foundation gobbets were plastered to my cheeks. There wasn't much time for a repair job so I simply scrubbed myself clean and nicked some of Gail's Wash and Go. I Washed and Went. There wasn't even any time for a hair-dryer, let alone breakfast, but who cared about that. I was so sick with grief I might never eat again.

On my way into work I caught sight of my naked face with its dark-circled eyes. Nice. I was pallid and about as grey as I felt. Not a single man whistled or even gave me a second look.

I wondered desperately if there was anything I could do to make amends. Call Snowy? And say what? She wanted to get Charlie in the bag, make him marry her while he was still panting for her like a dog. Then announce it in *The Times*, and Tom would have to spend the rest of his days in silence. Charlie Drummond wouldn't want to admit he'd married a prostitute. Oh hell, what if Snowy were pregnant? Ten p gets you a pound she hadn't been using anything. The Drummond boys are old fashioned. Charlie would marry Snowy if he knocked her up – at least he would if he were anything like Tom.

The thought of Tom made me want to crawl away and die. I buried my head in my hands all the way to Bank. Nobody asked me, was I all right, love? like they did when I looked decent. Nobody gives a monkey's about ugly girls.

As Ellen Jones was now finding out.

I twisted my hands in agony. Tom's words rang in my head with the horrible sound of truth. 'I've never seen anybody more sorry for themselves.' It was true, wasn't it? Just because I was in a bad mood about Seamus and my other boyfriends, I'd deliberately tried to screw things up for Ellen – I hated her for getting married before me. I winced when I thought of my fuss about the dress. It was Ellen's day, and I'd acted like a spoilt brat. And I'd cheered when Snowy started her seduction routine, even if I didn't think it would go as far as it had.

Would Tom believe that? I doubted it. Oh Christ, I thought as I was squeezed into the sardine pack coming out of the Tube, why even ask? He told you: he loathes you. And he fancies your little sister.

I was tormented by a horrid fantasy of being a bridesmaid at Gail's wedding, as she floated down the aisle like a wisp of thistledown on Tom's arm, gazing soulfully up at him, and me clumping wretchedly behind her in the frilly magenta thing. Gail was delicate and feminine like I never could be – she knew better than to swear like a navvy when a man is around. She would agree with Tom, not argue with him. She would say little and be a woman of mystery and let him do the talking. She would not discuss the relationship. She would let him order for her and pick the movie. She would not return his calls, and would accept his bouquets with diamond earrings in them with a casual insouciance.

She would be eating organic live yoghurt in the Carrefour pantry in no time, and I would be the in-law outlaw, crazy Alex, a fucking dinner party anecdote!

A sob caught in my throat as I ran up the steps to Hamilton Kane.

'Morning, Alex,' said Tina on Reception. 'Dragged-through-a-hedge look in vogue, is it?'

'Don't be so superficial,' I snapped. Attack was the best form of defence, since I could see my hair in the lift doors, and it had dried into rasta rats' tails, plastering itself to my scalp.

'Well, don't go outside, you might frighten some children,' Tina said smugly. 'Mrs Huntington wants you to go directly up to her office. What *have* you done? Glorious is truly on the warpath.'

What indeed? I got into a mercifully empty lift and opened my handbag, grabbing for my hairbrush. I scuffed it through my hair as fast as I could. Riiii–iiip, went my hair, the sound of a thousand ends splitting like all my boyfriends. But what could I do? I had no time. Damn, Tina was right, you could probably use me as an exhibit in the London Dungeon.

'Get in here,' barked Glorious crossly as soon as I knocked on her door. I trembled as I sat in her big pink chair, tilted backwards to make you feel like you're in an inferior position (a special Personnel tactic for people they're telling off). She obviously didn't realise I needed no help in that direction. If I were any smaller, you'd need a microscope to see me.

Glorious let off a terrific angry fart. Then she let off a volley of small ones, for emphasis. It sounded like pistol shots, but I was too scared to snigger.

'I have received a very telling memo,' she began. 'Yes, a *very* telling memo. From Mr Mahon downstairs.'

My heart stopped.

'He says he needs to see you about unfinished business,' she went on. 'I must say, I expect my new team to give *one hundred and ten per cent* to this department!'

'You can't give one hundred and ten, it's impossible.'

'Don't be facetious,' she snapped. 'If you're going to be flitting between office and mine, there is *no place* for you in Human Resources. I hope I make myself clear. Now get down to see him, and I want you back here by nine forty-five with an assurance that this will not happen again.'

'Mmm, yeah, sure.'

'You know, Alexandra, dear,' she said, leaning her huge boobs forward on the desk and getting all motherly, heavens preserve us, 'when you leave one place for another, you should really have all your loose ends *tied up*. I'm sure you agree.'

'I really do,' I muttered, getting the hell out of there.

I slunk down to Seamus's office.

'Ah, Alex, it's yourself.' He was all smiles. Like the crocodile in *Alice*. 'Come into the office, there's a girl.'

As soon as the door shut he was on me. Smiling broadly for the benefit of Jenny, watching him outside, he said, 'Thought some more about my little idea? I hope you have. Because you can't decide to drop me like some hot potato, you know. Are you going to play nice?'

'I don't know what you mean,' I stammered.

'Ah, sure you do. You were all over me from the first moment you saw me,' he said obnoxiously. 'I want you to be at the flat tonight. Eight thirty sharp.'

I looked in amazement at the flat keys, which he was pressing back into my hand. He loves this, I thought as I saw the flash of pleasure in his eyes. The mean little bully, he loves it. He knows I can't talk.

'It's a cruel world out there without a job,' Seamus told me. 'Your mother doesn't play golf with that many people. Everything you've got I can take away like that.' He snapped his fingers. 'Of course, it's your choice, darlin' –' like hell, I thought – 'but I'll tell you this. If you don't turn up tonight, don't bother turning up tomorrow. Because you're fired. History.'

'I don't believe you,' I blurted out tearfully.

Seamus grinned. 'That's your problem,' he said.

Chapter 27

'But *why* are you resigning?' Glorious demanded. She glowered at me like some 'fifties headmistress who had caught a prefect with a gardening boy. 'It's not easy to find a job, you know. You have a total lack of experience. And sticking at something for a couple of months isn't much of a commitment.'

'I know, but I can't help it,' I said, my eyes brimming over. 'I've just got to go.'

'With no explanation?'

I shook my head mutely.

'Then you'd better get out. No, don't bother getting your things,' she added darkly as she saw me heading to my office, 'someone will send them to you. We're not having you stealing confidential employee data.'

Oh yeah, like the dental health plan for directors' wives. Or maybe the expensive report on why exciting lime green was a good colour for walls in the equities department.

'And don't expect a reference, either. I can't imagine why Mr Mahon recommended you for promotion,' Glorious said archly, raising one eyebrow to suggest that she imagined why very well. She farted loudly at my departing back.

'You'd better be careful, Mrs Huntington. If someone lights a fag in here, the whole place could go up,' I said, grabbing my bag.

Two of the secretaries burst into muffled giggles and Glorious went puce with rage.

'Really!' she said.

I slunk out, ignoring the catty comments from Tina in the lobby. She would probably miss having someone to trade barbs with once she found out I was gone. Or maybe not. I hadn't exactly been winning friends and influencing people.

I was so depressed on the Tube ride home. It was surreal, the empty Tube pulling out of Bank, with space to breathe and actual empty seats. My hollow-eyed reflection with its ratty hair stared back at me from the windows. My shitty job hadn't been much but it had been mine. I would rather sign on than face Seamus torturing me every day, but God, was that really my choice? Apparently it was. I had no experience – true enough. I'd quit after five minutes, also true enough, after an affair with my married boss who turned out to be one of the greatest scumbags of the 'nineties.

You can say what you like about my choice of men, but at least I'm consistent.

'Darling, I hope this is a joke,' Mum said breathily when I called her later.

''Fraid not. My boss was coming on to me,' I said, conveniently forgetting the rest of the story.

'But men always do that. You should see Dr Richards with me. Such a goat. Anyway, sweetie, if you'd married that wonderful Justin, you wouldn't have to worry about the "work world", as I call it.'

I sighed. 'Mum . . .'

'Well, you're not getting any younger. At your age I was practically a grandmother. Why can't you be more like Gail? You're always clumping around in your wretched clumpy shoes, so tall you look like an Amazon, darling, and men like a bit of *femininity*.'

'I can't grow any smaller, Mum.'

'If you'd wear florals it would cut your height, you know. And if you curled your hair, yours is so straight and lank.'

'I've got short hair now.'

'*Short* hair? Oh Alex, why will you persist with this tomboy attitude? You won't be able to find another job. After all I've done to get you the last one, and you just *throw* it away. It's not as if I don't have enough on my plate. Had you forgotten I'm doing the Tory tombola again this year?'

'As if I could. I'll get another job.'

'Well, if you don't, you'll just have to come home here where I can keep an eye on you. Your father can find you something to do in the office.'

Oh God help me, anything but that. I saw my future at home in the Surrey estate agency, answering my father's calls in an ankle-length smock from Country Casuals, with bright pink lipstick and blue eyeshadow, until my spirit is so thoroughly broken I wind up calling Kevin the postboy and begging him to marry me.

I'd follow Snowy on to the game before I'd do that.

Then I caught another glimpse of my reflection and concluded that the pimps' union would probably send me home in disgust.

'Gotta go, Mum,' I said.

'Remember, darling, florals. And always put a bit of perfume on the places you wanted to be kissed.'

I had a vision of myself at Harrods, spritzing Allure firmly on to my ass.

''Bye.'

'Toodle-pip,' Mum chirped.

The Indian summer gave up the ghost. Overnight it turned into winter, freezing, bloody, slushy, filthy London winter. The pelting rain and icy drizzle matched my mood perfectly as I tramped round the city, fingers and nose freezing, trying to scrunch up even a dot of enthusiasm for job interviews. Nobody was hiring – or to be exact, nobody was hiring me.

'You don't even have a referee at Hamilton Kane?'

'Can you type? What's your speed per minute?'

'I'm afraid an Oxford degree is far too grand for this job, love. You're overqualified.'

'I'm not, I'll do anything,' I pleaded, 'filing, coffee, anything, I'm a really hard worker.'

The bloke looked at me over the tops of his wire-rimmed Lennon glasses. 'Darling. It's a job for an office junior. We want seventeen, not twenty-seven.'

I wondered if I should hire a schoolgirl uniform from some Soho sex house and wear my hair in plaits. But it wouldn't work. My bloom had vanished along with the first five or six rungs on the job ladder.

I ignored my sister Gail's jeering and Keisha and Bronwen trying to be kind. Keisha told me to try and sell some of my new sculpting. What a joke, but I was so desperate I actually did. In between trying not to think about Tom Drummond, and going for jobs advertised in the back of the *Evening Standard*: 'On Target Earnings, Ninety K Per Annum!' You turn up, and it's some shitty tower block in Hackney, with a bunch of sad bastards in polystyrene non-iron shirts, desperately

trying to flog double-glazing to old ladies before they get hung up on.
Or advertising space in French technical journals to Arab arms dealers.

(I tried that one for a day. Sheikh Somebody was so annoyed by me
he put a fatwa on my boss, so that was the end of that.)

And Not Thinking About Tom Drummond. That was a fulltime
career in itself. Trying to squish the memories of myself at Carrefour:
ignoring Ellen and ruining her life, whilst helping a prostitute to run
off with Tom's brother. I hadn't looked in *The Times* for the
announcement of the cancelled wedding. I didn't dare.

What a bitch I'd been. Oh why, why didn't I tell Tom the truth
about me and Seamus? He must have thought I was jumping his bones
right there in Tom's house. I'd let the coven annoy me so much that
getting my own way was all that mattered. And I'd blown it with
Tom. Not that he was interested anyway, he'd only wanted my help
in getting rid of Snowy.

You see? I hardly thought about him at all. I didn't think about him
as I tramped through snowdrifts to another crappy job agency. I didn't
think about him as I filled in the forms offering to work Christmas
shifts in Selfridges. I didn't think about him as I took my new
sculptures to every gallery that hadn't yet split its sides laughing me
out the door. I didn't think about him as I contemplated waitressing at
the National Gallery café, so at least I could see art on my breaks.

'What can you offer me?' I asked them morosely.

'What can you offer us?' they asked me.

Well, if you're going to hit me with trick questions . . . I slunk off
to Piccadilly, pieces in my bag, and tried to find someone, anyone, to
take me seriously.

I failed. And failed. So I tried and tried again, and what do you
know, I failed some more.

I wouldn't say it got you down, but even Anthea Turner would
have come home depressed.

'Cheer up, Alex,' Keisha said, 'you'll come through.'

'It's OK, Alex, you'll find somebody to buy the ferrets,' Bronwen
said kindly.

'They're owls,' I pointed out. Bronwen blushed and said she meant
owls.

Gail tossed her blonde hair and smiled patronisingly. 'I think you
should seriously consider working for Dad, you're not going to find
anything here.'

'Thanks a bunch, Gail.'

'I'm only being honest,' Gail said nastily. She was always being 'honest'. You want to watch out for your friends who say that: it mostly means 'I'm only being spiteful.'

I slunk off to bed. I looked like rubbish, my snappy haircut had grown straggly and my expensive cosmetics had run out, and I couldn't afford to replace them. It was back to the seven ninety-nine blow-dry special in the unisex salon (by Safeway), and Boots No. 7, and then only if I was lucky. Even scrimping every penny I was still behind in my subsidised rent. Signing on was a total ordeal – try telling your dole police you want to be a sculptor some day.

I was getting desperate. And Not Thinking About Tom got harder every day.

The Ted Younger Gallery on Ship Street was the last on my list that Friday, so I tried to put some effort into it. One more hurried door slammed in my face and I would be done for the week. It was a grey-skied afternoon, with dirty, slick snow crammed on the pavement. The Ted Younger Gallery had an empty Coke can rattling around on the pavement outside. Dull landscapes in antique frames and a boring brass figure, like a rubbish Henry Moore.

I entered. I had unwrapped one of my owls before the door had been opened properly. Sometimes they would throw you out before you even opened your bag.

'Don't tell me,' a waspish voice came from behind the counter.

I looked up to see a flat, flabby old geezer with a burgundy velvet smoking-jacket, soft white hands and a sardonic smile. The white hair on top of his head was sort of bushy and his cheeks were florid. He was so camp you could have rented him out to the Boy Scouts for an overnight stay on Dartmoor.

'It's the new Damien Hirst. The next Rachel Whitread. I'm being offered to see a work that generations will one day admire in its glass case in the Tate.'

'It's the first Alex Wilde, actually,' I said, rather miffed. I mean, spit in my face all you want, but don't compare me to Damien Hurst. Chopping off a cow's head and letting flies eat it isn't my idea of art. More a matter for the Health and Safety Inspectorate. Or possibly the RSPCA.

I limped up to the counter and shoved my owl under his nose.

Bastard. He was going to look at my bloody owl if I had to jam it into his eyeballs. My shoes were pinching my toes, I think they'd shrunk from all the water they'd taken in. So I could get Tarantino about this, if pushed.

'Interesting,' he said.

I just stood there. I actually thought I hadn't heard him right. His line should have been 'Piss off or I'll call the cops,' but he seemed to have a different script.

'Interesting. You've got a flair for motion. Although I think it would work better with wood.'

I burst into tears.

'But clay's not bad,' he said hastily. 'Good Lord, girl, don't take it so personally.'

'Oh! Sorry, it's just the kindest thing anyone's we said to me,' I sobbed.

'Then you must have had a rough time. Please turn off the waterworks, you're drenching my floor as it is. And it's a real imitation Persian you're ruining,' he said, plump fingers handing me a Kleenex.

'So do you think you can sell it?' I asked, through a mist of tears, blowing noisily.

'Absolutely not,' he said cheerfully, 'no demand for it whatsoever. I can't imagine anyone I'm acquainted with could sell something like that.'

I burst into more tears. Although this time I tried to mop them up with the tissue. I'm not in favour of girls crying. I'm in favour of bottling up your feelings and repressing them as deeply as possible.

'Perhaps you'd like a cup of tea,' he said.

His name was Gordon Farrell. He was gay and charming and he hated his job. So I knew where he was coming from.

'Wretched,' he said, 'rheumatoid arthritis. If the bloody global warming is going to fry the planet, I just wish it would hurry up.'

'Why do you do it?'

'A marvellous question. Why indeed? This is little more than a bric-à-brac shop with fancy prices. Our clientele is strictly out of town, of course. Sweet old ladies from Shropshire, whom we invite once a year for private viewings. Usually one gets enough business that way to stay afloat, but it means I have to man the ship. More's the pity.'

'Why didn't you stay at Sotheby's?' I asked curiously. It's always good to hear about other people fucking up their lives. Makes you feel you're not alone.

'Some regrettable business with the chairman's son.' Gordon sighed. 'All I can say is, he *looked* eighteen. At any rate, my career in the big leagues was sadly foreshortened.'

You couldn't call Glorious Thunderbum's department the big leagues, but I told him my Seamus story anyway. He leant his pudgy body forward, fascinated.

'Dolores Mahon's husband? How delicious. But then you're in the same boat as me. One really shouldn't shit on one's own doorstep. First rule of business.'

'Pity you can't use my stuff,' I said glumly. 'At least I'd have been safe with you.'

Gordon cackled. 'If I may say so, Miss Wilde, you'd be quite safe with a straight man. You aren't exactly heading for the cover of *Vogue.*'

'Cheers,' I said.

'Now, don't pout, it doesn't suit you. I have a proposition for you, though not a sex one, I'm afraid. It's too boring for me to sit here all day staring at the walls. I don't mind paying you to do it.'

I gaped at him.

'Shut your mouth, dear, if the wind changes direction on the moon it'll freeze that way. You took art at Oxford, you can blither on about Impressionism and wear long skirts.'

'What's the money like?' I bartered.

'Terrible. Slave wages,' Gordon countered.

'I'll take it,' I said eagerly.

Chapter 28

He wasn't kidding.

About the money, I mean. He wasn't kidding. It came to about two hundred and ten a week – a bit less than eleven grand a year. I tried asking for more, but all he did was look hurt and shocked.

'Do I resemble Richard Branson?' he would say. 'Or Bill Gates, perchance?'

It simplified things, anyway. I didn't have to agonise over the sassy Drew Barrymore crop versus the kiss-curled Winona look, or whether to tip my hairdresser ten quid or twenty. I would not be visiting Joel at John Frieda again any time soon. Nor did I waste time wondering whether Marks & Sparks grilled vegetables on tomato bread had enough protein in it for lunch. It was Asda all the way for me, public transport, Rimmel cosmetics and those shops by Oxford Circus Tube that sell you two sweatshirts for a fiver.

Who cared? My boot was stuck on the Old Kent Road in the Monopoly board of life. Do not pass go, do not collect two hundred pounds. I just about managed to make my subsidised rent. But on the plus side, my tax bill dropped through the floor.

'I don't know why you bother,' Gail said airily. 'That shop's bound to close soon. You might as well take up Dad's offer, it would suit you.'

'Why don't you take it up, Gail?' Keisha suggested sweetly. So Gail flounced off to Harvey Nichols and stopped tormenting me.

Without Keisha and Bronwen I think I might have gone mad. Bronwen kept me decently clothed by deliberately ripping the odd shirt in her photo sessions, then she got to keep them. And Keisha implicitly let me nick her shampoo and musk bath oil by leaving them out when I was due for a shower, and then not bawling me out when they were an inch lower in the bottles. She wouldn't overly give me permission, of course. It's the principle of the thing. Her Kanebo

213

Milky Facial Soap was sacred, though, you have to know where to draw the line.

But it was tough. Gail flitting in and out on her endless round of parties, constantly speculating on Snowy's whereabouts, and what Tom might be doing, until Keisha told her to shut her face or she, Keisha, would shut it for her. And Keisha and Bronwen off to their exciting jobs and new boyfriends. Bronwen had finally hooked up with Dan, Dan the Man (actually Dan the Dentist), who treated her nicely and ignored her efforts to shock him by popping 'e's in the Met Bar.

In fact, Dan told Bronwen that most people stopped taking drugs at twenty-six, and he supposed she wanted to cling to it. He said very sweetly that that was fine, some people needed a bit more time than others. Then he chuckled and said wouldn't it be funny if she wound up an old pop-picking fart like Jonathan King.

Bronwen came home that night and threw out every Class A substance she possessed. If there were any spiders lurking in our plumbing they were a happy bunch that night, I can tell you. She also ran round like a madwoman, ditching the tartan mini and the long purple skirt with the mirrored circles, the 'Mad for It' T-shirt, everything emblazoned with 'Girl Power' and 'Design for Life'.

Tony Blair should get him in as the drugs czar, is my opinion.

Anyway, Bronwen got some new styling commissions and got herself a whole new image. She was still funky, but now she was funky in favouring Alexander McQueen and John Galliano over those rock-wife staples of Prada and Gucci. She asked for a raise and got it. And her skin improved, since she occasionally slept during the night-time now.

Keisha was kicking ass at *Up and Running*, where, amazingly enough, she had spent one full season without telling her bosses they were useless pieces of shit. She got good guests and started talking about doing something different next season, 'Because I don't want to get pigeon-holed into kids' telly.'

'Heaven forbid,' I said heavily, looking at her schedule, which read things like 'Pick up Spice Girls at Hotel. Write questions Alan Shearer. Film report on *Doom 4*.'

She had also dropped the teeny popstar and started dating a record company executive. He wasn't sixteen and he wasn't famous and

Keisha never spoke about him. This gave me the sinking feeling that it might be serious.

So the girls weren't *that* useful. I mean, it's great when your mates are having a good time. But do you really need them to be lucky in love, lucky at work, stylish and rich, when your own life is going down the loo faster than Bronwen's 'doves' and 'elephants'?

Well, do you?

The lead cloud did have a silver lining. A very, very small one, almost as small as Seamus Mahon's penis. Small enough to require the old microscope. But it was there.

I was working in a gallery. OK, it was indeed a bric-à-brac shop, full of schmaltzy pictures of unidentifiable ancestors, and rural church spires. But it was better than Hamilton Kane. Better than typing Seamus's letters, and better than organising rotas for Personnel.

I learned a couple of things. How to tell the browser from the buyer. How to make anybody with even a couple of hundred quid feel valued. It was disgusting, actually, what a good sucker-up I was. I didn't let the hours drag. I couldn't, because that meant thinking about Tom, and having the horrid despair start dragging at me all over again. I organised their dreadful records, and badgered Gordon until he bought an Applemac, and started to log profit and loss and provenance and things like that. I cleared the backlog of post, and looked up a few likely London prospects to invite to a new private view. I also got the window-cleaners in, and hung a new sign outside the front door, in suitably sombre navy lettering.

I was a one-woman revolution in that shop. I switched the window display every week and wrote price-cards in calligraphy, in case a Japanese tourist came past and wanted to impulse buy. I designed smart new boxes to put our stuff in, pale blue cardboard like Tiffany's, with silky sheets of tissue paper.

'Darr-ling, I don't know why you bother,' Gordon said kindly.

I liked being creative. OK, so it wasn't exactly Oscar Wilde, but what the hell. If we ever sold anything, maybe I could work my way up to a pittance.

But I had to face the sad truth. Once I'd tarted the place up, it was still a tarted-up place that sold old junk, as opposed to a dingy, filthy little place that sold old junk.

Younger's was an answer to my darling mother.

'Oh, do come out of that fleapit and come home, sweetheart, you know you're not fitted for life in "the Smoke",' she said.

'Mum, I'm doing OK,' I lied.

'I hope you're growing out your hair. Has the owner offered to take you to dinner yet?'

'Not yet.'

Heavy sigh. 'What's the *problem*, darling, you're not still wearing trouser suits, are you? Who do you expect to find if you sit in that dust bowl all day? And Gail tells me you never go out at night.'

'I can't really afford it,' I said stupidly, prompting another twenty minutes on why I should take the King's shilling and do my dad's filing for him.

'You could live at home rent-free. And there are so many *tremendous* young chaps down here.'

Like Nigel Feather of the Woldingham Young Conservatives? Spare me! 'Mummy, women don't need to have a boyfriend to make them feel complete,' I said righteously.

'What utter, utter nonsense,' my mother said swiftly. 'A woman without a man is a failure, darling, and she becomes bitter and twisted like your aunt Caroline.'

I shuddered. Aunt Caroline was my mother's younger and uglier sister, who was indeed as bitter as a sloe and twisted as a pretzel.

'Well, I'm nothing like Aunt Caroline,' I said firmly, 'and I really must dash, Mum, 'bye now.'

I put down the phone and looked at my reflection miserably. I was thin and drawn, not so much Kate Moss as a scrawny chicken. Misery had robbed my skin of all its bloom, my hair was a mess and the highlights out of a packet had an unpleasant brassy quality to them. My bank had taken to sending me nasty letters, but they should be grateful I was making anything at all.

I wondered if I should truly jack this in and go home.

The thought came to me that Tom Drummond would have cheered me, would have told me I was doing the right thing. This shop had an old yard in the back, where Gordon kept a potter's wheel, and let me throw sculptures on my breaks. Some of the stuff was drivel, but most of it was pretty good, fuelled by my depression and sickness of heart. Gordon kept telling me he could never sell any of it.

Tom would tell me to do it anyway. I remembered with a pang how he'd always been so keen on being true to oneself.

That filled me with such longing I started to cry. I was doing a lot of that lately. I'd told Gordon my hayfever was chronic.

'In December?' he asked, but I pretended not to hear him.

I'd sold two paintings all week when I came home on Friday. One to a woman who asked if a ship scene from the Staithes Group could be attributed to Turner. I thought I deserved a medal for not giggling even a tiny bit.

'Well, no, but very much in the *spirit* of Turner,' I said.

'Yes. The artists had much in common,' she said decisively. I'm always told I have a good eye.'

I bit my tongue. I did not say, for example, that if she had a good eye it was the duff one that was looking at pictures. Or that what Turner and and this guy had in common was that they were both painters.

(I know I said it was in his spirit, but I was being paid to talk crap. What was her excuse?)

At any rate, money changed hands, so everybody got something out of it.

Gordon had been shouting at me because he had deleted last month's sales from our computer, it was hailing outside and it had cracked our front window, so I was cross and freezing and soaked, because Green Park station was shut down due to a security alert, and the bus was late. I hadn't bothered to tart up my make-up, and my white slacks were now cuffed with dirt, and I generally looked like shit.

So no change there.

At any rate, I got home and found the light in our flat was on and there was a general noise of revelry. Bloody brilliant. I did so want to socialise merrily with Dan the Man or Dave the Rave, or Gail's latest conquest. I did so want to pretend I was having a terrific, Swinging London time, talking about media or fashion and trying to make up stories to make my job seem interesting. Yes, that was what I wanted to do, as opposed to something unsatisfying like sinking into a bubble bath with a family-sized bar of Fruit and Nut.

Perhaps if I waited out here for a bit Keisha would sod off to the tapas bar in Camden or something, conquest in tow.

But it was too bloody cold for plan B, so I had to bite the bullet and walk up the stairs.

When I got to the door, the loudest laughter was Gail's. Actually, it wasn't very loud. It was just persistent. It sounded like a very tinkly brook, or a sweet infant chuckling in an endearing fashion. It was her Force Ten Man Attack laugh. I hardly needed to get into the flat to see the expressions that accompanied it, such as the Shy Di glance up under the fringe, the girlish flick of the hair, and the Light Gesture, for example resting her manicured nails very lightly on the coat sleeve of the target.

There was no escaping the conclusion that the worst had happened. Gail, too, had got herself a bloke. So now it was only I who was single in the whole flat.

Topping myself would take far too much energy, so I got out my keys and opened the door.

And stopped dead. Because standing in the middle of the room, her hand resting lightly on the cuff of her conquest, was Gail, looking stunning in a wispy John Rocha piece of nothing. She was laughing and flirting and genuinely lighting up the room. I could sense the pleasure and happiness flowing from every pore of her exfoliated skin. She'd pulled out all the stops. Her make-up was so good it looked like a pro had done it at Harrods counter an hour ago, and maybe they had. Her hair was done up in a very stylish and complicated French pleat, giving her a classy, if still girlish, look. She was teetering in high heels that made her look even slimmer than normal, her bum had almost completely disappeared. And she was drenched in Chanel No. 19, I could smell it across the room.

None of this was much of a shock. Gail takes her bloke-hunting very seriously.

But her man took me a second to get used to.

'Hello, Alex,' said Tom.

'Tom,' I said.

I wished the ground would open and pull me into its gaping maw, but it stayed annoyingly firm under my feet. I became painfully aware of my red nose, watering eyes, stringy hair and drenched trousers. The last time he'd laid eyes on me I'd looked like rubbish, and now I was looking even worse.

I could not think of one dry or witty thing to say. 'Tom,' I repeated. 'Tom Drummond.'

'Very good, Alex, you get full marks on the recognition test,' Gail giggled. 'Can't you say anything else?'

'What are you doing here?' I asked weakly.

'Picking me up for a date, what does it look like?' Gail said, not without a note of triumph.

'Oh,' I said, as waves of jealousy rocked through me. This was completely surreal. This did not compute.

'I expect you're a bit surprised to see me here,' said Tom, responding to my sister's squeeze. 'I've been talking to Gail for a couple of weeks, actually. Ever since the wedding.'

'The wedding?'

'Yes. After all the fuss, they had it quietly in the family chapel, but I don't think Ellen minded. We –' he looked hideously embarrassed – 'managed to find Charlie and persuade him he was making a dreadful mistake. He came to his senses. He had to win Ellen back, naturally, but it worked out all right in the end.'

'Win her back? That must have taken all of two seconds,' Gail giggled.

'Where's Snowy, she hasn't been back here?'

'I believe she's going to sell that flat and live abroad somewhere,' Tom said. His voice was very measured, but I could hardly look at him. Even though things had worked out all right, it must have cost his family. The shame. The scandal. God, I thought with my heart in my mouth, how he must adore Gail to associate himself with this place. With us. With *me*.

'That's nice,' I managed. 'You – you never said you were talking to Tom.'

'Oh, I knew how you felt about him,' Gail said airily, 'so I didn't want to tell people we were going out until it was serious. But I'm afraid it is, rather, so you'll just have to kiss and make up.'

Tom looked about as sick as I felt. Oh God, I couldn't bear this, I just couldn't. The greasy burger I'd had for lunch was suddenly clamouring for a return appearance. Tom hated me and he loved my sister, and Gail looked blissfully happy about it. I wondered what stage they had got to – was she already picking out her own wedding gown?

'Will you excuse me? I need a bath,' I heard myself blurt out. 'Do have a wonderful time.'

'Oh, I *will*. Tom's taking me to *Romeo and Juliet* at the National. I can't believe you never told me how romantic he is, Alex—'

But I had already rushed past her and shut the door.

Chapter 29

I tried to put a brave face on it.

I did, really. I started getting up earlier, making sure I had time to wash and brush my hair. And I always put on a layer of make-up, no matter how cheap.

I don't know why I bothered. Nothing was going to get me back to my usual self, not unless the Good Looks Fairy dropped a two-week holiday in the Seychelles, all food and cosmetics provided, into my lap.

Funny how I now wanted to get back to my usual self. Prior to that, I hadn't thought my usual self was much cop. Too fat, breasts too small, thighs too big, bum too squishy. Generally undainty and unGail-like. It was only now I'd taken a downhill turn that I realised I hadn't been all that bad. OK, so I wasn't cool, and prior to being revamped by Keisha I wasn't stylish. But I'd had a certain fresh young prettiness, the kind that all women overlook but most men think is cute.

Of course, that had all changed now.

I was about as fresh as last Easter's eggs.

And all the freshness that had been sucked out of me had been sucked into Gail. She primped and preened like a supermodel. She had her hair cut in a blunt, sexy curtain, she spent ninety quid on make-up, she bullied my mother into giving her extra money for dresses.

'Alex!' she cried, bouncing into my room in a slinky scrap of red. 'What do you think of this? Would Tom go for this look?'

A corpse would have gone for that look. Gail at her best could turn a statue on.

'I'm sure he'll love it,' I muttered.

'No, no, it's too much,' she decided, 'I'm going to go demure, I bet Tom likes demure.'

I'd sort of been crossing my fingers that she would stick with the hot red thing, because Tom hated girls who looked cheap. It was always fun watching him squirm out of the drunken embraces of various Yanks at Oxford, murmuring, 'How kind,' and 'Thank you so much.'

But Gail is a pro. She takes no prisoners. Her radar, locked on target, is incredibly accurate. Out went every short skirt and tight top she owned. In came virginal white, enchanting pastels and sweet twin-set cardigans. Her spike heels gave way to pumps and maryjanes. And not a pair of trousers survived.

Her bedroom, once home to hunt-saboteur leaflets and annoying books on macrobiotic cooking, was transformed. Out went *Only Sadists Wear Leather* and *The Organic Dinner Party*, in came mounds of fluffy teddy bears. She hung an Athena print of a simpering infant over her anti-vivisection poster, and filled a crystal vase with roses to put on the windowsill.

'Why don't you just get a copy of *How To be a Good Wife and Mother*, and leave it on your bed?' I suggested sourly.

'Ooh! I will!' Gail breathed. 'Where do I get it?'

I would like to be able to say that Tom saw through this. I supposed I cherished a very faint hope that he might still resemble the man I knew at college. Tom had been a perfect gentleman himself, but the way I remembered it, he *liked* my independence, he didn't want a Stepford Wife.

But then again we had only been friends.

Maybe he was looking for something quite different in a girlfriend. Like Linda . . . she had been a real girls-in-pearls heroine. The kind of chick they feature in black and white on the inside page of *Country Life*, you know the one, 'Miss Claudia De Vere, engaged to be married to Lord Richard Hamilton.' Linda would have shopped, and decorated, and organised holidays, and supervised the nanny, and pretended to have lots of headaches. A bit like my sister, only better bred. But what Gail lacked in blood, she made up for in looks.

Tom was just like the rest of them. He had fallen for that startled-fawn look, and God help him now, he was in trouble. Gail was manicured and feminine enough to make Barbie look butch. I thought miserably of what a great couple they would make: ex-Army, take-no-prisoners Tom Drummond, and fragile Gail Wilde.

And there was no hope for me. Tom was in deep enough to call

Gail, to be round here, to take her out to dinner, and the theatre, and the ballet. After all the trouble we – I – had caused at Carrefour, he was *still* here.

'Look at the lovely flowers!' Gail screamed, squealing for joy the day after their date. Tom had sent a huge bunch of yellow roses from Lavender Blue, the designer florist. I'd prayed they were for Keisha, but no such luck. 'Wow! Can you believe it!'

'He's got you bad,' Bronwen said, admiringly.

'Mmm.' Gail ripped open the envelope. ' "Thank you for a delightful evening, Tom." Oh, how adorable, it's so romantic.'

'It's not that romantic,' Keisha said coolly. 'He doesn't say "love". And they're not red.'

'As if that mattered! What do you think, Alex?'

'I – uh –'

The phone rang. Bronwen jumped on it, and then her face fell, like it did any time anyone who was not Dan the Man called. 'It's Tom Drummond for you, Gail,' she said.

I quietly grabbed my coat and headed out the door.

'Why so down?' Gordon asked when he came in at lunch. 'Always look on the bright side of life. You're never fully dressed without a smile. Whistle while you work.'

'How do you know I'm down?' I mumbled.

'How?' He threw an expansive arm around the shop. 'You're not cleaning, stacking, moving, packing or typing. Nor are you mooning over sculpture books or throwing clay birds in my back yard.'

'Just a bit of man trouble.'

'Don't *talk* to me!' Gordon said fiercely. 'Men! Who can understand them? Doesn't he like you?'

I shook my head.

'Maybe he's gay,' Gordon said with satisfaction, 'yes, he must be gay, and you don't want to wind up a fag-hag, too demeaning, so you'd better hand over his phone number. I promise not to be too rough.'

'Tom's not gay,' I said morosely. 'Tom's as straight as a laser. He used to be a soldier.'

'*Truly* butch, how thrilling.' Gordon looked at me, and stopped himself. 'Oh, spoilsport, perhaps he isn't gay, well, it's his loss. Why doesn't he like you?'

'Because he's in love with someone else. With –' I forced it out – 'my kid sister.'

'Ahh.' Gordon tried to look sympathetic, but he was gripped, the gossip hound. Who could blame him? If it was anybody but me, I'd have been gripped too. 'So the arsenic in the teacup option is ruled out? Tampering with her brakes is a non-starter?'

''Fraid so,' I said. I couldn't help it, a big tear welled up over my lashes and splashed on to my cheek.

'Come on now. This too will pass,' said Gordon, coming over all profound. 'Plenty more flesh on the street.'

'Don't you mean—'

'I know what I mean,' said Gordon with a jaunty wink, going into the back.

All I wanted was to be left alone with my heartbreak, but Gordon wasn't having any of it. He had plenty of advice, and since he signed my wages, I had to listen to it.

'You're going to have to mend your quarrel. You know you are. He likes your sister—'

'Big time.'

'And she likes him, so I expect wedding bells will start to chime. Love and marriage, love and marriage, go together like a horse and carriage . . . OK, OK, no need to look so upset.'

'You're taking things a bit fast, aren't you?' I asked, my heart thudding. 'They've only been going out for a couple of weeks.'

'Yes, but she wants him, you're telling me she's making all the little girly moves.' Gordon crinkled his eyes delightedly. 'And if he's keen on her . . . Tom Drummond doesn't sound like a chap who mucks a girl about.'

My tummy lurched. That was true! I'd never thought of that. If Tom acted serious, he *was* serious.

'So. You can't keep avoiding him.'

'I can! I can keep avoiding him,' I cried desperately. 'I've managed to be out every time he's come over so far, and out or in bed when he brings her back. He doesn't want to see me anyway.'

'But you want to see him. Not with Gail, I know, but there it is. You're going to have to be brave,' Gordon said soulfully. 'If love has passed you by, at least you can behave with honour, with quiet dignity, like Josephine after Napoleon divorced her, or that girl in the *Lord of the Rings*, when Aragorn spurned her, or—'

'Oh, all right,' I managed. 'Maybe.'

'You can't hide your head in the sand for ever,' Gordon said.

I thought about that. He was right, but I didn't want him to be. I had changed my mind about the ostrich: it seemed like a remarkably clever bird, with a neat way of confronting a crisis.

'Put on your glad-rags and throw a dinner party!' Gordon enthused.

'Oh, get lost,' I said, 'you've got to be kidding.'

Throw a dinner party? What did he think I was? The sodding orchestra on the deck of the *Titanic*?

But Gordon had a point. I repaired my tear-smudged foundation, sold a couple of watercolours, and got out of the shop as early as I could. There was no point trying to make myself pretty, I was like a candle next to the sun of my beauteous sister. God, it had been bad enough growing up with Gail, listening to all the jokes, watching all the mothers crowd round the elfin little girl instead of the big clumping gnome that was me. If you ask me, the Ugly Sisters were more than fair to Cinderella. They only made her sweep the bloody cinders. They didn't sue her for mental distress, or even mutilate her, I thought they were most restrained. I knew where they were coming from.

My only comfort, growing up, had been that Gail liked different men than I. I had my shopping list – sense of humour, charm, poetic looks, Byronic dashingness, etc. And Gail had hers – money.

Funny thing, that – Tom satisfied Gail's list, but he scored a big fat zero on mine. I mean, OK, he had a great sense of humour. He was about as sensitive as a prison guard. And he wasn't lean and curly haired, the slight, Byronic look I used to fancy. He was a whopping great beast of a man.

But I wanted him.

I thought about it all the time. How it would be to go out with a bloke *capable* of carrying me across a threshold. To be folded up in arms with huge biceps attached to them. When Tom was fat, he was a teddy bear, and he'd been cute, if that's your bag – like the bloke in *Roseanne*, you know the one. But now he was in shape, he was a grizzly bear. It was a whole different deal. It was sensuous.

Remember those lines in *Julius Caesar*? 'Let me have men about me

225

that are fat. Yon Cassius has a lean and hungry look; Such men are dangerous.'

Right on, Bill, now you've got me dredging up my O-level English, and that's when you know it's serious.

Oh, what the hell. Tom was going out with my stunning, amazingly annoying little sister. He wanted the kind of passive, wifely girl I could never be. What heartbreak, but there it was. Even as sad as I was, I knew I could never change. It would be like asking a penguin to fly; I'm just not that sort of bird. Even though, agreed, my own career was a lesson in how not to do it, and my audience as an artist consisted of my mirror.

I missed two buses thinking about this, jumped on the third, and had a row with the conductor about the right change. So that took my mind off him for a good two minutes.

By the time I was trudging up Elgin Avenue, I'd come to a reluctant decision. I had to face this situation. Otherwise Tom might think – might possibly think – might just maybe get an inkling that I actually fancied him.

I gritted my teeth. That would be worse than anything yet.

'Hey, Gail,' I shouted as I let myself in. I pasted a smile on my face like Happy the Dwarf. Was there a Happy? Well, I was going to be Merry, Cheerful, Detached, Happy, Joyous, Perky and Gay. Unless Gordon bagsied that last one.

It was clear from the buzz of the hair-dryer that Tom the target was not yet in firing range. Also, Gail's knickers were draped all over the sofas.

'Hi, Alex, you're early. Got anything on this evening?' Gail asked. 'Stupid question, you never go out, do you?'

'I might go out,' I said.

She laughed loudly. 'Oh right, good one, yeah. Anyway, Tommy's coming round to pick me up quite soon.'

'Where are you going tonight?'

'Out to a party at the French embassy, I think. Or is it in the British Museum, and the embassy thing next week?' Gail turned in front of our mirror, brushing out her gleaming gold hair. She wore a fishtail silver dress that clung to her minute curves, and some glittery eyeshadow and palest pink lipstick. She looked like a mermaid. 'He takes me to the most wonderful places.'

I grunted.

'Tommy will be pleased you're home, he always asks about you.'

'What do you mean?'

'Oh, if you'll be there when he arrives, or when we come back. Oh gosh,' Gail put her manicured nails up to her lips, 'maybe he doesn't want to bump into you, Alex, maybe you should leave.'

'He can bloody well lump it,' I said furiously, wretched at the thought that that might be what he meant. 'I live here!'

'God!' Gail pouted and threw her Mason Pearson across the room. 'You're so selfish, Alex, if you do anything to muck it up for Tom and me I'll kill you.'

'Do you really like him, then? You've only known him for a month or so,' I said desperately.

'Oh, you know – I think he's *the one*,' Gail said dramatically, 'I really do. He's a perfect gentleman and I love his house, and we fit so nicely, and anyway – I'm ready.' She retrieved her hairbrush for a few extra strokes. 'Yes, I think it's time.'

'Time?'

'Time to settle down. Marriage, children . . . Mum always says that's what really fulfils a woman.'

'But do you love Tom, though?'

'Oh, masses, I love him loads,' Gail said emphatically, 'he's my baby elephant.'

'Your what?'

'My ickle Babar, that's what I call him, because he's so strong, and he never forgets to call,' Gail explained, drenching herself in Dune.

The doorbell rang, and I was grateful to hear it. The sound of the gates of hell clashing shut behind me would have been a welcome change from this conversation.

'You get it, Al, I want to look busy,' Gail squealed, running into her bedroom and slamming the door.

Reluctantly I got up and let Tom in. I couldn't see what he was wearing, because of the two dozen pink roses he thrust in my face.

'Gail,' Tom said warmly.

I stepped aside. 'Sorry, only me.'

Tom had on a dark, charcoal-grey suit and black shoes. It picked out his eyes and his black lashes. He looked so muscular, so purely male. I had a hateful image of that barrel chest cradling my sister's fragile body. Jealousy rocked through me; I would like to say I fought it down but I didn't, I blushed a rich crimson.

'Alex, how are you?' Tom asked gently.

'I'm fine,' I muttered.

'And how's work? You resigned from Hamilton Kane?'

'Gail!' I yelled frantically. 'Gail, Tom's here! Er – yes. I'm working in a gallery down in Piccadilly. Younger's.'

'Oh. Much more your speed,' he said neutrally.

There was a hideously awkward pause.

'I'm – uh – I'm sorry for the misunderstanding at Carrefour. I had no idea,' I said, and any redder and the blood vessels would have exploded of their own accord.

'Don't give it another thought, entirely my fault,' Tom said, so fast and so smooth the words tumbled into each other.

I couldn't take it, it was such a polite dismissal, exactly the kind he used to give to the drunk Yanks who had hit on him, when they apologised the next day. He was clearly as uncomfortable as I was. He hates being here with me, I thought, he just wants to get Gail and get out.

Chapter 30

'Tommy,' Gail breathed, emerging from the bedroom. Her voice had gone up an octave. 'Flowers for me, ooh, how sweet.'

'Gail, you look wonderful,' Tom said. 'Like a fish.'

'A fish?' she asked.

'A mermaid,' he said hurriedly, 'and, um, Alex, you look marvellous too, sort of like . . .'

'A whale. Ah-ha ha ha,' Gail giggled. 'Has Alex been boring you to death? Sorry, I was busy with my embroidery.'

She held up one of those awful round frames of a kitten playing with a ball of wool. Jesus.

'It's charming,' Tom said, looking perplexed. 'No, Alex was telling me about her new gallery. We're looking for art for the office, perhaps I should drop by some time.'

'It's a very small gallery,' I said, 'it really wouldn't suit you.'

'And are you seeing someone?' he asked awkwardly. God, this was horrible, I was hating every bloody second.

'Don't be silly. Alex! She lives like a nun,' Gail giggled.

My face flamed back up. 'But I am,' I said. 'Seeing someone.'

'You never said,' Gail accused. 'Who?'

'Gordon Farrell, he owns the gallery,' I said triumphantly. Tom raised an eyebrow, but I ignored it. There was no way I was going to let Tom Drummond walk out on me all superior and forgiving. 'He's very successful and from an excellent family.'

'Have you been going out long?' Tom asked, his face working a little.

'Mmm. Well. He's been asking, but now I've said yes,' I lied, 'so you won't be catching me in all that often, because Gordon likes to take me to new openings and the theatre and that sort of thing.'

'What sort of thing?' Gail challenged, her smoky lids narrowing.

'The cinema. Foreign films. Ones with subtitles,' I concluded, folding my arms for extra emphasis.

The phone rang, and I jumped on it.

'Hello, is that 555 2237? This is Mr Brines,' said Bronwen's boss.

'Oh, hello, Gordon darling,' I said brightly, 'yes, I was just talking about you, I hope I'm not too late for *Manon des Sources*. Maybe tomorrow. And thank you for the lovely roses, red ones are definitely my favourite.'

'Hello? Hello?' asked Mr Brines.

'Oh, me too, darling. Goodbye,' I said sweetly, and hung up.

'Oh well,' Gail announced. She looked slightly miffed, one–nil to me! 'Don't let us keep you, we don't want to be late.'

'Where are your roses?' Tom asked.

'In the office,' I said, 'Gordon always likes me to have flowers on my desk. He says I'm far more beautiful than they could ever be. Anyway, have a good evening.'

Tom nodded at me and shepherded Gail out the door.

I fled into my bedroom and collapsed.

Keisha arrived back with Bronwen in tow. Both of them were deliciously excited: Dan the Man was making 'move in with me' noises. Keisha had met Jeremy, her current man, for a drink, and was still saying zip. So it sounded like both of them were on the move.

I thought about what it would mean if they moved out. Oh please, not yet, I couldn't face drinking soya milk and eating tofu burgers. Although with Tom in the frame, maybe I wouldn't have to for long.

'So how's it going, girlfriend?' Keisha asked me, when the 'Dan is great' stream of conversation had run its course. 'I met Gail and Tom outside, she said you're going out with Gordon.'

'Mmm, yeah, I am.'

Keisha blinked suspiciously. 'Is that a lie?'

'I suppose you could call it a lie,' I admitted, 'on technical grounds.' She gave me The Look, so I had to add, 'The technical grounds of its not being true.'

'Now why did you do that, *cariad*,' asked Bronwen, 'when you'll have to go to all the bother of faking calls and flowers and stuff?'

'I couldn't bear Gail getting all smug,' I said, deciding not to mention my declaration of passion for Mr Brines just yet.

'She'll check up on you,' Keisha warned, 'you're going to have to tell him.'

This was sadly true. Oh, what a tangled web, and all that.

'Better yet, get yourself a man,' Bronwen suggested. 'A real one this time.'

I hate it when my girlfriends say this. 'Get yourself a man.' How? Where? You can't walk into the Man Supermarket and just pick one up, despite all those stupid articles about fresh produce counters being the new singles bars. There's the threat of Aids. And the threat of Assholes. Trying to find a decent man in a nightclub is like trying to find a decent batsman on the English cricket team. And the hallowed environs of Younger's were not exactly full of thrusting specimens of manhood, unless you counted the pretty young things who swung by for Gordon.

Gay men have got to be doing something right, I tell you. Gordon wasn't even that attractive, and he saw more action than Patsy Kensit at a rock festival.

And you have to remember the environmental factors.

Such as I looked like shit (did I mention this one before?).

'No, really, we'll help,' Keisha said eagerly. So eagerly, I realised how badly I must seem to need it. 'We'll throw a dinner party. I know loads of—'

'Stop right there,' I said, 'haven't you read *Bridget Jones's Diary*? Don't you know the Karmic Law of Dinner Parties? Everything that can go wrong, will go wrong, only this time in public. I don't need to spill the redcurrant fool all over my white dress. Or put salt in the crème brûlée by mistake.'

'What crème brûlée?' said Keisha.

'What white dress?' said Bronwen.

But they were being deliberately obtuse. Ha! What did everyone take me for? I wasn't going to be tricked into that old one.

I went to bed quickly, so I could try and get to sleep before Gail got back. No chance. I sat in my bedroom, I lay on the bed, I counted sheep, I counted Seamus Mahon's ex-girlfriends. I was still awake at quarter to one, and there was no mistaking Gail's sweet, girlish giggle, or the low tones of Tom trying not to wake everyone up. They talked for a little while at the door, but he didn't come in.

It didn't make it any better. I bit my pillow, it would never do for Gail to hear me snuffling.

I told Gordon of my little deception first thing the next morning.

'My,' he said unflatteringly, 'we are scraping the barrel, aren't we?'

'Will you go along with it? If you need to, I mean?' I begged.

He looked at me witheringly. 'It better not get back to Heaven, you'll ruin my reputation.'

The phone trilled its lazy trill. Gordon had bought one with a specially melodious tone, he thought it was the gadget of the universe. I thought it was one up from those doorbells that play the *Close Encounters* theme when you press them.

'Hello, Younger's, oh, hello, Mr Drummond,' he went on, as I made frantic 'not in' gestures at the receiver. 'Oh yes, my darling sugar pumpkin is right here. It's Tom for you, sweet cakes.'

'Er, hi Tom,' I grunted, my face and neck purple with shame. Thank Christ they're not using videophones yet, can you imagine, no woman would survive a week. Plus, you'd have to have neat hair and make-up twenty-four seven.

'Don't be long, angel eyes,' yelled Gordon, 'you know how I hate you talking to other men.'

'Gordon sounds the jealous type,' said Tom's neutral voice.

'Oh, mad jealous, I don't know what to do with him,' I replied, making enough shooing motions for Gordon finally to bugger off.

'I was just wondering if you'd thought some more about selling me a piece for our lobby. Or several pieces, in fact. We look very drab at the moment.'

I bit my lip. There were plenty of bland, corporate paintings in here, and I knew Tom had money. But he was doing this for charity; to ingratiate himself with Gail.

'I told you, there's nothing here for you,' I said shortly.

'But it won't hurt for me to have a look. Come on, Alex, you don't want to deprive your boyfriend of a sale,' Tom insisted.

'Can't you look somewhere else?'

'If I didn't know better, I'd think you were giving me the cold shoulder. What's the matter, you don't think I'm right for your sister?' asked Tom blandly.

'I think you and Gail are perfect for each other,' I said stiffly. 'Come by any time.'

Then he hung up, and I bit my carefully cultivated nails raw.

★

I repaired my make-up a million times, pushed my sleeves above my elbows, and ran round the corner to buy two dozen red roses, which I stuffed into a milk jug and put on my desk. They were a bit manky, but they were the best I could come up with. Lunchtime came and went, and no sign. I was just beginning to feel off the hook when the doorbell jangled, and my heart did a slow flopover in my chest.

I breathed in and poked my head out from behind the roses.

'Hello, darling,' said my mother.

I did a double take, but unless Gordon had slipped a tab of acid into my peppermint infusion, it was Mum, resplendent in a hot-pink woollen coat and dress with matching tights, black pumps, and a black hat with a vomiting spray of feathers.

Gordon had heard the jangle and re-emerged, like a piranha scenting blood.

'Mum, this is Gordon Farrell. My boss. Gordon, this is Emma Wilde.'

'Mrs Wilde,' said Mum instantly in case he tried to call her Emma. 'Alex's mother. I had to come up to "the smoke" today, so I thought I would check in on my little girl. I don't know what you think you're wearing, Alex, you look like a workman.'

'Whereas you look devastating,' said Gordon with a courtly bow, 'and may I say that the crow did not die in vain.'

Mum simpered flirtatiously. 'It's rather dashing, isn't it? If only we could persuade Alex into something a little feminine.'

'My thoughts exactly,' said Gordon, the leeching traitor, but Mum was not to be fobbed off with such obsequious grovelling.

'Although how she can afford it on her pathetic salary, I'll never know.'

'Mum . . .'

'You don't have a head for business, Alexandra, it's about time you realised it. You should be home with us, meeting some nice young men.'

'It's the harsh nature of capitalism, Mrs Wilde,' Gordon said, beaming. 'We give Alex job satisfaction, that's very important.'

'Real satisfaction comes from the *family*,' my mother said. 'What is this?' She picked up my latest effort, a slinking panther. 'A snake? Snakes don't have legs.'

'It's the idea of a panther,' Gordon said defensively.

'It's *my* idea of a mess.'

'Mum, I really must ask you to—' I began, braving the thunderclap that would inevitably emerge, but was saved by the bell, or the doorbell, to be precise.

Or maybe not. Because Tom stepped through the door. He was wearing a charcoal-grey business suit, and a blue pinstriped shirt, and he was all that and a bag of chips.

'Oh my God!' hissed Gordon under his breath. 'Are you *sure* he's not gay?'

'Shut up!' I hissed back. 'You're my sodding boyfriend!'

'Ahh,' said mother loudly, a radiant smile threatening to split her jaw in two. The feathers wobbled wildly. 'Tommy Drummond, isn't it? You are courting my little Gail.'

'Mrs Drummond, how nice to see you again,' said Tom, with perfect poise. I don't know how he does it, not one flicker of embarrassment showed up on his face. I was dying a million deaths, it was worse than the time we went to buy school uniform in John Lewis. Mum bought two of everything, and then when the total was read out to her she screamed, actually screamed. '*Four hundred and fifty-eight pounds?*' she shrieked. Then the assistant made the mistake (red alert! red alert!) of telling her it was actually pretty reasonable. She screamed again and then she started taking a poll of all the other mothers. 'Do *you* think it's reasonable? Do *you* think so?' Gail and I both scarpered and pretended to be trying on hats. It was one of the few times we've ever agreed on anything. Oh man, that memory has made me come over all shaky now.

'I always knew you were sweet on Gail,' said my mother dreadfully. 'I thought you were necking the time I walked in on Alex in the Oxford Union.'

'Mum,' I gasped, weak with shame, 'Tom doesn't need to hear all about that.'

'Well, so long as your intentions are honourable, young man. You'll have to work fast, you know, all the boys have crushes on her. She's a catch.'

'She certainly is,' Tom agreed.

'Now Alex here, I despair of. With that dreadful short haircut and these frumpy clothes. Don't you think young women should dress femininely, Tom? You'd never find a girl like Alex attractive, would you?'

'Ah . . .' Tom said.

'Of course not. You see, Alex, if you won't listen to my generation, perhaps you'll listen to your own.' She looked at her watch. 'Oh my, I must be off, I shall miss my train.'

'Lovely to meet you,' said Gordon, sniggering, the bastard.

'Allow me to get you a taxi,' Tom offered, holding open the door and blessedly escorting her out. I watched as he flagged one down and most courteously handed my mother into it. Then he gave the man twenty quid, Christ, he was a gentleman.

I shuddered. The only way it could have been worse was if she'd arrived with bags full of Country Casuals shopping and made me try them on, one ghastly outfit at a time. I almost felt for Gail. Surely Tom wouldn't want to be connected with that.

Tom walked back in before I could remind Gordon he was meant to be my boyfriend, and should therefore stop looking at Tom like a starving Labrador faced with a rump steak.

'Your mother seems on good form,' he said politely.

'Ummm,' I said in a fury of shame. 'Shall I show you some nice brasses?'

'Certainly.' Tom eyed Gordon with distaste, so I defiantly kissed Gordon on the cheek.

'Alex has been such a blessing,' Gordon said faintly, 'to the gallery, Mr Drummond.'

'I'm glad you're doing something to make you happy,' Tom replied. 'Look, you have masses of stuff here we'd be interested in, but I need a while for Alex to show me round properly.'

'Come to the private viewing,' Gordon burst in eagerly. 'Alex is hosting the next one. On Sunday!'

This was news to me.

'Terrific, love to,' Tom said neutrally.

'And bring your girlfriend,' Gordon added, 'it'll be a double date.'

Chapter 31

'I can't do it,' I said glumly.

Gordon was firm. 'You can, darling, and you will. Let him see you shine. Think how much better everything will seem.'

I gathered up my panther and slunk off home. Why, when your heart is breaking, does everybody insist you put a brave face on it?

I didn't want to shine. I didn't want to buck up. But I went home anyway.

Gail got home late, clutching an exquisite Hermès silk scarf.

'I surprised Tom at work and took him shopping,' she squealed triumphantly, 'and then I admired this so much, he bought it for me.'

'Lucky you.' Bronwen admired it.

Gail tossed her blonde hair. 'It's not luck, it's destiny. He needs someone like me, you know. Just wait 'til I get into Carrefour, I'm going to completely redecorate. All those fusty old tapestries and lead windows, I'm going to knock a few of the walls together and create some really interesting spaces. Very white walls, chrome furniture . . .'

'I think it's a listed building,' Keisha pointed out dryly.

Gail pouted. 'I bet Tommy could get that overturned.'

'He wouldn't want to, he loves Carrefour,' I said.

Gail marched up to me. 'How would you know?'

I shrugged. 'We were friends for years.'

'Yes, well,' she said shrilly, 'you were a friend, but *I'm* his girlfriend. Tom likes feminine women, you know.'

'So Mum was telling me,' I agreed.

Gail wasn't listening, her narrow face had flushed pink. 'I know Tom came round to your office today,' she went on. Bronwen and Keisha had pricked up their ears, anticipating a sisterly row. 'It was only professional, you needn't think it was anything else. He wants some art—'

'For his lobby.'

'And if he *is* being nice to you, it's only because he wants to impress me.' She shoved the scarf rather fiercely under my nose. 'This was six hundred quid, Alex, I mean, he's mad on me.'

'I can see that,' I said.

'Well, I'm just saying,' Gail concluded.

I looked back at her. 'What are you just saying?'

She frowned. 'Stay away from my man. We all know you don't care about nicking other people's husbands, I've discussed the Seamus thing with Tom.'

I flushed. 'What?'

'Well, it's only the truth. Anyway, you stay away from my man.'

Gail stalked off into the bathroom before I could say another word.

'She's jealous, she must be insecure,' Keisha said. 'Anyway, you'd hardly make a play for your own sister's bloke, Alex, would you?'

I said nothing. Chrome and white paint? It killed me, Gail was so wrong for Tom, even if she did look like a delicate buttercup. Was that what Tom wanted? Clearly it was, so there was nothing I could do, except what I did, which was to pick up Gail's new scarf and blow my nose on it, with Bronwen bursting into shocked laughter.

'Come on,' Keisha said, 'let's go out and get hammered.'

After I'd locked up my room (or who knew what revenge Gail would come up with) we sodded off to the Rat & Parrot in Camden and ordered six Moscow Mules.

'How stupid, thinking you wanted Tom,' Keisha said comfortably. 'You can't stand him. Frankly, he must be nuts about Gail, if he actually came round to buy something of yours.'

'Maybe he did want to see me,' I suggested faintly, because the booze gave me courage. 'Maybe he wants to bury the hatchet.'

Keisha laughed and went to put on Mary J. Blige. When she came back, she asked, 'In your back or in your head?'

'What do you mean? He can't still be furious.'

'You know about the money, right?'

At my blank look, Keisha raised an eyebrow. 'God, didn't Gail tell you? The reason Snowy hasn't come back here? Tom found her and paid her off. He told her if they *did* marry, his brother would divorce her if he found out the truth, and to stop the scandal, he gave her money to fuck off abroad for six months. Charlie was gutted, really ashamed. He grovelled to Ellen, quiet registry-office wedding, happily ever after. Part of the deal was that Snowy moves out of her flat. We wondered about that, but now I see it was to protect Gail.'

The drink wasn't slipping down quite so easily now. 'How much money?' I asked.

'It's s'posed to be a secret,' Keisha slurred, 'Gail only found out 'cause she went through his letters.'

I'd gone icy cold. 'How much money?' I asked.

'Three quarters of a million,' said Keisha.

Oh my God. Three quarters of a million! *Three quarters of a million?* As in seven hundred and fifty thousand quid?

'Alex, why are you breathing like that? Alex, stop gasping! Excuse me, c'n we have some water here, please?'

The cab roared home through the drunken streets of North London. God, Friday nights here is like rush hour at Piccadilly Circus, with the ravers and all the Japanese tourists walking eagerly round with their shiny plastic backpacks, eyes peeled for a Gallagher brother.

I shut my eyes and tried to stop the world spinning. Tom had spent that much money, and he was *still* seeing Gail? It's not my fault, it's not, I thought desperately. I mean, I wasn't a prostitute, I wasn't responsible for Snowy . . .

But I kind of was. I'd brought her along – or that's how it looked – and I'd done nothing to stop it. Tom had money, we all knew that, but still, it must have been a huge chunk of his net worth.

And he hadn't tried to make me feel bad about it. He hadn't said a word. If Gail hadn't been snooping round his place we still wouldn't know now.

His behaviour made me feel absolutely light with love. It was so brotherly, so generous. And the fact that I'd been the worst guest in the history of guestdom, and he still hadn't dropped even the smallest hint – Tom was so gallant.

I flashed on him driving a tank the way he'd driven the car back from Gloucestershire. I saw horribly attractive images of him as an officer, in uniform, whenever I closed my eyes. The thought that he could knock Seamus over just by breathing on him refused to go away.

I'd always wanted a lefty, sensitive, poetic type – how come I had fallen for this macho, upper-class slab of beefcake?

And now Gail was going to marry him and turn his lovely old home into a postmodern airport hangar. It was a good job she couldn't clamber into my head, I thought, I'd never see another birthday.

When we arrived home there was a note propped up on the kitchen table. Keisha poked her door into Gail's room and saw that her wardrobe was empty, the fluffy teddies had vacated the building.

'She's gone, she's gone,' Keisha said, clapping her hands with glee, 'excellent, it should be on Ricki Lake.'

I ripped open the note.

'You darned cow –' darned cow? Fucking bitch was more her style, maybe she thought I would show it to Tom, and she didn't want to leave any evidence of herself as a Woman Who Swears – 'how could you do that to my lovely present from Tommy? Just because you are a pathetic old maid, you want to ruin all couples' happiness, well, it won't work with me. I have moved out and am going to live with Tommy.'

'I wonder if Tommykins knows about that,' Keisha giggled. 'I hope he isn't in bed with some serving wench when Gail arrives with her suitcase.'

I thought of Gail, tiny shoulders shaking in faked distress, turning up at Tom's with a toothbrush and a plea to stay the night, and a plan never to move out. Tom would be delighted to see her, and I had given her a perfect excuse.

Then I thought of something worse. I saw Gail weeping girlishly on Tom's manky shoulder about what a bitch I was, and Tom kissing her tears dry, and scooping her up in his arms and taking her to the bedroom.

'I don't think there's much chance of that,' I said, trying not to show Keisha that my hands were shaking. I put down the trembling slip of paper.

'Well done, Alex, you win the Flatmate of the Year award,' Keisha announced drunkenly. 'No more Gail, and at least you won't have to put on that dog-and-pony show for Tom any more.'

I turned up at Younger's the next morning and savagely cleaned the place. Boy, if there were any happy dust mites in our shop they'd had their chips that morning, I can tell you. Then I went into the back and started to throw a new sculpture.

The clay turned this way and that under my fingers, moving so fast it seemed to be liquid, not solid. Long, wonderfully turned legs with tiny calves appeared out of the grey; an A-line skirt, a hip thrown forwards.

My obsession was giving wings to my fingers and thumbs. I was sculpting my sister. Gail emerged out of the slab, hazy, then better defined, as I pulled and cut and tugged and sliced, her oval face, her gleaming hair (I spritzed varnish on to catch the light). Gordon wasn't in, and with no one to interrupt me, I worked solidly all morning, even missing the eleven o'clock chocolate break. The phone rang a few times, and I steeled myself to hear Tom say he wasn't coming, but it was only Lady Tim Haydn and Mrs Ponsonby, two of my stupider customers, promising their attendance on Sunday.

About two Gail was finished. I looked dumbly at what I had done; my sister to the life, leaning against a tabletop, the delicate features and snub nose smiling tauntingly up at me. It might have been the best thing I'd ever sculpted.

I burst into tears. Wretched, massive sobs, the kind that make your chest heave and your eyes and nose run like Linford Christie. I couldn't stop crying, for about ten minutes I just cried and cried, until my hanky got so sodden I had to throw it away. I tried to pull myself together and start making calls to the caterers, but I just couldn't. Eventually I crawled out to the loos and wiped my streaming eyes and blew my nose, and if the loo had had Gail's scarf wrapped around the loo roll I would happily have used it about a million times.

Someone was ringing the little brass bell at the front of the store. I blew my nose again and hoped they'd go away, but they didn't, which just meant I had to go out there, bloodshot eyes and ruddy nose, and try and look human. The magazines all tell you to go with your instinct, but I don't think shouting 'Fuck off, fuckface' would have been the best sales technique right now.

It was Tom Drummond. He was wearing another suit, this one plain black, and carrying a very smart briefcase. His mouth opened a touch – just a touch – at the sight of me, before he remembered his manners and shut it, pretending nothing whatsoever was wrong.

Yesterday he'd come in here and seen me with my mother. Today he got the full-on hysterical female look. I would love to say I was now past caring, but amazingly enough, I was still behind caring. I cared a hell of a lot that he saw me like this.

In fact I gave a strangled yelp and ran back into the loo.

'Alex?' came Tom's gentle voice. 'Alex, are you OK?'

'I'm fine,' I yelled back, frantically wiping and slapping on the old concealer and blusher. Oh God, a bottle of Optrex, my kingdom for a bottle of Optrex.

'You haven't split up with Gordon, have you?'

'Certainly not, we're very much in love, as if it's any of your business,' I shrieked, giving up the unequal struggle and opening the door. 'I'm very busy, so you'd better get on with it.'

'Mm. Rushed off your feet,' Tom suggested, looking around the empty shop.

I scowled. 'I suppose you've come to tell me you're cancelling for the view on Sunday. Which is fine; we hardly have the space for one more.'

'Not even when he's looking to make a major purchase?' Tom asked lightly. 'Because I'm not cancelling at all. I wanted you to know that. I realise you've had a quarrel with your sister.'

'You're living together now,' I said, struggling to keep the dejection out of my voice.

Tom nodded. Oh shit, he was good looking. The man is *fine*, as Keisha would say, he has got it going on. 'Just until she finds another place of her own. But I told her, my promise to you must stand, of course.'

'Hey, don't do me a favours, OK?' I snapped.

Tom frowned. 'Damn, Alex, just when I was thinking you'd mellowed out a little.'

'Mellow is for coffee,' I snarled. Then I remembered that I'd indirectly cost Tom about half his savings, so I blushed and looked away. 'But you can still come, if you want to.'

I was staring fixedly at the wood when Tom reached out and took my hand. The contact of his skin on mine was so surprising, so electrifying, I jumped out of my skin, like a pheasant clattering away from his gun.

'Alex, do you have to tense that way?' he asked softly. 'We've known each other for years, can't we still be friends?'

''Course,' I grunted, because I didn't trust myself to say anything else. Friends? Why? So you and Gail can torture me? I've got enough friends, thanks.

241

I sneaked up a look at him. He was regarding me so warmly I feared I might start blubbing again.

'What's Gail going to say?' I asked.

He shrugged. 'Gail and you – Charles and I fight all the time, it's just siblings. I'm sure you'll make it up. And anyway, I pick my own friends.' He chuckled, and I noticed the way his eyes went all crinkly at the corners when he did that. To think, I could have had this guy, I thought to myself.

'I can't believe you blew your nose on it,' he said.

I grinned. I knew I should apologise, but who cared, she was asking for it.

'Look.' I said it before I thought hard enough to stop myself. 'Do you have a few minutes? We could go and have tea.'

Tom looked at his watch. It looked expensive.

'I've got a meeting in an hour.'

'Sure,' I said, feeling crestfallen.

'But I'll put them off. Hold on a second.' He took out a mobile, looking rather shamefaced at carrying something so modern, and rang his secretary. She was putting up a bit of a fight but Tom was having none of it, and I felt my mood lift, just a little. It was probably super-masochistic, but I wanted his company. Without Gail, or Keisha, or Ellen, or anyone else around.

I bolted off to the loo to try some more last-minute repairs. It wasn't great, but you do your best with what you have, I suppose. At least I looked presentable. The plain black Warehouse trouser suit hid my scrawniness and actually came off as quite bohemian, with the severe crop. Right now I couldn't hope for much better.

'I know a greasy spoon round the corner,' I said enthusiastically.

'Greasy spoon? Don't be ridiculous,' Tom said, 'I've booked us into the Savoy.'

Twenty minutes later we were seated on a chintz sofa, a plate of scrumptious little finger sandwiches in front of us, with minute cakes on the tier above and scones with clotted cream and jam on the tier below. An obsequious waiter had seated us in five seconds flat, and another was pouring the Lapsang Souchong. God, but these things were delicious, and the atmosphere had slowed my pulse rate the moment I walked through the door.

Lucky, lucky Gail, I thought jealously.

The pianist struck up 'Let's Call the Whole Thing Off'. It was a bit

'England for American tourists', but still. You didn't enjoy this, you were made of clay, like one of my sculptures.

'I was sorry we quarrelled,' Tom said tentatively.

'Me too,' I gabbled, 'really, because I swear I didn't know—'

'Oh, I know you didn't.'

'But I behaved so badly, I know I contributed, I can't tell you how sorry I am,' I said, and felt my throat knot again. Oh no, I hate this, I tend to cry when I'm embarrassed. I may not even be in a crying mood, but when I'm severely embarrassed, I get weepy. I forced it down – not again.

'Nonsense,' Tom said, also rushing his words out. Probably because he was one of those Englishmen who looked on discussions about feelings, apologies and such like with the eye of a six-year-old looking at a visit to the dentist's. 'I was an oaf! As if you were responsible for what my brother did! As if I had any right to tell you how to live your life!'

I bit my tongue. Seamus! Oh man, what had Gail been feeding him?

'Seamus and I—'

He held up a hand. 'You don't need to explain, like I said, it's none of my business.'

'Honestly, he was jumping on me. I couldn't get him to go away,' I said in a small voice, 'and he'd told me his marriage was dead. I know it's no excuse, but I felt so miserable. That's why I was bloody to Ellen. I felt like no man would ever want me.'

Chapter 32

'No man would ever want you,' Tom repeated. He looked thunderstruck. 'Don't be ridiculous.'

I smiled softly. I didn't want Tom feeling sorry for me.

'So how's life with Gail?' I asked.

He squirmed a bit. Maybe he thought she'd have his guts for garters just for talking to me. 'Fine. I was – a little surprised when she turned up so suddenly.'

'She's very beautiful,' I said encouragingly.

'She is,' he agreed. 'Extremely attractive.'

Well, I don't know about *extremely* . . .

'Wonderful hair,' Tom said. 'Fabulous eyes, they're absolutely huge. And she's very delicate. Lovely hands.'

OK, OK, I get the message.

'When we go out, all the other men seem distracted by her.'

'That must happen a lot,' I speculated.

'She doesn't seem that interested in her work. I believe she wants to be a novelist?'

'So she says,' I replied. Oh hell, this conversation was getting worse by the minute. I certainly didn't want to talk about me, but did I really want to talk about Gail?

'Were you close, growing up?'

'About as close as Margaret Thatcher and Arthur Scargill.'

Tom laughed and my stomach gave a lurch. I'd always loved his laugh and now it reminded me of the lion in the MGM logo. Huge and male. Ridiculously good natured.

'Now you say that,' he told me, 'I must admit, you two have nothing in common. You have such a different outlook on life. Totally different senses of humour. And you look nothing whatever alike.'

God, he was worse than my aunt Mary, who used to say 'two peas in a pod' with less and less conviction every year, faced with the fairy and the gnome, until she finally gave up and started saying I was clever instead.

'So things are pretty serious between you two – living together?'

'Not that serious,' Tom said hastily, 'I'm nowhere near ready to settle down.'

That's what you think, I thought gloomily, but with Gail on the case you haven't a chance.

'What about you?'

'The Pope has a better lovelife than me,' I said glumly.

Tom looked surprised as he offered me a chocolate square. 'I thought you were madly in love with Gordon?'

'Apart from Gordon,' I said furiously. Then I had to look away as Tom bit his lip to stop himself from laughing.

'You've always had loads of men after you, Alex,' Tom told me when I'd calmed down.

'No, they all dumped me, or ran off with scoutmasters,' I said, and suddenly felt a big surge of relief. I just couldn't be arsed to keep up the pretence any more. Tom was gone, so why bother? This was almost like the nice, honest chats we used to have when he was a ballast balloon. Except, of course, that now I was in love with him and he was practically married to my sister. But what the hell, you can't have everything.

'I think you've got a bit of a selective memory, kiddo,' said Tom. 'What about Jack?'

The teacup paused on its way to my mouth. Jack Sullivan, the lovelorn dentist from Witney?

'Forgot about him,' I admitted.

'And Quentin?' he pressed.

Oh yeah, Quentin Dean, the young Fellow of Medieval Icelandic, he'd been a bit keen. And he'd even had his own car and flat.

'Quentin was too mushy,' I said sulkily.

'But what about Robert? And Edward?' Tom went on.

'They were all at college,' I protested. 'You can't count them.'

'Well, you certainly didn't. But not all of them were at college,' Tom Drummond, Counsel for the prosecution, went on. 'When you moved into that frightful squat of Marxists—'

'It was all right,' I lied.

'And you had a crush on that oaf with the matted hair—'

'Dreadlocks.'

'And a dog on a string.'

'You mean Crispin,' I admitted, sounding surly. Crispin was a middle-class dropout like me. He was mad on me, too. I had dumped him because I couldn't face the embarrassment of going out with someone named Crispin, I mean, it's worse than Dwayne. And after a while, personal hygiene had assumed a new importance in my life, although I didn't want to admit that, since it didn't seem very bohemian.

'And let's not forget Malcolm,' Tom went on, 'nor Philip, who took you to Paris for walks on the Champs-Elysées, and when you dumped him didn't you see Peter—'

'Fine fine, don't remind me,' I snarled.

'But it looks like you need reminding,' Tom said gently. 'You're only thinking about the men you wanted who ran out on you. What about all the other ones you *didn't* want?'

I didn't say anything. Those boys hadn't made my heart stop, so I'd ignored them. Maybe – if you twist my arm – there had been quite a few.

'Loads of men are keen on you, Alex, you need to stop feeling sorry for yourself.'

'You said that before.'

'And it's still true now,' Tom said.

I wanted to throw myself into his arms and pour out the truth. Who cares about those other men? I want you, you, you!

But I'd had my chance and I'd blown it.

'I'd better get back to Gail,' said Tom, a bit regretfully, 'but I'm glad we're friends again.'

'Me too,' I agreed, over the knot in my throat.

'I'll be at that showcase Sunday. And I'll bring Gail along, how's that?'

'Fine,' I muttered.

'Good.' He lifted his head and a waiter materialised at once. Nobody ever ignores Tom Drummond. 'We should spend more time together, don't you think?'

I made it home, not knowing whether to laugh or cry. Part of me was squirmy with excitement at the thought of seeing Tom again so soon. And part of me dreaded it, because he'd be with Gail. The thought of them together made me want to puke up all the cucumber sandwiches.

Keisha was thrilled. 'Ooh, we must make it a big deal. I'll bring Jordy. And Dean.'

'Dean the pop star?' I asked doubtfully. Jordy co-presented *Up and Running*, he was one of those kids' TV presenters who look so squeaky clean they poo toothpaste. Add Dean from Red Alert, another Keisha old flame, and you'd have a *Smash Hits* convention in my gallery.

'It's all publicity,' Keisha said firmly, 'I'll call the *Daily Mail*, we'll get your place in the papers.'

'All right,' I said uncertainly.

'And I'll bring Davina Darling!' Bronwen enthused. 'You know, the supermodel—'

'The junkie,' Keisha sniffed.

'The anorexic,' I agreed.

'The highly rich young woman who professes to like art,' said Bronwen, 'and I know Eric Fortune the photographer . . .'

I looked blank.

'He's the hot guy at the moment, Alex, really, don't you *read* the *Face?*'

'Oooh yes,' said Keisha, warming up, 'and we'll make it really fabulous, Alex, you'll wow everybody, and Sotheby's will poach you.'

'You just make sure the party is fantastic,' said Bronwen blithely.

'You want to do what?' Gordon asked in horror.

'Special catering – pigs in blankets, little pizzas – er – crêpes Suzette,' I suggested. Gordon had gone pale and was clutching himself in the wallet area.

'Do you *realise*,' he said heavily, 'how much that sort of stuff *costs?*'

'But we're going to have all the stars there,' I exaggerated madly. 'And I've phoned all our best customers. And Bronwen is spreading the word.'

'Who is Bronwen?' Gordon demanded. 'Look, if you want to do it you'll have to do it yourself.'

'Fine,' I said crossly. 'You'll have to give me a budget.'

'A hundred quid. Including wine,' said Gordon, triumphantly.

I wasn't going to be defeated. I ran out to Marks & Spencers. That all cost way too much, so I tried Safeways. And there I was triumphant – got strawberries on special offer, bananas too, smoked salmon, cheese and small sausages. The wine was tricky but there seemed some good-value stuff around, so I got Spanish, French, Italian and Australian just to be safe. And you can't argue with that!

'I'm not sure about this, Al,' Keisha said dubiously when I got home.

'What's wrong with it?' I felt flushed with triumph.

'The Scotch eggs go off tomorrow. And the bananas are a bit brown.'

'And the strawberries are a bit squashed,' Bronwen added.

'Look. We *freeze* the perishable stuff, stupids,' I said eagerly, 'and the fruit will be fine because I freeze that too.'

'It'll taste weird,' Bronwen guessed.

'No! I'm going to do Mum's special tipsy fruit salad. Defrost the fruit –' well, I wasn't sure about this bit but doubtless it would work OK – 'and then soak overnight in brandy, so it doesn't matter if it's a bit bruised. Everybody will love it, just alcohol and sugar.'

They helped me cut up the cheese and mini sausages, well, OK, we ate most of the cheese and mini sausages, but they looked so cute, what could you do? I was thrilled at how many people the girls had got to come along. Maybe there would be so many people there that I wouldn't have to see Gail at all.

'We'd better try on our outfits,' Keisha said. 'Oooh, what about my white leather jeans and that Joseph silver silk shirt?'

I was just wondering what I could wear when Bronwen chimed in, 'You can borrow some of my stuff, Al.'

'Or mine,' offered Keisha with a reluctant sigh.

But I shook my head. This was my night – I had to do it my way. I'd got it planned, anyway. Sadly anything I'd taken to Carrefour was out – bad vibes in the area – but Tom would still love my white Emporio Armani dress that took off five pounds round the ass area, which is why it cost five pounds per square inch, I suppose. Anyway, that, and the neutral lipstick and blusher and a touch of moss green on my lids for drama—

The doorbell rang. Bronwen bounded to answer it, but it wasn't Dan the Man. It was Gail.

'Oh, hi,' said Bronwen sadly.

'Come for your stuff?' said Keisha. 'You left an essential oil dropper in the bathroom.'

'No, I haven't come for my stuff,' said Gail terrifyingly. She tossed her blonde hair and folded her stick-insect arms. 'I've come for Alex.'

'Well, I'm staying here,' I said.

Keisha sniggered but Gail was Not Amused. She was giving me Mum's death stare, and believe me, you don't want to be around that.

'You'd better keep away from my man!' she spat. 'I've told you before!'

Keisha and Bronwen both hovered expectantly.

I felt a surge of bravery all of a sudden. 'I was his friend before you ever knew him,' I said.

'You saw him yesterday!' Gail spat. 'And you had *tea* with him!'

'You never said, Al,' Keisha reproved. She hates it if I withdraw Gossip Privileges.

'And we had a great time, and I'm going to see him again, on Sunday,' I said.

'You're bloody *not*!' Gail screeched. 'I won't let him!'

I folded my own arms. My hands were clammy, but so what? I wasn't going to let her see that.

'Why don't you tell him he's not allowed to see me, and see what he says,' I told her.

Gail looked wildly from Bronwen to Keisha and back to me. 'He won't listen!' she wailed, and burst into angry tears. 'I hate all of you, you horrible bitches.'

'Don't you mean darned cows?' Keisha asked snidely.

'Especially *you*, Alex!' she raged. 'My own sister! Keep your thieving hands off my boyfriend! He doesn't want you anyway, you're just making a fool of yourself!'

'Come on, Gail,' Bronwen reasoned with her, 'she only wants to be friends.'

'She doesn't fancy Tom at all,' Keisha laughed.

I didn't say anything. I was feeling horribly lanced through with guilt. She was totally annoying but she was my little sister! And if she and Tom were happy . . .

'I *forbid* you to see him *any more*!' she squealed.

'Well, he's coming on Sunday,' I said tearfully.

'I know.' Gail's eyes were like chips of ice. 'And I'm going to be with him, so you needn't think you can try anything funny. And you'd better not embarrass me in front of him, I want to marry him, you know.'

'It'll be fine,' I muttered.

'Yes, well, it better be,' Gail snarled, 'because I've told Mum what you're doing and she's going to come along as well! Probably with Dad! So if you try and steal *my boyfriend* from under my nose she's going to know all about it!'

'We're having tipsy fruit salad,' Bronwen told her happily.

'We've got stars coming,' Keisha said loyally.

'I don't care *who's* coming, just you keep away from my Tommy!' Gail spat. 'And now I'm going home to my lovely dinner with Tom and we're going to have candles and flowers!'

'Sounds disgusting. All that wax gets in your teeth,' Keisha said.

Bronwen giggled and Gail stormed out of the flat, banging the door behind her.

'How ridiculous,' Keisha laughed. 'You better watch your back, Alex, she thinks you're really after her man.'

Chapter 33

I spent the rest of the week in a frenzy of preparation.

You've never seen anybody work so hard, I mean, it was obscene. I called every customer our little shop had ever had or nearly had, even the ones in Scotland. I sucked up to Mrs Ponsonby and Lady Paula and Miss Featherington and Tom Tucker and Dwight S. Limo, the insurance broker from the United States. I pulled off all the addresses I'd tapped into our new computer and went to it like one of those bond salesmen on Wall Street.

Obviously it got a bit annoying at times (Dwight wanting to spend ten minutes on the dress code) and embarrassing at others. I invited three people eagerly whom Gordon had sold fakes to.

'Is this some kind of a joke?'

'Do you realise we have a lawsuit pending?'

Well, some people can be so fussy, I ask you. Anyway, that was nothing to me ringing Judge Wapter's number.

'Ooh, I'm sure he'd like to come,' I said ardently. 'We've got some pieces he'll be *especially* interested in.'

'Really,' said Mrs Wapter dryly.

'Oh yes, they're – uh – just his style,' I babbled, looking at the manky collection of rubbish filling our windows. 'Um – really, there's going to be lots of stars and press and society, he'll truly enjoy it.'

'Will he?'

'Yes,' I said, warming to the theme. I was a born saleswoman, no doubt about it. 'Gordon was just saying the other day how much this private view would interest the judge. We must talk to Mrs Wapter and make sure she brings him down, he said. It'll be right up his alley. He's one of our most *valued* customers.'

'How kind,' Mrs Wapter said.

'So you'll bring him?'

'That would be fairly difficult,' Mrs Wapter told me.

'Oh,' I said, disappointed, 'has he got something else on?'

'Not as such,' said Mrs Wapter, 'since he died six months ago.' She hung up on me.

But on the whole, I got a fairly enthusiastic response. And Bronwen and Keisha were doing their bit, so we could pretty much say the shop would be full. Easy-peasy, I thought, trying not to think about Tom, you can do it.

The next step was to have something to sell. Of course there would be a market for our scruffy eighteenth-century filing cabinets and gloomy oil paintings of boys in knickerbockers, but I hankered for just a couple of decent things to display.

'How about the de Kooning?' I asked Gordon. 'And the Jackson Pollock?'

'The *de Kooning*?' he asked in an artificially strangled voice. 'The *Pollock*? Have you gone mad?'

It was the pride of Gordon's life that he owned two pieces by these modern masters. He'd paid vast sums for them, 'In the high six figures, darling,' and he liked to keep them in the basement, in shrink wrap, where no one could see them. This was because he was afraid that someone might buy them. Whenever I suggested a client might be shown our jewels in the crown, Gordon shuddered with exaggerated horror.

'Oh, not Mrs *Richards*,' he would demur. 'She's only into the classics . . . no, not Dame Agnes, good God, that woman has no sense of colour.' Or 'Richard Tyrant? He has about as much aesthetic sense as Dale Winton.'

'But he's got pots of money, Gordon.'

'Alexandra, no means no,' Gordon would say firmly, and then stride across the room with his cheeks clenched very tight, as though carrying a leek using only his bottom.

He looked at me balefully right now. I hardened my heart. It was the immovable object and the unstoppable force.

However, Gordon didn't have my secret weapon: fear of looking stupid in front of Tom.

'You've *got* to, Gordon, if you want to be a serious dealer, just think of all the press there, and anyway, none of the old dears will want to buy it, but you'll *look* like a player and it will seem awfully strange if you don't have your best stuff on show . . .'

'They're such Philistines,' Gordon wailed, 'you're such a bully, Alexandra, and we don't have any other moderns to go with them.'

'We'll look marvellously iconoclastic,' I wheedled. 'Think what all your friends will say when it passes off so wonderfully.'

'As long as they're out of harm's way,' Gordon moaned reluctantly, 'and I'm holding *you* responsible, Alex.'

He went downstairs to dig them out and I went home, flushed with triumph.

It didn't last long: I had a wonderful call from Mummy on the answer machine when I got in.

'This is Mrs Wilde calling for her daughter Alexandra,' Mummy said, in a fake posh accent she uses purposely to embarrass me (on answerphones, when buying school uniform, when potential boy-friends rang to ask me out). 'Alexandra, will you please call home at once, there is something very important I must discuss with you.'

This would have been even worse than it sounded, but Keisha and Bronwen were both out with their nice, available boyfriends. It's hard not to resent people in couples when you're on your own. After Mummy's message I had to listen to some puke-makingly sweet talk from Dan the Man and Jeremy the record executive. Bleuurgh! 'So looking forward to tonight, darling. Wear that red dress – or don't bother with any dress.' 'Can't wait to see you, Keish, been thinking about you all day. Did you know you were this distracting?'

I went straight to the cupboard and ate Keisha's Sweet 'n' Spicy Pot Noodle, just to be mean. Also Bronwen's M&S Lite Toffee-Apple Layered Dessert (only 115 calories, no artificial sweetener), so that showed them.

What right did my flatmates have to a life when all I could do was organise a stupid party?

To reassure myself I went to the fridge and checked the fruit, salmon, Scotch eggs etc. were still there. They were. Well, it was going to be a top bloody party. For a second I thought of ringing up Crispin and my old mates in the squat but rejected it as a bit *too* bohemian. Stimpy 'two bellies' Jackson would stand in front of the de Kooning all night belching and asking who'd spilt the paint.

And yes, they had a phone in the squat – some anarchist hackers had rigged it so all their calls got charged to *Hello!* magazine.

Finally I knew I couldn't put it off any longer, so I opened the bottle of peach brandy I was going to use for the fruit salad to let it breathe – I read that somewhere once. Alcohol needs the fresh air for flavour. I thought maybe I'd better help ventilate the bottle by having just a small glass before I called my mother back.

Anyway, it was medicinal. For courage.

I dialled Mum's number and got only my father, who is super-bad on the phone, going for the world monosyllable record (sample conversation: 'How are you, Dad?' 'Fine.' 'How's work?' 'Fine.' 'How's the tennis elbow?' 'OK, thanks, love.' You get the drift. Sometimes I would attempt to break the pattern by telling Dad all my news – dumped by latest boyfriend, promoted, starting work on new sculpture, cut hair, etc. – and Dad would listen in pained silence, concluding with either 'Hmm, oh dear,' or 'That's good,' depending on tragic/ecstatic nature of news. He would then get off the phone as quickly as possible. Not slow to take a hint, after only fifteen or so years we started asking Dad to pass the phone to Mum, only to be told by a family friend that Dad got upset at this, and puttered round with a long face asking why his daughters never wanted to chat to him).

Of course this is a blessing sometimes, like now. 'Is Mum there? She rang earlier,' I said brightly.

'Oh no. What time is it?' he asked, a bit eccentrically I thought.

'About half seven,' I said.

'Right. Well, she should be there any minute.'

'Where?' I asked, mystified.

'There, in the flat, silly,' Daddy said patiently. 'She caught the five forty-three, so I'm surprised she's not there already.'

'Mum's coming here?' I gasped.

'That's it,' he agreed. 'Said she wants a word with you, darling, and she feels like staying the night.'

'But how did she get the keys?'

'Oh, Gail gave them to her,' said Dad blithely, presumably unaware how his words were stabbing daggers of fear into my shrivelling, alcohol-induced bravery. 'She stayed here last night. With her nice boyfriend.'

Despite the surging panic, my curiosity got the better of me. Tom must have made quite an impression for Dad to be so chatty.

'Did you like him?' I asked.

'I thought he was terrific, darling,' Dad said warmly, 'and they seemed very keen on each other, hope I shan't have to fork out for *too* big a wedding, ha, ha.'

'Ha ha,' I said. 'Anyway, gotta go, Dad love, got to tidy the place up for Mum.'

'Now Alex, I hope you and your friends have been keeping the flat in good condition,' said Dad severely.

I gave a strangled laugh. "Course! Just going to, uh, freshen the pot pourri.'

Oh God! Oh God! It wasn't fair, of course we have our tidy sessions once a week – OK, once every fortnight but who's counting – but the difference is, the others are here to help. My mother, aka the Wrath of God, was descending on me like a wolf on the fold, and me running around like a blue-arsed fly trying to figure out where to start. Obviously the kinky Nancy Friday/Joy of Sex pop-up editions had to be removed from various tables and cunningly hidden under the bed. Then there was the filthy crockery to be shoved in the sink, with me hastily turning on the taps and squirting with the Pine Fresh Concentrated, because bubbles are better to look at than dried-on kebab. Having done that I made our dirty knickers top of the priority list but only got as far as scooping them off the bathroom floor (pausing to throw three empty loo-rolls with bits of pink Andrex stuck on them in the bin) when the doorbell went like the Crack of Doom at the Day of Judgment.

I wailed and flung everything in the washer-dryer. I could run away, but there were no back exits.

The Hour was upon me.

'Darling!' said my mother, as she swept through the door.

I've heard people say 'Bastard!' in a friendlier tone of voice.

'What do you call this?' she asked majestically. 'Is it a science project? Are you trying to grow a mushroom crop in the filth?'

'Ha, ha,' I said weakly.

Mum picked up a Walnut Whip wrapper from last night's chocolate run and dropped it in the bin. 'It's totally disgusting, completely repulsive. I certainly didn't raise you to live like this . . .'

She went on like that for several minutes until I was forced to blame everything on Keisha.

'Well!' Sniff. 'I bet when Gail was here it wasn't like that. You'd better show me her room. Yes, I see it's tidy in here, and it smells of lavender.'

Gail had blitzed it with Laura Ashley Asphyxiating Pong whenever Tom was due round.

'Alexandra,' Mum rolled my name, 'we are going to have to talk about your fixation with Tom Drummond.'

'Tom is a friend of mine.'

'You've got plenty of friends, and Tom is your sister's boyfriend. You had a chance with him, you know.'

She bustled into the kitchen, putting everything in the wrong place and starting to cook with Bronwen's groceries. 'He was a wonderful visitor.'

'What's that got to do with anything, Mum?' I asked crossly.

My mother ceased crumbling the Oxo cube into the water and fixed me with a deathly stare.

'The way you talk, anyone would think you *were* after him,' she said. 'I hope you're not going to embarrass Gail at your do this weekend. I can tell you, my girl, your father and I have been very patient, but if you hurt her chances, you'll just have to find somewhere else to live. Fiona Kane hasn't forgiven me, you know.'

At that moment the door burst open and Bronwen stumbled in, drunk as a skunk.

'Hey Alexsh – gesh what, caught him wif anuvver woman, motherfuggin bastard, complete blurry *cunt* – oh, hello, Mis' Wilde, nish to shee you . . .'

Gail played hardball. Mum stayed for two nights and made my life a living hell. The word 'shame' is not in her dictionary.

'Now come along, Keisha, you can't go out looking like that. No, Alex, be quiet, Keisha's wearing so much make-up she looks like a clown.'

'Where's my collection of *NME*s?' Bronwen asked after one nightmare day.

'Oh, those scatty old papers?' Mum said brightly. Our drawing room was now so sterile you could operate in it. 'I threw them out.'

'You did what?' asked Bronwen silkily.

Mum was unfazed. 'I threw them out, dear. They were a fire hazard.'

'I've been collecting them since I was twelve,' Bronwen gasped.

'Then it's high time you grew out of them. No wonder your young gentleman preferred another girl. Nobody likes a tomboy,' said Mum, 'look at Alex.'

'What about me?'

'Well, you are on the shelf, dear, aren't you? You can't deny that.'

I begged and pleaded with Mum to go away, which she agreed to do only after she had confiscated my Joseph pant suit – 'Feminine women let the *boys* wear the trousers, darling.'

She paused to tell Keisha that men liked long hair and to warn me again: if I screwed up Gail's patch, I was out.

I would have loved to tell her to jump in a lake, but she was my mother. And at twenty-seven, I was still dependent on my parents. Without Mum, it was hello Crispin, hello squat.

Isn't it amazing? Just when you think things can't get any worse, life takes a major bloody dive.

'You needn't think we're going to help you prepare,' Bronwen said darkly, 'daughter of the psycho mother.'

'Yeah, you brought her here,' Keisha added.

The two of them were primping and spritzing and selecting darling little dresses, Keisha going it with her Mac nearly nudes and Bronwen ladling on the Shu Umera. I was trying not to be frazzled, I had two hours to get the food ready and drive it there. Gordon had already called in a panic so many times I had to take the phone off the hook.

'Oh please, pleeese, I've got to do my hair,' I wailed. T minus fifty and my face was pale and stressed, my eyes were red and my tights were ripped.

'Oh well, I guess I can do the fruit salad,' Keisha grumbled.

I tapped it dubiously. 'It seems a bit hard.'

'It'll thaw out,' Keisha promised, 'you just get ready.'

I dived into the bathroom and started wrestling with my appearance. I had a stress-related zit right in the middle of my chin. Hastily I covered it in eight layers of Rimmel but it still showed through. Never mind.

'Do what you can with what you have,' I breathed, trying to be Zen. My crappy No. 17s repaired some of the damage, but my eye pencil went a bit wonky, and it was the Stay-on For Ever indelible kind. Shit. Visions of Gail, radiant in her fresh-faced beauty, danced before me.

'The cheese is a bit hard,' Bronwen yelled.

'Well, put it in the microwave.' I grabbed my dress, the long, white Emporio Armani number, forgiving in the bum area and you can't really ask for more. It swept all the way down to my ankles, so I decided to go pantyless. VPL would be a total nightmare. I wanted this to be the smoothest, coolest night ever.

My reputation was riding on it.

Chapter 34

I recklessly jumped in a cab and went round to the gallery. Only a minicab, and it did smell of spilt beer and old fags, but what the hell, it seemed like the height of luxury.

Bronwen and Keisha were bringing the food later. Fortunately I was not going to have to wait for Keisha to be ready before I got out of the door. Apart from wanting my chocolate on the chocolate run, her most annoying habit is her lateness. Her make-up and dress have to be changed fifty times. Her jacket at least three times. In fact if Keisha says, 'OK, Al, let's go,' you can say it'll be at least another half-hour before she gets from the mirror to the door.

I used to counter this by hovering in the vicinity of the door and hefting my bag backwards and forwards in a deliberate manner, but this only tipped her off to my impatience and made her purposely take longer. What you should do is take up *Vogue* and read it in a bored, laconic manner, at which point she will start rushing and get all annoyed and tell you to shift it.

Bronwen is ready to go in thirty seconds flat. She makes up for that by always forgetting something by the time we are four streets away, so we have to go back and sometimes trip the burglar alarm because we are stressed.

Anyway they are both better than Justin, who used to leave restaurants if I was over fifteen minutes late, and then say 'Punctuality is the politeness of princes' if I complained.

The cab screeched into Piccadilly and down towards the gallery. I hugged myself and thought of how brilliant it was going to be. I had a gold and silver theme worked out, with gold and silver thin ribbons to drape everywhere, glitter for the tablecloths, and gold and silver sugared almonds to be scattered in an opulent-looking but actually very cheap manner. People pay such ridiculous amounts for parties, I don't know. I had splashed out on a few white and yellow chrysanths;

the florist had shown me great huge balls of petals, they would look marvellous and complement the theme, plus they were discounted because the ones he was sending were 'not the freshest'. Fine with me, I only needed them for one day.

I got out and haggled with the cabby over the fare; maybe he thought I was a rich girl in swanky white dress, because he tried to rip me off. I only gave him five pounds and he called my mother a leprous whore and said he would insult my father if I could tell him which of my mother's customers my father had been.

'Is he being rude, Alex?' Gordon asked stoutly, coming out to defend me. 'We could call the dole people,' at which point the cab roared off in choking belch of exhaust smoke.

'Darling, you look wonderful.'

'Do I?'

'Mmm, like an angel,' Gordon said, 'the zit doesn't show at all. Anyway,' ignoring my crestfallen face, 'you'd better get into these coveralls to go down to the cellar.'

'You want me to get out the paintings?' I asked horrified.

'Well, you can't expect me to do it,' said Gordon reasonably, 'I've just had a manicure. I'll call the florist and organise the ribbons.'

I pulled on the coveralls and stomped downstairs to the cellar. The de Kooning was no problem, if you don't count the hernia and heinous back injury I must have done myself as I staggered upstairs – 'Good-oh, Alex, keep going!' Gordon yelled as he delicately laid out our miniatures on their black velvet. The Jackson Pollock was another matter. When I pulled off the bubble wrap three dead spiders fell out on me. Gordon rushed downstairs at the sound of the screaming and then yelled at me for raising his hypertension.

'They're perfectly harmless, child!'

'*Aaaaargh!*' I shrieked. I hate spiders more than anything, even Justin. Gail once dropped one down the back of my neck in the car, on the way to Alton Towers. I screamed inconsolably and Dad nearly spun the wheel into oncoming traffic, and they gated *me* for a week, the bastards.

'Bring that painting up here,' thundered Gordon, 'and it's more than your life is worth if it so much as brushes against the walls.'

Once I had staggered upstairs with the Pollock, and stacked it against one wall, I surveyed the room. The gold and silver ribbons didn't look quite as impressive as they had on the packet photo. They looked a bit like our dining-room table after the cheap Christmas crackers had been pulled. The sugared almonds were great, but there weren't really enough of them to make an impact. Gordon was playing with them earnestly, balancing one in the lap of a porcelain shepherdess, another on the lock of a writing cabinet, etc.

'Where are the flowers?' I asked plaintively.

'Here.' Gordon pointed to some wilting blossoms in a white jug.

'That's it?' I gasped. 'Where's the job lot I ordered?'

'Oh, he said he didn't have enough. But these are complimentary.'

They looked rather insulting to me, with their limp heads and limper leaves. And they weren't white and yellow. More orange and neon pink.

'Oh my God, it's going to be a disaster,' I said.

'Not if you've got the food and wine right,' Gordon reassured me, 'and you look wonderful, apart from the zit and the hair. And the eyeliner.' He went out to the back and got out six of my latest sculptures, including the little statue of Gail, then arranged them around the de Kooning.

'They're modern,' he said dubiously, 'maybe'll they'll set it off.'

The doorbell rang. Gordon and I both jumped out of our skins to see Mrs Ponsonby, with three old dears in huge purple knitted hats, come imperiously through the door.

'Am I early?' she said. 'Good God, child, what are you wearing?'

There was a sound of screeching tyres and I heard Keisha's voice yelling, 'And you can fuck off too, you fat blind bastard.'

She staggered inside carrying a hefty tray of food. It looked very nice, all laid out on little sticks like something from Marks & Sparks, but Mrs Ponsonby was staring horried at Keisha and the gold stud in Bronwen's nostril.

'God, some people just don't know they're born,' Keisha said. 'Fucking assholes. Where shall I put it down?'

Twenty minutes later the private view was in full swing. I had pulled off my coveralls and now was floating round ethereally like some kind of angel or spirit. That was the best thing that could be said for the evening.

It was jam-packed. The special printed invitations had done their work – a bit too well.

'Get *off* me!'

'Get your elbow out of my ribs!'

'I beg your pardon, my elbow was nowhere near you!'

'Air!' gasped Lady de Winter. 'I need air! Open the windows, Alexandra!'

I hastily clambered on top of an antique bookcase to open the window, getting dust all over my knees and a death stare from Gordon, who was trying to chat up one of Bronwen's colleagues in a corner.

'Young woman, do you mind getting your arse out of my face?' demanded Miss Featherington. My bum was indeed brushing against the white whiskers that sprouted from her warts, but there was no other way up there.

'Just a second,' I gasped.

'Y'all leave her alone, ahm enjoying the view,' said a thick Georgian accent, 'ah lahk a girl who enjoys her food!'

With horror I glanced down to see Dwight S. Limo placing his orange-rimmed glasses next to my knickerless bum, protected only by the thin white rayon of my dress.

'Nothing lahk a bit of rump stake,' he continued, giving a loud laugh and patting my bum in a manner likely to cause an international incident. 'Y'all keep lookin' after those curves.'

I flung open the window and scrambled down, my hair messed and my face beetroot. Dwight gave me a lascivious wink.

'No panties,' he drooled in a stage whisper. 'Ah lahk a girl that knows how to dress.'

'Ha ha,' I stammered, edging away as fast as I could.

'Close that blasted window!' shrieked Mrs Ponsonby. 'Do you want us all to die of hypothermia?'

I panicked and pretended not to hear her. Keisha rescued me by sticking glasses of our cheap red wine in everybody's hand.

'How disgusting,' said Lady de Winter, 'and the cheese is all hard and brown.'

'Roasted cheese and sausage, traditionally burnt,' said Bronwen, 'it's an old Welsh recipe.'

'Try some brandy instead,' Keisha offered, splashing some into her wine glass.

'Brandy and red wine?' Lady de Winter squealed.

'It's a new South African cocktail, it's very chic,' Keisha said without turning a hair. 'Oh look, what a pretty oil painting, I expect you can't afford it.'

'Excuse me? I could buy everything in this gallery!' Lady de Winter said, drawing herself up to her full height, which was only five five. Keisha, to my horror, blew a thin line of smoke down into her face.

'That's what they all say,' Keisha told her.

'Mmm, Keisha can I have a word?' I hissed. 'Don't talk to the customers like that!'

'Well, I don't mean to be funny, Al,' Keisha said, 'but the old bag was getting on my tits. Anyway, she loves it.'

'What are these ugly clay figurines?' someone said loudly, holding up one of my sculptures. 'My four-year-old can do better than that!'

'Oh, let me see,' said Jack Herman eagerly.

My heart sank a bit lower, through my shoes and into the floor. Jack Herman was the art critic of the *Evening Standard*, probably the foremost expert in England on modern sculpture. I wanted to scream, 'No! Not that one! Let me make a better one!'

'Look, Jack, aren't they ridiculous?' the woman was snorting.

Outside the window I could see a chauffeur-driven Mercedes pulling up. A uniformed driver got out and opened the door, helping out first my mother, swathed in an electric-blue coat with a peacock motif in orange sequins, Tom Drummond in beautifully cut black tie, and my sister Gail, in a platinum chainmail mini dress that looked like a T-shirt with pretensions. Her hair had been cut and lightened since I saw her last, and now it swung in a choppy, sexy curtain around her cheekbones – she'd done a bit of dieting too, by the looks of it. Those cheekbones were sharp enough to chop out cocaine. Gail's long, silky smooth legs teetered up from strappy silver sandals, and she had a tiny Prada bag swinging from one shoulder.

She looked at the heaving mass inside with amazed disdain.

'Come along, darling,' Mum said loudly. 'Maybe you and Tom can get something for the house.'

I backed away into a corner. I just didn't want to deal with the Little Mermaid and Prince Charming right now.

Gordon saluted me over a glass of brandy. He had one arm draped over the blond chap. At least he wasn't noticing quite what a disaster it was turning out to be.

'This fruit salad is freezing!' said an old biddy loudly.

'Ow!' I turned to see old Dr Kettle, one of our big spenders, glaring balefully at me. He had his gums clenched tightly shut.

'What's the matter, Doctor?' I asked tremulously.

'Somebody shut that bugger of a window!' roared Mrs Ponsonby.

I turned a fraction just in time to see a glass of red wine tip slowly over an eighteenth-century miniature. Oh man!

'My fors teef have stuck in your fugging banana,' Dr Kettle mumbled, and as I looked down I saw something pink and white locked into a yellow mush. 'Ish bloody freezin' in the middle! Lucky if I don' *sue* you!'

'Having fun, Alex?' came a soft voice at my elbow. It was Tom; he'd edged through the room to find me and now he was standing right in front of me. The crowd packed around us, pushing us closer together.

In my misery, I suddenly felt a hot wave of lust wash right across me. I was close enough to see all the muscle under his shirt.

'What a great turnout.'

I looked at him suspiciously, but he seemed to mean it.

'Your sculptures are out too, I didn't know you were so talented.'

'Really?' I asked.

'Really. You have such a gift. I'd actually like to buy one.'

'You don't have to do that to make me feel good,' I muttered.

'I'm not. I'm doing it because I want to. And also as an investment – they'll be worth much more one day.'

This was a bit of a facer, as I hadn't expected actually to sell any sculptures, I had never thought of putting a price on them. Another wave of pleasure surged right down to my toes. Tom truly thought I had some talent, then . . .

I felt my nipples involuntarily erecting through the thin fabric of my gown, and foolishly looked down, to see Tom staring at the same thing.

I blushed richly. 'Isn't it cold in here?'

'No,' said Tom.

His eyes locked on mine.

'Er . . . which sculpture did you have in mind?' I asked quickly.

He reached his long arm over the heads of the quarrelling women behind him and pulled out – the statue of Gail.

My heart did a sick little flip in my chest. Tom palmed it one way and another, cradling it like it was an eggshell. I looked at her there in the clay, alive with life and movement.

'It's incredible, it's so like her,' Tom remarked. 'You've captured her perfectly.'

I wanted to capture my sister with a big-game net and drop her into a piranha swarm in the Congo. Tom was gazing at the statue with perfect admiration. I felt all the small tendrils of hope I'd had growing in my heart wither and die like Morning Glory at sunset.

'She was easy to sculpt,' I muttered.

'I'll give you two for it, if that's acceptable,' Tom went on.

I tried to look happy. Two hundred pounds. Maybe I could buy some nice make-up . . . if there were anyone worth making up for.

'Alexandra,' cried my mother, squeezing her ample bulk next to me in defiance of the basic laws of physics, 'the food is utterly inedible, what are these wretched sweets everyone's grinding into the carpet, and nobody can see anything to bid on it.'

'Thank you for pointing that out, Mummy,' I grunted.

'Get *out* of my way!' roared Mrs Ponsonby at Jack Herman.

'You fat old bitch, you've made me drop my cigarette,' snarled Herman.

Gail came pitching up, like a siren swimming in the wake of a battleship. 'Hello, Alex, it's not going awfully well, is it? I think the crowd are damaging the antiques, although they mostly look like replicas to me.'

'You're an expert now?' I replied feebly.

Gail shook her sleek golden mane. 'Don't be bitter, Alex, it's *so* unattractive – oh Tommy, what's that?'

She peered at herself.

'It's me! Who did a statue of me? Alex? Gosh, that's not too bad . . .' She looked up at Tom in the manner of a startled doe, or Nancy Reagan gazing adoringly at Ron. 'And you're going to buy it, Tom? How sweet! You are a darling . . .'

'How much?' asked Mum eagerly. Too eagerly.

'Two thousand,' said Tom, kindly pretending not to notice my flush of shame.

Two thousand? I'd really got it bad, because I didn't feel thrilled, I felt gutted. He loved Gail so much he was prepared to pay two grand for a clay figurine of her?

'Oh my God,' said Mum loudly, 'what is that?'

I spun round to see thick smoke blooming up behind a Grecian urn. There was a distinctly nasty crackling sound.

'*Fire! Fire!*' screamed Lady de Winter.

There was a general howling and everyone tried to leave at once.

'Oh my God, the de Kooning,' I gasped. It was propped against one wall just inches from the blaze.

'Fire! Fire!' Gordon wailed.

I shoved back through the stampeding customers and tried to reach the painting.

'Don't worry, Alex, I've got it,' Tom yelled.

I stood up on a chair so I could see over the heads of the crowd.

Tom came back into the main body of the gallery and flung a huge bucket of water at the fire, which fizzled out nicely.

It also did a damn good job of soaking me. Everybody halted in the scramble to the door and gazed transfixed at me, wet, no underwear, with a see-through, white, soaked, rayon dress plastered to my body like cheesecloth on a porn model.

'Outstanding,' said Dwight S. Limo, grinning broadly.

And at that moment, the chair teetered slowly and toppled backwards, flinging me against the wall, right through the canvas of the Pollock, which broke apart with a pop like the paper on a new jar of Nescafé.

Chapter 35

Well, I was mature about it. I did the only sensible thing. I crawled into bed and refused to answer all phone calls the next day.

Keisha and Bronwen kept me supplied with life's essentials, such as the *Sun* and bars of Caramac. They made feeble attempts to tell me everything would be OK.

'It'll probably clear up very nicely.'

'It wasn't your fault you were naked.'

And 'Everyone will have forgotten it soon.'

'Really?' I asked, perking my tousled head out from under the sheets.

'No,' said Keisha, who couldn't resist, laughing hysterically. 'Ha, ha, ha!'

'D'you know what Gail said to me when we were giving you our jackets?' Bronwen jumped in eagerly. ' "If I had a body that fat I'd have worn a corset, let alone no underwear." '

I buried my face in my hands. Oh God, I was never, ever going to be able to show my face in London ever again.

'I've got to get away,' I said, 'maybe I could go to Australia, except I don't have the money.'

'Maybe Gordon will sue you and send you there in a convict ship,' giggled Keisha.

I'd forgotten all about Gordon. Last thing I saw before I dived into a taxi, sobbing with humiliation, was his darling little face all shocked and staring woefully at the ruins of the Pollock. Not to mention the rest of his shock. Gordon had been calling all night but Keisha told him I was out. I didn't need to speak to him to know that I was fired. Toast. History. Kaput.

I always believed I was not an average girl, and now I was being proved right, because I had the worst employment history in the history of history. What would my next triumph be? I wondered.

Janitor at the Natural History Museum, where I would somehow knock over that big dinosaur skeleton, reducing it to dust after a billion years? Au pair, so I could poison the children and turn the house into a fire hazard? Secretary, so I could mix up envelopes and spill corporate secrets wherever I went?

Perhaps I could become a nun. In one of those contemplative orders where they don't even speak.

Let's face it, my lovelife could not be any worse in there than it was out here.

Of course, they did have the annoying requirement that you love your fellow man and do not covet your neighbour's wife. They said nothing about coveting your sister's boyfriend, but I had a nasty feeling it might be included.

'You've got money,' Bronwen said.

'Yes,' Keisha reminded me, 'Tom is giving you two thousand for that statue of Gail. You could go anywhere with that.'

'Wow, two grand just for a statue of her,' Bronwen sighed, 'how romantic, he must truly love her.'

'You'd better call him and tell him to send the money right away.'

'Wire-transfer it.'

'Then you can get the hell out of Dodge,' Keisha concluded.

The phone rang. Keisha let the answer machine pick it up, which was just as well since it was my mother.

'Alexandra, this is your mother – Mrs Wilde calling for Alexandra, and I know you're there, you had better pick the phone up at once.'

I sighed and held out my hand for the portable. 'Hi, Mum,' I said.

She was cross. Very cross. I've seen charging rhinos in a better mood.

'I don't know how you could put me through that humiliation,' Mum shouted, 'standing there naked like a tuppeny whore . . . don't tell me you didn't know you were going to get wet! And such a scrimmage, and that revolting food, my goodness, with me your mother and everyone thinking "There's her mother, not much of a cookery teacher!" '

I doubted that was what they were thinking but refrained from saying so.

'And what do you think you did to poor Gail's chances with Tom? Do you think he wants to be associated with such an exhibition? You'd make a terrible person to be related to, so embarrassing.'

This was true but she could talk!

'Poor Gail is in floods of tears, she wants to change her surname so nobody connects you to her. Although how they could do that I fail to see, with Gail so feminine and always nicely turned out. Anyway –'

Here it comes.

'Your father and I want you to move out of the flat, you're doing nobody any good with this silly, "staying in London" business, you're to come home here, where we can keep an eye on you.'

'But Mum, I hate Surrey.'

'That's something you should have thought about before you disgraced the whole family. No, I won't hear another syllable, Alex, you can come back home and help your father in his business, it'll be good for you to do something useful.'

'I won't,' I said defiantly.

'Well, you can't stay in the flat,' said Mum heavily, 'and remember the last time you tried to make it out there on your own.'

'This'll be different.'

'You ended up with lice and living in a house with rats.'

'They weren't rats, they were very small dogs,' I said, but sadly, because she was in fact right. Why is it that most people are perfectly capable of looking after themselves by the time they're eighteen, and my mother wanted me to be chained up at home at twenty-seven?

Sometimes I think I'm OK, I'm quite pretty and a bit of a laugh, and then I go home and they lop twenty years off my age and make me feel like that awkward schoolgirl with pigtails I was in Mrs Minchin's class.

'Well, if you think you can take care of yourself, be my guest,' Mum went on in outraged tones, 'but you're not doing it in our flat.'

'Can I speak to Dad?'

'Your father agrees with me one hundred per cent,' said Mum. Poor Dad, that meant Mum had chewed his ear off for four hours until he was too cowed to do anything but agree. I made a mental note to remember to call Dad at the office if I really needed some money. Then I thought, how sad was I to be thinking this way?

'We're not having you hanging around London ruining things for Gail,' Mum said annoyingly.

I wondered idly if I had in fact been so embarrassing that Tom would finish with Gail in order not to have me as a sister-in-law. That would have been a silver lining, but unfortunately, Tom was too honourable to do that, and anyway, he wouldn't give a damn what people thought of anyone he liked.

'I want you out of that flat by the weekend, Alex, and—'

I hung up on her. Then I quickly took the receiver off the hook. This kind of thing is a scorched-earth tactic with my mother, but what the hell. I was going to run away to sea so she'd never find me to exact her fearsome revenge.

'She wants me to move out,' I told the others, 'and go back home.'

'To the commuter belt?' Keisha asked with as much horror as if I'd said 'the gulag'.

'You don't have to do that,' Bronwen said. 'If you can type you can get good money temping.'

'I can't type.'

'You did it for Seamus Mahon, of course you can. Look, I'll ask Personnel if you can come and work for me at *Up and Running*,' Keisha said.

'Or you can be a stylist's assistant for me,' Bronwen said bravely, looking at my utterly unstylish clothes that were strewn about my bedroom.

I gave them both a hug. They might be annoying when it comes to chocolate, clothes and having a life, but they're good girls. Without my friends I would be a pancake by now. Crushed by the oncoming trucks of despair and poverty.

'Thanks, you guys, but I have to find something myself,' I said resolutely.

There was a knock on the door.

'I bet its Jeremy,' said Bronwen jealously to Keisha.

'I bet it's Dan come to apologise. Don't take less than two dozen red roses,' Keisha said.

But it wasn't, it was Tom Drummond.

I barely had time to pull on a dressing gown and wrap my hair in a towel. It was perfectly dry, but it was also greasy and tangled. This is a top tip for when men you fancy drop in unexpectedly, when you always look shit unless you're my flatmates, who are the supremely awful pulled-together females. The definition of a pulled-together girl is that she puts on make-up in the morning – whether she's going out or not.

Tom came in and I refused to look him in the eye.

'Alex, I've brought you your cheque,' he said.

The trouble with this situation was that I couldn't very well say, 'Piss off and leave me to die of a broken heart, you sister-dating bastard,' when he was handing over a cheque for two grand.

'Thanks,' I said, and then some gremlin taking over my better judgment added, 'You're paying far too much for it, you don't have to give me that much.'

'That's where you're wrong, it's a steal,' Tom said. 'Can I sit down? Any chance of a cup of coffee?'

'Please, please do,' said Bronwen, .

'Of course, let me put the machine on, I've got some Jamaican Blue Mountain,' said Keisha, most unnecessarily I thought. They both *had* boyfriends and they professed to hate the English upper classes, so why were they all of a flutter now Tom was around?

'I s'pose,' I said grumpily.

'I've never seen a more lifelike sculpture. You got Gail so wonderfully. She breathes in the clay.'

'Yes, well,' I said nastily, 'you can think of it as Pocket Gail. It twirls, it flicks its hair. You can take it with you whenever she's not there and kiss it – "Good night, Pocket Gail!" Or if you've got any questions about organic goats' cheese pizza, or whatever bloody veggie crap she's got you eating, you can get it out and focus on what Gail would say – "What do you think, Pocket Gail?" It's just like the real thing: it never has anything interesting to say and it never puts on an ounce.'

Tom looked at me in total amazement. 'Are you and Gail, er, fighting, Alex?' he asked.

I shrugged and died a little bit more. Where did that come from? Well, I know where it came from, but the point was, I might as well wear a big T-shirt with 'I AM JEALOUS' stamped across the front.

'I expect she's too ashamed of me even to speak,' I grunted.

Tom laughed. What a sexy laugh that boy had. 'She did use some rather choice language. She told me I wasn't to see you any more.'

'But you're here,' I pointed out.

Tom shrugged. 'I don't like being told what to do. Oh, thanks, Keisha, terrific coffee. Anyway, I wanted to make sure you got your cheque.'

'You could have put it in the post.'

'Well . . . Gail mentioned to me that you wouldn't be staying here.'

'I see,' I said blankly. 'Well, she's right. I'm going to cash your cheque and go to Australia.'

'You are?' said Tom, looking alarmed. 'But I've only just found you again, you can't run away from me like that.'

'I can do anything I want to,' I said miserably, 'Girl Power.'

'But you're one of my best friends,' Tom objected.

I looked at him sharply. 'I am not one of your best friends. I'm your girlfriend's sister, that's all. I've got enough friends, actually, thank you very much.'

'And your boyfriend, Gordon, of course,' Tom said sarcastically.

I recalled that Gordon had been openly snogging the svelte blond man. 'My relationship with Gordon is none of your business,' I said with dignity.

'Why are you being so awful, Alex?' Tom demanded sharply. It was the kind of question I usually asked with a sort of whining tone. Tom barked it at me like he was still in the Army and I was a private who'd failed the boot-shining.

'I'm not,' I said, snatching the cheque before he could change his mind. 'I just don't need another male friend, Tom. Anyway, Gail wouldn't like it.'

'Who gives a damn what Gail would or wouldn't like?' said Tom. 'I'll be buggered if I'm going to let you slip away again.'

'Well, bend over and grab your ankles, then,' I grunted.

'You can't just disappear, what about your job at the gallery?'

'What gallery?' I laughed. 'It was burned, soaked, crushed, knocked over . . . and it's got a Page Three girl for a gallery assistant.'

Tom grinned. 'Actually I thought it was great fun. And I enjoyed the last bit most of all.'

'Yeah, well, you've always wanted to see me naked,' I challenged.

He lifted one eyebrow. 'Very true. And I wasn't disappointed.'

'How can you say that?' I screeched at him.

'Because it's true,' Tom replied calmly. 'Oh come on, Alex, you know any red-blooded male is going to enjoy that.'

'Hmm,' I said furiously. 'Well, you might have looked away.'

'And I might not. Of course, Gordon didn't seem too interested.'

'Yes, well,' I said after a pause when I couldn't think of any rejoinder, 'I feel a bit tired, in fact I've got PMS, so if you wouldn't mind leaving me alone I'm going to bed.'

'But I haven't finished talking to you,' Tom protested.

'I've finished talking to you,' I said firmly, 'so thanks for the cheque and goodbye.' I got up and stomped off towards the bathroom. 'I'm going to wash my hair now.'

'But you've just washed it,' said Tom, pointing to the towel on my head.

'That's as maybe,' I said haughtily, 'but now I'm going to give it, um, a hot-oil treatment. Do give Gail my love next time you're taking her to Le Gavroche.'

'Alex!' Tom said, springing up. 'Wait! I must say something to you.'

This sounded pretty promising. He was speaking in dramatic, Jane Austen tones. In fact I could see Keisha and Bronwen, pretending to drink coffee at the table, and read *Hello!* but actually hanging on his every word.

'Go on, then,' I said, and foolishly, despite myself, I allowed my heart to beat a bit faster and my palms to get a bit sweaty and my hopes to rise. You'd think I'd have learned my lesson by now, but you would be so, so wrong.

I'm the kind of girl who reads Mystic Meg every week and truly looks out for Destiny carrying a large pot plant, even though last week Destiny did not, in fact, take me to a pet shop, nor did Destiny the week before wear polka dots.

Perhaps Destiny kept getting me mixed up with my sister.

That must be it.

Because Tom's impassioned reply was, 'It's about Gail.'

Oh my God, I thought, he's going to tell me they're engaged, I just can't bear it.

'I've told you before, I don't want to hear about her,' I snapped. 'I'm sure you're both very happy, and no, I won't turn up to Carrefour and ruin your wedding too. Now *just go away.*'

And I ran into the bathroom and quickly turned on both taps very loudly, so he wouldn't hear my undignified crying.

Chapter 36

When I woke up on Tuesday, Keisha and Bronwen had already left for work. I was glad because this made it easy for me. I hate goodbyes.

I packed up two suitcases full of my best clothes: my Donna Karan suit and Joseph leather trousers and stuff. I also took one block of clay. I have no idea why; obviously my art career was over, strangled at birth, but somehow I knew I'd still need to sculpt.

I also took a Marks & Sparks bag full of groceries. If there's one thing I've learnt it's that a broken heart and wanting to die does not, in fact, result in cardiac arrest or death. This means you get hungry. As a result, Keisha's specially purchased reinforced carrier bag was nicked city. She'd kill me if she ever caught me, which she wasn't going to. I took some Frankfurters, some seedless grapes, a jar of peanut butter and a packet of Ritz crackers, along with two cans of Cherry Pepsi, so you can't say I didn't cover all major food groups.

The rest of my stuff I moved into Bronwen's room with a begging, grovelling note. If it had been Keisha, she'd have read the begging, grovelling note and promptly thrown it all away. I wanted a clean new start and was trying to persuade myself that this was a good thing – first day of the rest of your life, new broom sweeps clean, too many cooks spoil the broth or whatever. It wasn't working particularly well but what the hell. I had a plan and it involved walking out of here with just the clothes on my back. And two suitcases full of designer clothes and make-up. And some peanut butter.

There was certainly no room for my fun collection of Whimsey miniatures, with only the walrus family slightly chipped. Nor for my long-suffering cactus plant, nor my file of pictures of Jason Connery as Robin of Sherwood, including a studio publicity shot personally signed to me by Jason with a kiss in silver pen.

Jason Connery was my entire love life for two years during my teens. Oh, how I pined for his clean-shaven, genital-free, non-threatening good looks. I used to kiss his pictures on the back of my door individually before I went to bed, but I used to wear glasses then, and his picture had to be the last thing I looked at before I went to sleep at night, otherwise – if I inadvertently glanced at a book or a teddy – it was put the glasses back on and do the whole thing over again.

I suppose I've always had a puppy-dog admiration for men I can't have. Starting at the age of five, when Mum has told me I had a big crush on Brian Cant from *Playaway*. Then there was Mr Johnson, the builder, who was big and rough and fat and about fifty-five, I used to make him endless undrinkable cups of sweet milky tea. And right before Jason there was the geezer who played Avon in *Blake's 7*, who was cruel and masculine and imperious. I blamed this guy for my current situation with Tom. I mean, if Avon hadn't always been forcing pretty women to their knees and then kissing away their resistance in a masterful manner, perhaps I wouldn't have a crush on that big brute Tom Drummond.

I stacked my papers under Brownwen's and picked up my cases, then I wrote them both a nice note. After all, they'd soon be sharing with Gail instead of me, that's if she didn't manage to cling on to her slot at Tom's house, and they'd need soothing.

I went to the hole in the wall opposite our flat. My heart beat a bit faster as I put my card in; sometimes the bastard eats my cards, whilst sneeringly ordering me to contact my bank. But no, Tom's cheque had cleared, so I was eighteen hundred pounds in credit, instead of being overdrawn. Even seeing the figure caused a bit of a pang, though.

Oh, I've skipped a bit, haven't I? I'm always doing that . . .

I suppose on Monday and Tuesday, every time the phone rang I kind of hoped it was him. OK, I know, pathetic to put your happiness in someone else's hands, etc., etc., but if you want the truth, that was how I felt.

This was different – yeah, we always say this time it's different, but this time it was. You see, I didn't have to go through the faint, squirmy-tummy thing like I had with Seamus, or Justin, or Peter, and then more and more gradually be let down and annoyed. I wasn't buying into a bloke just 'cause I liked his looks and my groin was saying, 'Oh, yeah, come to Mama.' I had known Tom when he was a big ball of lard and I didn't fancy him at all. I knew him then and I knew just what he was like, and I loved him, I loved being with him, I laughed so much with him, and even when I fought him about most stuff ('What's the Story, Morning Tory?' I used to yell at him) – I still really liked him.

So here's a pig not in a poke. Very much out of the poke and on full display, in fact. Rolling around eating acorns.

Only now he's lean and brilliant and a high-flying City millionaire.

And he's a man whose brother's life I nearly ruined and whom I cost seven hundred and fifty grand.

And who's dating my sister.

And he still likes me, he still wants to hang out with me even though I did all that and then treated the whole of London to an all-nude girly display. Even though I am only a failed secretary and failed sculptor and failed gallery person and, well, just failure, period.

I don't know what I expected. I had made him bugger off; did I really want him to ring so I could hear his important news about Gail? Yes and no: I didn't want to talk to him, it hurt too much; I did want to, though, just to hear his voice, just to be in contact with him. Anyway, that was impossible.

Normally you ring a guy's answer machine while he's at work. Making sure to dial 141 first, of course.

That didn't work because Gail was there. I could imagine her picking up the phone, her voice going specially breathy in case it was Tom, or some other man. I swear Gail goes to some kind of Living Barbie school for girls. You know that forty-year-old woman who remodelled herself to look exactly like Barbie, well, that's Gail, except Gail is prettier and girlier and didn't need to spend fifty grand doing it.

Anyway, the point is that Tom didn't ring. In fact, once Gordon got the message that I wouldn't speak to him, the phone stopped ringing for me at all. It was like I had vanished from the face of the earth. All my mates were probably reading up on the hysterical pieces in the gossip columns (Keisha refused to let me see them) and asking themselves why they'd ever talked to a prat like me.

I wondered how much it cost to change your name by deed poll?

I got out two hundred quid and went to Waterloo in a taxi. There I caught a train for York. Bloody hell, it only cost sixty-five quid return, what was it made of, solid bloody gold? I loaded up on

Quavers and *Private Eye* and the *Guardian*, and one of those flaky apple pastry things and I was all set.

In Smith's I walked determinedly past the trashy novels and copies of *Bridget Jones* – God, what a bonding experience that is for women. Bronwen got sick when I first moved into the flat, and six different hospital visitors bought along a copy of *Bridget*, foolishly asking if she'd read this. Read this? What are you talking about? Of course she's read it, she's female, isn't she, she's past the *Are You My Mother?* stage, of *course* she's read it. You might as well ask if she's ever been let down by a man. There's one empty plinth in Trafalgar Square, you know, and I think there ought to be a statue of Bridget Jones on it. We could take a vote and Britain's women would rise as one. So I walked past *Bridget* and on to the self-help section. *Awaken the Giant Within, The One Minute Manager, Do it Now!* all that sort of stuff. I loaded my basket next to the Quavers. I was determined, this was going to be a new start for me, this was where I was going to change my life. The only way was up, baby, and all that jazz.

Yes! I am woman, hear me roar!

See me go over to the phone bank and phone my answering machine to check if Tom called!

See me listen to messages of undying devotion from Dan and Jeremy!

See me slink off to the train, gutted, tail between my legs!

When we finally pulled out and headed off to the frozen north I unwrapped my pastry, but it stuck in my throat. I wanted Tom. Not even fat and refined sugar could take the pain away any more.

I got three quarters of the way through *Private Eye* before the crying started up again. But that was OK, because most of the people in the carriage just shook their papers and ignored me, like I had drunk an invisibility potion. When the ticket collector came round he took one look at my red face, streaming from every orifice, and decided he didn't need to see my ticket after all.

Bloody waste of sixty-five quid, I shouldn't have bothered.

I stumbled out at York with legs that had gone to sleep and a face like a baboon's arse. I told myself that I was the only one conscious of the flushed face and puffy nose, but sadly, when I turned up at the Hertz desk with my driving licence, the old bag looked at me highly suspiciously and said had I been drinking on the train.

'Stick out your tongue,' she said.

I complied. 'Uuurgh, it's purple,' she shivered. 'Drink is demon, it'll ruin your liver.'

'It's Ribena!' I said indignantly.

'Oh yeah? Well, put one finger on your nose and walk in a straight line,' she insisted.

I did so.

'Say, "the tip of the tongue, the teeth and the lips", she demanded.

'The tip of the tongue, the leeth and the tits . . . thips . . . lips,' I stuttered crossly. 'Gosh, you're worse than my choir mistress.'

'Hmm,' she said suspiciously. '*Are* you drunk?'

'Not a drop, here, let me breathe on you,' I suggested.

She recoiled, which was some compliment, from a check-jacketed, purple-hatted Monster from a Thousand Fathoms like her. 'Uuurgh, get away from me with your nasty Southern germs!'

'As opposed to your nice Northern ones?' I asked sarcastically. That didn't sit too well, but fear of losing some commission made her grudgingly give me the form anyway. She stared at me like a passerby leering at a traffic accident as I filled it out.

'Gone for the Mini Metro?' she said scornfully. 'The cheapest option, I see.'

'Yeah, well, it's 'eighties revival chic,' I lied defiantly.

I gave her the money and she gave me the car keys.

'Better bring it back without a scratch,' she said threateningly.

'I will. I'm a brilliant driver,' I lied again.

Her parting shot hit home.

'For someone who's not drunk, you certainly look awful,' she said.

Thus cheered, I got into the car and headed out towards Rosedale. The scenery was beautiful – once I'd got away from all the honking, yelling, screaming drivers, I mean, all that fuss just because I misjudged my entry into a couple of roundabouts. And turned right instead of left once in a while. The city fell away behind me and I finally hit the moors, which were astonishing, if you didn't mind the odd rotting sheep carcass amongst your purple heather.

OK, so it wasn't all Wuthering Heights. I did get a bit lost – went fifty miles down one wrong road, and then discovered I'd got the map upside down, and had a bit of a sense-of-humour failure. Not to mention the radio in the car was permanently stuck on Radio Two, where the programmers are sadists. Who the hell can take three hours of Simply Red and Andrew Lloyd Webber? This is Cool Britannia, remember (copyright, T. Blair).

I finally pulled into Pickering, which was great. There was one of those small market town shops with a faded yellow polka-dot dress stuck optimistically on a mannequin in its window, with the wonderful, if not entirely true, statement 'If it's happening in Paris, it's happening in Pickering' plastered in front of it.

I stopped for fish and chips in the local pub. Everything felt much better once I got my chips. At least as far as my physical body went. I'd like to say my heart was so shattered I just pined away, but if it was, it didn't stop me eating the chips. Despite the obnoxious presence of some likely local lads who obviously fancied their chances.

'Tuck in, lass.'

'Yer nobbut skin and bones, I reckon she's enjoying that, Peter.'

'Aye, Jack, aye, she is that.'

The sad thing was they were in their forties and fat as houses, and they obviously thought they could pull me if they were only loud enough.

Was I so sodding ghastly that Jack and Peter reckoned they were in with a chance?

Apparently so. I finished my chips, smacking off the last of the vinegar. It was great vinegar too, real gut-rot, not that wussy crap you get with balsam and white wine and herbs. Then I got up and decided to call the cottage and see if the phone was working.

It was. Then I just thought I'd call the flat's machine, to see if anyone had left a message.

Anyone had not left a message.

Nothing. Zip. Zilch.

'Don't look so sad, love,' Peter told me with a fragrant belch, 'might never 'appen.'

But the fact was, it already had.

The last part of the journey took less than twenty minutes, which was just as well, since it was getting dark and bloody freezing. In my break for freedom I realised I'd forgotten to pack any thermal underwear. Oh well, maybe my misery would be over when I died of hypothermia.

Rosedale is a tiny village in the North Yorkshire moors, if you can count it as a village when it only has one pub and a sub-post office.

The reason I was scarpering there was that my family owned a tiny cottage on the hill. It used to be a miner's hovel, and Mum thought it was 'picturesque', then discovered that there was no golf to be had for miles and never came back there. Twice a year we paid a cleaning lady to come round and 'do' the place for filth, thus allowing my parents to keep up the fiction that they were going to rent it out as a holiday cottage. The point of it was, I think, so Mum and Dad could bang on at dinner parties about their 'country hideaway'.

It was so well hidden they'd probably forgotten where it was.

But I knew where we'd buried the keys, and also that we paid our minimal phone/electric charges by direct debit.

I planned to use it as a base. I was going to job-hunt around here; get work as a turkey plucker for Bernard Matthews, or a boot cleaner for Leeds United, or something. After all, up here nobody would recognise me. Nobody would know of my utter disgrace and idiocy and lack of romantic success. Maybe I could marry a rugby player and farm whippets.

I found the key under the mat, rusting (no one can say the Wildes lack imagination), then I let myself into the cottage. It was thick with dust, really filthy, I felt quite at home.

First thing I did was phone the flat and fend off Bronwen's questions.

'I'm in a secret hidden location,' I said mysteriously. 'Anyway, has anyone called for me?'

'Yes,' Bronwen said. 'Tom Drummond called five minutes ago.'

'He did?' I gasped.

'Yeah,' said Bronwen. 'He says he needs to talk to you about Gail – could you give him a call?'

Chapter 37

I had a brilliant supper of peanut butter on Ritz crackers, then tried to fix the heating. Nothing doing, I'd have to work on it tomorrow. For tonight, I could crawl under eight layers of blankets. It was so heavy I could hardly breathe, but at least it'd keep the cold out.

The sooner I could get to sleep, the sooner I could start in on my new life.

'Don't you want me to give him your number?' Bronwen had asked breathlessly.

'No. I don't want to talk to Tom Drummond,' I said, a big tear splashing on to my nose. 'Really. I'll call and tell you everything once I've got a new job.'

'Can't you tell me now?' Bronwen begged. 'Oh please, Alex, you know I can keep a secret.'

'Later,' I promised and hung up.

Keep a secret? Yeah, right, talking to Bronwen was as good as baring your soul for the *News of the World*. Why advertise when you could simply talk to Bronwen, and she would do it for you, free of charge?

So I crawled into my heavy bed, and cried, and tried to be upbeat, but I was about as upbeat as a Leonard Cohen single played at 33rpm in a funeral home. At first I couldn't get to sleep because there was no noise. No gentle honking of horns. No police sirens duh–duh–ing smoothly in the distance. Not even drunk revellers to lull me off to dreamland.

Nothing but the chill silence over the vast stretches of heather, and the faint bleating of a stranded sheep. Totally unnatural, a sort of lack of noise pollution. But eventually the crying did wear me out, and I slept very soundly and had no dreams. Probably just as well.

Next morning I scrubbed my teeth and tried to get clean with kettle water. Have to ring the cleaner, I thought to myself. But the first thing was to find a Job Centre and see what they had going. I'm not proud, I told myself as I jumped in the car, I'll take anything.

'Are you taking the piss?' the woman – sorry, Career Realignment Operative asked at the Job Centre.

'No,' I said defensively. 'Why?'

She regarded me as if I were something unpleasant she'd found on the sole of her shoe. Her name was Mrs Donaldson, she couldn't have been more than thirty-odd, but she was already dressing in a way my mum would have been proud of. A ghastly floral frock with front pleating was crowned by a necklace of fake pearls and a scary hairdo that must have ripped a hole in the ozone layer all by itself. Man, it looked as though it would chime if you tapped a spoon against it.

'You come in here, all fancy-like, and you say you want a job?'

I realised I was wearing my Donna Karan. It was true, I hadn't actually packed any casual clothes. Er . . . maybe a mistake.

'But I really do,' I protested. 'I'll take anything.'

'Hmm.' Her face relaxed just a minute touch. 'Well, there's not much round here. This *is* Yorkshire, you know.'

'I know.'

'And the moors towns are a high unemployment region.'

'I'm sure,' I said humbly.

'There are sixteen applicants here for every job going,' she continued balefully.

My heart sank a bit. That didn't sound good. I couldn't live off Tom's eighteen hundred for ever.

'Aah,' I muttered. Oh God. I was going to become a homeless person, and wind up frozen to death in the streets of Pickering with my meths bottle and a dog on a string. I wondered where I could get the dog on the string? Hmm – maybe I would run into Crispin in a chronic alcoholism centre somewhere, and I could borrow one of his? And I could nick a trolley outside Safeways for my baglady must-have, then I could go round to all the hotels very early and nick their deliveries of papers and eggs and milk . . .

I was cruelly interrupted from my successful baglady fantasy by Mrs Donaldson waving a sheet of paper in my face.

'Maybe this would suit you, though. Seeing as you got a fancy degree from Oxford.'

An art degree, I almost said, but stopped myself just in time. If she didn't know I was thick, why burden her with the knowledge?

'It's just down the road from Rosedale,' she said, 'in Kidlington. The Christian Library of North Yorkshire, run by Dr Barry Gallagher. They have a position for a reputable librarian, with good morals, a single woman preferred. Could you be a librarian?'

'Me? Oh yes. Love to to read. Er, Jane Austen. Vikram what's his name. Er . . . Agatha Christie,' I floundered, '*Men Are From Mars, Women Are From Venus.*' She looked doubtful. 'Are you a single woman?'

'Well, I'm not a single man,' I said, which went down like a lead balloon.

'Of good morals? You're from London, aren't you?'

Clearly Mrs Donaldson thought London was on a par with Sodom and Gomorrah. And who could say she wasn't correct? It would be right up there if I'd ever had a chance.

'Oh, I never miss mass on a Sunday morning,' I told her eagerly, cowering only very slightly in case God had a thunderbolt handy.

'Well, we don't get too many in 'ere from Oxford, so I *suppose* I can put you forward for it,' she said slowly. 'You can go along there now.'

'What, right now?'

'Why?' she said, looking at me scornfully. ''Ave you gorranything better to do?'

You could say one thing for her, beehive or no: she was sharp as a brass tack. As they probably say round this neck of the woods.

I picked up the car, reluctantly put some petrol into it – God, it's a bloody scandal what petrol costs, we should have killed Saddam while we had the chance – and bought a few groceries and essentials. The price of everything seemed ludicrously high. I kept imagining my money dropping down, like the life force bar on Sonic the Hedgehog or something. I was so depressed about Tom that it almost didn't matter, but not quite. I knew I had to get this job.

The afternoon was crisp and cold as I drove down to Kidlington, great swathes of heather blazing purple and gold across the moors. A couple of birds plunged across the sky in long, looping arcs. It was beautiful but desolate, a bit like me, if you take away the beautiful.

The Christian Library of North Yorkshire was a crummy little brick building covered with faded posters of soppy-looking American boys with those annoying pudding-bowl haircuts. The kind of kids I sincerely hope, in the unlikely event of my ever having a child, my kid will beat up in the playground. They were wearing white socks and knickerbockers and grinning at the camera under a curly text, 'Let the Little Children Come Unto Me.' There were also a couple of balloons that had seen better days, with 'Kumbaya, My Lord' printed across them.

Alex Wilde, welcome to your future, I thought.

I pushed open the door and walked up to the reception desk. Well, at least there wouldn't be much to do here. The place was deader than Queen Anne.

'Hello, I'm Dr Gallagher,' said a voice.

I looked up to see a podgy little man with ginger hair and a wet bottom lip. Little bubbles of spit blossomed on it as he spoke. He stared at me through glasses thick enough to light a fire with.

'You must be Miss Wilde. I hope it is Miss, none of that feminist "Ms" nonsense.'

'Umm, right.'

'Because that's really why I'm looking for a single woman,' Dr Barry went on. 'None of this "working wives" nonsense.'

I bit my lip and smiled like Aunt Sally on *Worzel Gummidge*.

'I think working wives are responsible for so much divorce and misery. They orphan their children,' he said, little bubbles of spit blowing up everywhere like he was a toad.

' "The husband shall be head of the wife like Christ is the head of the Church. Wives, be subject to your husbands as to the Lord." That's St Paul, the great apostle.'

'Are you married, Dr Gallagher?' I asked, treading on my own foot to remind myself not to say anything.

'No,' he said bitterly. 'I was.'

'I see.'

'She ran off and left me. She left me for a deaconess.'

I stifled a choking laugh.

'Did you say anything?' he demanded, glaring.

'Dreadful cough,' I said, hacking one out to cover my back.

'Yes, well, a woman should not raise her voice in church. I do not suffer a woman to teach men! That's St Paul too. What do *you* think of priestesses? That's what I call them, priestesses. Pagans.'

'Well, I've never wanted to be a woman priest,' I said truthfully.

Dr Barry's wet smile broadened. Aah, I understood now, he *was* a toad, that explained it.

'I can see you're a good Christian woman, and you went to Oxford, hmm, how soon can you start?'

'Er – what's the pay?' I asked timidly.

The smile dimmed a little. 'It's eleven thousand a year – but your reward will mostly be the modest, decent service of God.'

Great – that was a new one for the bank manager. 'I know I'm three hundred quid overdrawn, but you see, I do have the modest, decent service of God.'

But let's face it, that was eleven grand more than I was getting at the moment. I took a good hard look at fat, woman-hating Barry, at the dingy little library stuffed full of crappy books nobody wanted to read, in this tiny little hamlet in the middle of nowhere, where I was being offered a rubbish job for rubbish pay.

'I can start this afternoon,' I said.

Barry told me I had a very good attitude. It was with great reluctance he agreed to let me drop off my shopping first.

'And maybe grab some lunch,' I suggested.

Barry gave a disapproving stare. 'Come now, Miss Wilde. You can have a sandwich at your desk. Lunch is for wimps! Ha ha ha!'

Back at the cottage I tried to be pleased. It was a job, right? It was a job. Hoo-fucking-ray.

I put away my stuff and then sat there and stared at the phone.

Obviously, I shouldn't call Tom. It would be madness to call him. Just so I could hear him tell me he and Gail were getting married?

No, it would be silly to call. Just because I was desperate for some contact, any contact. Just so I could kid myself that there was a hope in hell I could have him in my life as a friend.

It would be far more dignified not to call.

I asked myself if I had any self-respect. Well, the answer to that one was no, so I picked up the receiver and dialled his London flat from memory.

Oh my God, I thought panicking, what if Gail answers, I'll have to slam the phone down, but I forgot to dial 141, oh shit, hang up right now and dial 141 and redial, but then won't Tom hear me making two calls and think I'm a real pathetic weirdo and—

'Tom Drummond,' said a voice at the end of the phone.

Somehow I'd forgotten how sexy, how rich and deep that voice was, well, not forgotten exactly, but it was so different actually to hear it.

'Tom, it's Alex.'

'Where are you?' he said hurriedly. 'Everyone wants to know. Your parents are frantic. They think you've been sold into white slavery.'

I could just see Mum, loving every minute of the drama. She was probably recording a segment for *Crimewatch* right now.

'I'm perfectly all right, I wish everyone would stop fussing,' I said, 'I'm just settling into a new job.'

'Where?'

'That's really none of your business. Bronwen said you'd called.'

'Yes.' Now he sounded hesitant, a bit wary, as though he didn't want to have to say this. My God, I thought, feeling nauseous, he thinks he's going to hurt me. 'It's about Gail – I've got some news and I think it might upset you.'

'You think what?' I raged at him. 'The bloody nerve of you, you think everyone is just breaking their hearts over you, don't you, you think everyone is just dying to hang around the big cheese Mr Drummond.'

'But Alex—'

'Well, let me tell you, Tom, nothing *you* could do could ever be upsetting to me, I'm doing fine, thanks very much.'

'Alex—'

'I don't want to hear it!' I yelled. 'I don't need to hear it! You insufferable bloody smug bastard, you always were and you still are.'

'I'm sorry if I've distressed you,' Tom said softly.

'Well, don't be, I couldn't give a fuck,' I said, then hung up, sat down and sobbed my heart out.

'Alex, you're late,' Barry said pompously as I arrived back at the library. 'You mustn't be late when you're a Christian soldier marching as to war.'

'Oh well, Dr Gallagher,' I said respectfully – I knew I was going to have to kiss this guy's ass until my lips turned blue, and what happened to 'Miss Wilde'? 'An army marches on its stomach.'

I hadn't eaten a thing, of course. I never wanted to eat again.

'Well, man does not live on bread alone, but on every word that comes from the mouth of God. Now, let's get cracking, shall we? We've got a very long evening ahead of us, I'm afraid, it'll be your first bit of overtime.' He licked his lips disgustingly. 'I hope you don't mind putting in *evening* work, unchaperoned.'

'Er – 'course not.'

'Because with two young single people like you and me, people might talk.'

'Er, I suppose they might, but—'

'People might say we'd find it hard to restrain our natural urges.'

'I don't understand, it doesn't look all that busy,' I gabbled desperately, 'what will we have to do?'

This distracted him from his natural urges from a second and back on to his pomposity. He leant forward and breathed a week's worth of garlic in my face. 'We're undergoing a major update. We're going to catalogue every book in order, and replace it on the shelves. This mess distracts from the good news of the Gospel, I'm sure you'll agree.'

'Yeah, right,' I said faintly.

'We don't use computers, there's nothing wrong with a bit of elbow grease, so you sit there and fill out these forms on these.' With that, Gallagher pulled out a thick pile of slips, a file, and a huge cardboard box of books. It had cobwebs on.

'Oh. I hate spiders,' I said forlornly, watching him huff and puff as he tried to drag the box to my desk.

'Well, they'll be dead by now,' he said firmly, 'so you crack on. No time to waste.'

Bloody hell, he meant it too. No wonder this job hadn't been filled: Barry was not only a prig and a toad, he was a slave driver who would have done just great whipping the labourers at the pyramids. I wrote and checked and filed until the dots swam before my eyes and I got writer's cramp. Barry confined his activities to 'supervising', that is, he yelled at me when I got a placing wrong.

'Can't you read? Ecclesiastes, *not* Ecclesiasticus!' he shrieked. 'We should know our Holy Scripture by now, shouldn't we?'

The shadows drew in and the dusty electric clock ticked loudly round and round, but the pile of books didn't get any smaller. Barry gave me more the second I finished one section.

'No slacking!' he warned me repeatedly. 'You know what it says in Proverbs: "Go to the ant, thou sluggard, consider her ways."'

'Maybe you could help with the stacking, when you've finished that Bible segment,' I suggested, weak with tiredness and hunger. Oh shit, what had I signed up for? Barry replied with a lengthy recital of Martha and Mary and how Jesus said Mary had chosen the better part by skipping the housework and listening to His Word. It sounded like a giant chizz to me, and anyway, nobody had given me a 'part' to choose.

'I just need to go to the loo,' I said, feeling my throat knot up and my eyes get blurry with hopeless tears.

'That's the second time in two hours. I hope you don't have a medical problem,' Barry sniffed.

I wanted to lean against the filthy cistern and have another cry, but Barry was probably standing outside listening with a timer.

When I re-emerged he pointed at the box of books.

'But it's seven p.m.,' I said faintly.

'This day was made by the Lord, we rejoice and are glad,' said Barry, monumentally annoyingly.

I sighed and plunged my hand into the box of tatty books. Immediately, three huge house spiders crawled up out the shadows and scuttled across my hands.

I screamed and jumped in the air.

'Don't *yell*!' shouted Barry, and then the glint in his eye changed, and he pulled me into his fat pudgy body.

'There, there, there,' he said, ostensibly patting my back but actually feeling me up. For a fat bastard, he could certainly move those hands when he wanted to. They were clutching my ass, grabbing my tits, slithering all over me like a plump string of sausages.

I burst into tears, struggling to get free. 'Get off me! Get off me!' I squealed.

'Oh, come on, you know you want it,' Barry said, his breath coming faster, 'otherwise you'd have left by now.'

'You wouldn't let me!' I sobbed. 'I need this job!'

'I know you do, the Job Centre told me you were desperate,' Barry said thickly, 'so you should be nice to me, you know.'

I screamed in misery as he lunged round the desk towards me. He had a small and unimpressive hard-on.

'Go away!' I yelled.

'Ugh,' he grunted, and then he was on me again, his puke-making erection pressing into me and those fat hands grabbing, his fetid breath hot on my neck, and I was panicking and trying to push him off—

And suddenly a huge male paw reached out, grabbed him by the collar and flung him across the room. I stared in blank astonishment as a bunched fist shot out and punched him in his fat face, leaving him reeling and bleeding against a bookcase.

'Come on, Alex,' Tom said. 'I've come to take you home.'

Chapter 38

Tom pulled me out of there, which was just as well, because I wasn't going anywhere. I was staring at him with my mouth hanging open like a stranded flounder or David Mellor. I was rooted to the spot so hard I would need watering, any minute now.

'And you,' Tom roared at the cowering Barry, who was standing there with his hands clamped over his gushing nose, 'you fat little bastard, if you ever touch this young lady again—'

'You broke by dose,' wailed Barry thickly.

'—I'll start breaking all the other bones. You disgusting little hypocrite, I should go to the police. Come on, darling,' he said to me, and slammed the door behind us so hard the glass shattered, leaving a web of cracks like the spiders' in the box.

What did he just say? I asked myself frozenly. I must have misheard.

'What – what are you doing here?' I stammered.

'I'm here to get you, of course,' Tom said, smiling at me softly. 'I didn't come to borrow a book.'

'But how did you know I was here?'

'I traced the call to Rosedale, then asked your sister if she knew a reason why you might be there.'

'Oh,' I said. I felt stupid. And the mention of Gail sent a whole flock of little geese padding over my grave.

'Well, I'm perfectly happy, thank you,' I said stiffly. 'I didn't ask anyone to come and get me.'

'Yeah, you look it,' Tom said, grinning in an annoyingly attractive way. 'Come on, hop in.'

He opened the door to his Rolls. The Silver Phantom looked so out of place here, alongside the derelict schoolyard over the road and the nasty modern council houses. It also looked warm and seductively comfy.

It was bitterly freezing out here.

'All right,' I said grudgingly.

'Why did you come up here?' Tom asked, spinning the wheel smoothly in the direction of my village. He'd done his research all right. I had a nasty vision of him discussing me with Gail. 'Mental,' she'd probably said. 'Nervous breakdown. Consumed with jealousy.'

'I wanted to get away, get a new job, OK? Start again,' I said defiantly.

'You came up here for a reality check,' Tom said kindly.

'Yes.' But despite myself, I burst into tears. 'It's just that my reality checks keep bouncing.'

'It's OK,' Tom said, looking over at me.

'It isn't.' I knew I'd lost it completely now, but I couldn't be strong one more second. I was so tired and so despairing, and here was the only man I'd ever truly loved and I couldn't have him. 'Nothing's ever going to be all right again.'

'This isn't about Gail, is it?' Tom asked. A note of panic had crept into his voice.

'Yes, it's about Gail. Of course it is,' I sobbed.

'I'm sorry, Alex, I'm truly sorry, I never knew you would be so upset.'

'Well, you know now,' I said, burying my face in my hands.

The car spun upwards towards the cottage, taking the steep hill smoothly in its stride. With no streetlamps or neon to blot them out, the stars prickled over the huge sky like diamonds scattered on a jeweller's velvet cloth. Tom had a hard set to his shoulders, like a man beleaguered. He looked utterly tense.

I don't know why; I had bowed to the inevitable, I wasn't going to give him any grief.

Who could blame him for picking Cinderella instead of the elder Ugly Sister? Especially when that Ugly Sister had shown herself to be such a prime bitch. Now I knew how Ellen must have felt, when I was encouraging Snowy to flirt with her man. Well, Karma was handing her its revenge now, with interest.

'Who told you?' Tom demanded bitterly. 'I wanted to do it, to explain—'

'It wouldn't have been any better if you had. It would have been worse,' I said.

'So who was it? Was it Gail?'

I thought of gritting my teeth and congratulating Gail, and trying to catch some desperate illness so I could wriggle out of going to the wedding. Maybe I could gnaw through my own leg.

'No. I haven't spoken to her,' I said. 'I just knew.'

'How can you just know? Are you telepathic?' Tom demanded.

'Stop here,' I said wearily.

He parked the car outside my front door. Next to my tiny little Metro it looked even more outrageously lavish. I bit my cheeks and tried to pull myself together; Tom had come all this way just for me.

'I'll get us some coffee and supper,' I said.

'Oh. It's . . . sweet,' Tom lied charmingly. 'What fun to have a little hideaway like this.'

'Yeah, well, it didn't hide me for very long,' I said.

To my horror, Tom crossed the room, pulled me down on to the sofa and took my two hands in his. Oh no, I'd just stopped crying and now he was going to make me start again. I get a grip, and then he gets tender and compassionate. That's what triggers the torrents.

'Gail was upset,' he said quietly. 'I won't tell you otherwise, Alex, I wish I could, but I can't lie to you.'

'Upset? At the thought of me being upset?' I said acidly, tears starting to blur again. 'How nice of her.'

'Well, not at the thought of you being upset,' said Tom, looking confused, 'I mean, she probably was, but mostly it was the actual split, I think, although maybe not, Alex, I know you think I have a massive ego, I suppose it might have been you—'

'Tom.' The fog of words stopped my tears for a second. Despite my concentrating hard on what he had just said, it still failed to yield up its significance. Like *Alice Through the Looking Glass*, where the sentences have verbs and nouns and *sound* like English, but—

'What are you talking about?'

'Gail.'

'Yes, I got that bit, I mean, what about Gail, what split was she upset about? Me splitting from the flat?'

That seemed most unlikely. The further away I was, with my tendency to set galleries on fire and bust up wedding parties, the better; Gail would be cheering.

'No. Our split. Mine and Gail's.'

I sat very still. Hope had tricked me like this a couple of times before. Well, I was nobody's fool any more.

'What do you mean, yours and Gail's – split what? Split your living room? Split your housekeeping rota?'

Tom looked at me as if I was barking mad. 'Split, Alex, as in broke up. As in we are no longer dating each other. As in, Gail has moved back to your parents'.'

I stared back at him for twenty years. Well, OK, probably a couple of seconds, but that's what it felt like.

Then the floodgates opened, and I burst into rivers of tears, great, wracking sobs that convulsed my whole body, I couldn't stop them or dam them, my shoulders were shaking, my ribcage heaving.

Beside me Tom was starting and jumpy like a panicking racehorse. Men hate a crying woman, I realise that, but there was absolutely nothing I could do about it. I cried and cried.

'Alex,' Tom said frantically, producing a big red handkerchief with white polka dots on it, 'please don't cry, please, Alex, darling, I'm sorry I hurt your sister, but I couldn't go on with it.'

I grabbed the handkerchief and wiped my streaming eyes and blew my nose. It sounded like an elephant trumpeting. Very attractive.

'Why not?' I asked. My voice came out a hoarse whisper.

Whatever he said, I told myself, I had to cope with it. Whoever else he'd met, whatever little popsy he was seeing now, doubtless a good, home-loving kind of girl with a polo-playing daddy and a job making lunches for City businessmen at Sloane Rangers catering – the kind of girl who would serve him home-made bread sauce this Christmas – it had to be better than to see him with my own sister.

Of course I was still a total bitch. Look at how relieved I was – poor Gail, only I wasn't really feeling poor Gail, I was really exploding with relief.

'Because I've met someone else,' he said.

'Who?' I asked bravely. I caught sight of my face in the mirror over the fireplace. Everything was so red I looked like an extra from *Attack of the Killer Tomatoes*.

'Can't you guess?' Tom asked, looking at me weirdly.

'Oh my God! You're not seeing Snowy, are you?'

'Of course I'm not seeing *Snowy*, you total goose,' Tom said softly, 'I'm seeing *you*, Alex, or I am if you'll let me.'

And with that, rather hurriedly, like he was afraid I'd refuse, he pulled me towards him and kissed me, red nose and all.

I want to say it wasn't that good. That we fumbled, or something.

That it was a bit awkward. Things are normally, aren't they, the first time at least. You suddenly wonder if your mouthwash was strong enough, or if he'll think you're a tart if you French kiss him back, or if you'll bite him a bit harder than you meant to. Because what actually happened sounds too soppy for words.

He kissed me, and I melted. I forgot all about the state of my nose and my foundation. I couldn't have cared less about mouthwash or the size of my butt or whether he would be shocked at the grey M&S bra-strap visible under the neck of my shirt. All I could think about was Tom, that handsome, slightly callous mouth bearing down on mine, the way he was kissing me with such passion and insistence, the way he was making me feel so beautiful and desirable. My nipples flooded with blood. They got so stiff and tender they started to chafe against the cotton. My groin, too, washed with desire, a burst of lust spreading under my skin like a ripple from a pebble thrown into a glassy pond. I kissed nervously, he kissed hard, then harder, then when he took his mouth away from me I didn't even care, because he put it on my face, kissing me over and over, kissing my eyes shut and the tip of my nose and kissing my neck, the side of it, and my chin, and kissing my earlobes, just drowning me in these light, butterfly kisses, until I was dizzy with pleasure and wanting.

'Sorry, Alex,' Tom said, gasping and pulling back from me. 'Sorry. I couldn't help it.'

'I didn't want you to,' I said.

He looked amazed. A soft expression of delight and disbelief was spreading across his face. 'I thought you hated me,' he said.

I couldn't speak so I just shook my head.

'Alex! I was such a jerk, I behaved so badly at the wedding, I just thought of you with that Seamus bloke and it made me want to throw up. I know he was coming on to you – pushing you – but I was so hurt, I just lashed out. I couldn't stop myself, I just wanted to hurt you, to get back at you for how you were making me feel.'

'Oh Tom, I'm so sorry, I pushed Snowy into it—'

'Hell, of course you didn't, Alex, you were too innocent to see her for what she was. It was all my fault. I'd worked it out long before and – I suppose I thought as a gentleman I shouldn't say anything, I should let her try to rebuild her life, if it was a secret. I didn't act, and I could have stopped it. I pussyfooted around and then I tried to blame you, and I was so miserable about what I'd done to you I didn't know what to do with myself.'

He took a deep gulp of air. 'I've been a total bastard.'

'How? You have not!' I said defensively.

'Yes, I'm afraid I have,' Tom said. He looked utterly shamefaced. 'I – I used your sister. Oh, it wasn't as blatant as that, I mean, I told myself she was attractive and beautiful – which she is –' he said hastily, but in the manner of one who thinks she's not, not really – 'and I said since there was no chance of you ever dating me, the way should be clear for me to go out with Gail.'

He ran a large paw rather distractedly through his hair. 'It was obvious more or less from the word go that it wasn't going to work out. We were so different. Our tastes were different. We didn't find the same things funny, and there just wasn't a spark. I tried to cover up my feelings by buying her more and more expensive presents, but the truth was – I tried not to admit it to myself – that I dated her in the hope I could see you. I came to your flat whenever I could. I was devastated when you had that row and she moved out, and I knew I was going to have to end it, but by that time I thought maybe you would agree to see me as a friend.

'It was that evening at the gallery that nailed it down for me. You were so stressed and so funny, and you looked so lovely, and when you were naked—'

'Soaked,' I corrected him.

'Right, soaked – you just had the most beautiful body I've ever seen.'

'But what about Gail?'

'Gail?' he snorted. 'Well, Alex, I never saw her naked but I'm sorry, your sister's positively scrawny. No offence.'

Oh, none taken, I promise.

'Anyway, that night we split up and she took it rather hard. I was afraid you'd hold it against me. As you had every right to do.'

'And that's what you wanted to tell me?'

'Yes.' He shrugged. 'You wouldn't hear me out, so I assumed somebody had already told you, and you were so incensed at me that you'd run off.'

I just grinned. I wanted to give him a soft, romantic smile, but I couldn't stop this huge, shit-eating grin spreading all over my face. I was so happy. The kind of happiness I've only ever had once before, as a child, waiting for Christmas morning, eight years old and too excited to sleep.

'I ran off because I couldn't face you being with Gail. And because of the embarrassment, too.'

'Nothing to be embarrassed about,' Tom said thickly. He was hard and I could see it. He was one enormous guy.

Suddenly the wet explosion of desire burst right through me again.

'Alex, I love you,' he said, 'I love you so much, I want to be with you, do you think we could go to bed?'

'Oh yes,' I said, lifting my arms to him, 'yes please.'

Chapter 39

He picked me up in his arms as though I weighed no more than Kate Moss.

'You'll give yourself a hernia,' I said, blushing because it made me so happy he was doing it. It was turning me on even more. I'm sorry, but I'd always gone out with Byronic, Jarvis Cocker-like fops. To have a man actually take me in his arms, to feel the muscles sliding around under his skin . . .

He was hot. The sexual heat was a literal thing, rising between the two of us, lust thick in the air like musk.

Tom smiled. 'I hardly even notice you're there. I might never put you down.' He kicked open my bedroom door. 'Unless I can find a very good reason,' he said, and then he laid me down, very slowly, very tenderly on the bed, and started to peel off my clothing.

I wanted him. A sweat of wanting him broke out all over my body. He didn't fumble, he didn't giggle. All those magazine articles about how to have 'fun' in bed with your man, you know the ones that tell you that a 'shared sense of humour is vital between the sheets', I mean, they're talking pants, aren't they really? If you're laughing in bed you're doing it wrong. Unless you're watching *Fantasy Football* together. If you're having sex, you don't want to laugh, you want it to be passionate, you want a man to look at you the way Tom was looking at me now. With dark, predatory eyes glinting with lust. Total desire and intent. I knew he loved me, but now, he was going to *have* me.

He undid the buttons of my shirt. The greyness of my bra was a matter of total indifference to him. I could hear his excitement, his breath shortening as he peeled it off my breasts.

'You are so beautiful,' he said with complete seriousness, so he made me believe it, and then he bent and kissed my nipples and sucked them, very lightly at first, then harder, tugging them erect until I almost wanted to cry from pleasure.

When that finished, Tom's hands were under the small of my back, lifting me up like a doll, so he could undo my skirt and then pull down my panties, forcing himself to do it slowly, and when a soft gasp escaped him at the sight of me I couldn't help myself, I started moaning with the urgency of my need.

'Slowly, sweetheart, take it slowly,' Tom said gently, but I could feel his hardness straining against me, and I found myself jerking under his hands like they were hot metal. I pulled off his jacket, I would have ripped open his shirt but my hands were shaking so much I couldn't do it, and he had to help me, kicking off his shoes and tearing off his clothes.

Then he was naked, and I found I could look at him without chronic embarrassment, shyness or disgust. I didn't want to turn the light off. I could stare at him and think him beautiful, want him inside me.

Tom reached forward and brushed his hands over my shoulders. It sent a fresh spasm of desire crunching through me. His knee pressed down between my legs, roughly shoving my thighs apart. His large hands crept up my inner thighs, trailing fire, and then he was touching me, palming me, feeling my slickness against his fingers, his eyes hot with wanting, telling me he could feel everything, he knew how ready I was for this . . .

And then he bent that great dark head to kiss me, and he was inside me, pushing in the first time with perfect accuracy, kissing me and fucking me, and the pleasure at being filled swallowed me like a soft cloud of brown velvet, as though I had been empty and now he was making me whole.

'You're so good,' he gasped, 'Alex, you're so sexy.'

'You're incredible,' I said, and we both meant it, but we were both a little disbelieving, because maybe with other people we weren't demon lovers, we missed and fumbled and touched wrong and moved badly.

And then I discovered the secret of sex. In that moment, with Tom moving on top of me, thrusting harder and deeper every time, and me bucking up and rising to meet him, until everything fell away but the movement of his hips and hands and the explosions setting off inside me, like a match had been dropped into a box of fireworks.

The secret of sex is love. I loved him. I trusted him. He drove me nuts. I had thought about this so long before it happened, I was primed for him. The love in my head spread through my heart right to my groin.

It was OK that I wanted this animal fucking. It was OK that I couldn't control my response. I was not a bad girl, a slut. I was just in love and it was OK, and everything was always going to be OK from now on.

'Turn over,' Tom said.

'What?' I gasped, shuddered, riding the wave.

'Turn over,' Tom said, 'we should try this, I want to take you as deep as I can,' and without a pause he just lifted me up, strong hands round my waist, and flipped me over, yanking me up like a bitch on heat on my hands and knees, which is exactly what I was, on heat for him, lost in it, and then he was running his hands over my butt, stroking and squeezing and suddenly his fingers were there, checking for me.

'Oh,' he said. 'You like this.'

I flushed, nodded. 'Yes.'

'Say it. I want to hear you tell me.'

'I like this,' I gasped, 'I want it – Tom, please . . .'

He shoved himself inside me, his cock slamming deep down in me, his hands pulling my thighs closer to him, and the pleasure just intensified and deepened and spread like a thick wall of pressure across my body, and I could hear his breath getting more and more ragged, and then suddenly it just happened and I came – thinking about who was in me, what he was doing – I exploded in shattering crunching spasms, a sort of white-hot, brown-tinged bliss that made me dizzy, I didn't know where I was or who I was, I couldn't see, and then it faded away and somewhere I heard him groan, and come for me, and we collapsed on to the bed in perfect silence, and he reached for me and kissed me, and I started crying all over again.

When I woke up he was beside me, and all I wanted to do was lie there and breathe in his scent. Tom sleeping next to me, and I could stare as long as I liked at his dark lashes, his set mouth. I felt tenderness like I sometimes flash on when I see a newborn baby in a pram.

But there are no happy endings, are there? Everthing last night had swept away was coming back to me now. Gail. He told me he'd left

Gail, and how could I do this to my own sister? However annoying she was, Gail was still my kid sister, how could I?

Tom opened his eyes and looked up at me. 'Best dream I ever had,' he said. 'Or are you real?'

I steeled myself. 'Tom, we have to talk.'

He sat up and sighed. 'Damn. The most scary phrase in the universe, after "Look behind you".'

I grinned. 'Or "It's your mother on the phone".'

'Can I at least get some breakfast?' Tom demanded. 'A condemned man is entitled to a hearty one, you know.'

I nodded and went off to shower. I was determined not to start bloody well crying again. I don't know what was wrong with me, it's like someone had turned my emotion amps all the way up to eleven. Which they had, but that was still no excuse. This was England, not Ricki Lake. Besides, when I cry my nose goes as red as Rudolf, Boy Scouts could use it on Dartmoor for a guidance beacon.

Gail. Tom said she took it pretty bad. So bad, in fact, that he'd thought my running away had been in sympathy. I'd been jealous as hell, and I had never actually dated Tom. Dumped for your sister?

And that wasn't all. What about me breaking the Pollock? I was probably being sued for millions right now. I was a laughing stock in London. I had no job – I think we could safely say that my tenure at the Christian Library was over.

Sure, Tom was a millionaire a few times over. But even without the Gail thing, I couldn't just ask him to look after me. I know some women do that, and good luck to them, but I've known since I was a tiny girl that that wasn't for me. I was destined for love and motherhood, at least I hoped so, but also for – what? For glory, I used to think. Now I would settle for self-respect. Anything.

I had to be able to look after myself, before I could let Tom look after me. As much as I loved him, and I knew I really did. If I said, 'OK, baby, you work and I'll look after the kids, that'll be my job,' I would wind up resenting him, even resenting our kids.

Oh, listen to me, one session of lovemaking and I had us married with three babies.

Except it wasn't going to happen that way.

I got dressed, I put on a slick of cover-up, and went downstairs. The house was suddenly gloriously warm, and there was a delicious sizzly bacon smell coming from the kitchen.

'I fixed the heater,' Tom said. 'Bacon and tomatoes do you? There's some Lapsang in the pot.'

I felt a wash of sadness. 'Tom, I'm so glad this happened—'

'But,' he said wearily. 'I know that tone, Alex. What's the but, it's not going to work? Why not? I thought it worked pretty well last night.'

'First of all, I broke a Jackson Pollock,' I said, 'so I think I owe Gordon like millions of pounds.'

Tom's face was inscrutable. He just laid the table and started pouring out the tea. Oh funk, this was so perfect, so domestic, don't cry again, Alex, for heaven's sake.

'OK, so that's one problem.'

'Not to mention I burned down the gallery.'

'Go on. Tea?'

Tea? Tea? Is that what he said? I'm trying to tell him there's no future for us and all he does is offer me tea? 'Black no sugar,' I said, a bit crossly, 'and then there's the fact of me being naked which gave everybody a good laugh—'

'I know what it gave me, but I wouldn't call it a good laugh,' Tom said.

I blushed, but ploughed on. Once he got on to sex I'd be back upstairs and devil take the consequences. 'I don't have a job any more, I'm a total failure and I can't get involved with anybody while I'm like that.'

Tom paused for a second, then he smiled. I knew he liked to look on the bright side, but this was ridiculous.

'What are you smirking at?'

'Only you,' he said. 'Alex, you never spoke to Gordon, did you?'

'Didn't need to,' I said sullenly. 'I knew what he had to say.'

'Did you really?' Tom said. 'How about the fact that the Pollock was a fake, and he collected a packet from the insurance?'

I stared at him. 'OK, so maybe I'm not a million quid in debt—'

'And the stock was also insured. In fact, the story of the crush ran in lots of gossip columns, and people wandered into the gallery to see what all the fuss was about. Gordon's snowed under, he's desperate to have you back. I rang him when Keisha told me you'd vanished.'

'Oh,' I said.

'But you can't go back there.'

'Why not?'

'Because you've had a better offer. You remember Jack Herman?'

'The *Evening Standard* art critic? Yes, he was looking at my crappy sculptures,' I said gloomily.

'Well, he didn't think they were so crappy. He ran a piece on them, with pictures, two nights ago. Gordon is preening himself that he has "exclusive Alex Wildes",' Tom laughed. 'Sorry, sweetheart, but it is a bit of a facer to find you're the new Rachel Whitread, or something. Somebody offered six grand for the one I have of Gail.'

My head was spinning, I couldn't think straight. 'Well – you bought that one of Gail. Why, if you weren't in love with her?'

'I had to have it.'

'Why?' I demanded again, feeling my Adam's apple thick in my throat.

'Because you made it, silly, because I could see you doing it. I could hardly take another of your works, when that one was there and your mother was right behind me.'

I felt like French dressing – impossibilities mixing together, happiness and sadness like oil and vinegar.

Tom took my hand, and yes, my heart was leaping, but how much of a difference could that really make?

'Alex, you got it all mixed up. Your job's safe and people want to see your work. You're not going to be Damien Hirst overnight, but isn't this good, isn't this something?'

Something? It was glorious, it was totally wonderful, it was just what I'd always dreamed of, but . . .

'It still won't work, Tom,' I said, softly pulling my hand from his. 'I still can't do this to Gail.'

I put the key back under the mat and followed him back to York, where Tom returned the Metro to wreaths of smiles from the old bag on the desk.

'I'll get a train,' I said.

'Nonsense.' Tom grabbed me and bundled me into the front seat of his Rolls. 'You're coming back with me, like it or not.'

It was purgatory. On the way back I tried to explain. Tom was, by turns, angry, sorrowful, garrulous, persuasive. And I wanted to be talked into it, I so did. But I was a woman. I knew what it would do to Gail if I ran off with her true love, I'd never be able to forget I'd done that to my own sister.

'If she finds someone else . . .' I ventured.

'Damn it, Alex, do you know how many years I've waited for this? Why do I have to put it on hold for what Gail wants?' he shouted.

'You just do, I'm not going to break my own sister's heart,' I said stubbornly.

'Shit!' Tom yelled. He never swears in front of a lady. He slammed his fist down on the wheel, causing the horn to blare. 'Shit! Do you think I'm going to hang around for ever, waiting? I love you, you love me, that's all there is to it!'

'No it isn't,' I said, and started crying again.

Tom looked mutinously angry. He set his mouth in a hard line, and we drove the rest of the way home in silence.

'You'd better take me to the flat,' I said bleakly.

Tom dropped me off and got out to open the door. I hoped he would relent, say something sweet, but he merely helped carry in my suitcase, then nodded curtly and drove off with a screech of tyres.

I took a shuddering breath and tried to calm down, then I went back upstairs.

'Alex!' Keisha said as I walked through the door. 'Where the hell were you?'

'Long story,' I said miserably.

'Is it as long as your face, *cariad*?' asked Bronwen. 'Come on, spill the beans, inquiring minds want to know—' Then she took another look at my expression and shut up.

The bedroom door opened and Gail walked out. Her face was drawn and suspicious. 'Alex, where have you been?'

'In Rosedale,' I said, 'and I need to speak to you—'

'It's Tom, isn't it?' she demanded. 'You've been with him, haven't you?'

Then she burst into tears. 'You bitch, Alex, how could you do that to me.' You knew I was going out with him!'

'He said you split up,' I said weakly.

'Because of *you* – only you. You were always angling to get him,' Gail said, 'and now you have! Well, I hope you're happy.'

'I'm not seeing him, Gail,' I said, but she wasn't listening.

'Go home to Mum and Dad and explain it to them!' Gail yelled. 'I'm sick of your lies, Alex Wilde!'

Devastated, I slunk out of the flat and got in a cab for Victoria. It was true, I might as well go home. I needed to think.

The house was prettier than I remembered it, great clouds of winter jasmine bright against the sharp holly bushes, and the dark green yew tree on the back lawn. There was a river that ran at the bottom of our garden, and when I was a kid I used to sit on its banks for hours, knotting little crosses out of the rushes. Once I'd said hello to Mum and Dad, and managed to wriggle out of their questions, I planned to go there. Just to sit and look. I felt too upset to cry any more.

Mum was surprisingly placatory. Apparently Gordon had rung to tell her of the interest in my work.

'He says you've made almost eight thousand already, once you tot up the money for the eighteen pieces. And the non-abstract one of Gail, someone offered—'

'I know, Mum, Tom told me,' I said and cringed.

Mum smiled. 'How is Tom?'

'Er . . .'

'Oh, I know about you seeing him,' she said, 'Gail's been on the phone, but Alex, you two were always such good friends.'

I stared at her in disbelief. Mum wasn't angry, providing I hooked up with Tom. She just wanted at least one daughter married off to a nice rich man.

'Anyway, Gail's coming down to stay at the end of the week,' she said, 'so you two can make it up then. Let's face it, it won't be hard for Gail to pick up another man, will it?'

Oh, cheers, Mum. It would be hard for me, was that it? But then again who cared? I didn't want another man, I wanted Tom, and he was still the only one who was forbidden to me.

Chapter 40

The wedding took place six months later.

Not my wedding, of course. Sorry, didn't mean to tease you like that.

Keisha's wedding. Jeremy finally popped the question and she came round to tell me, which is to say she casually dropped the information in the middle of *Brookside*.

'*Brookie*'s dreadful these days,' she sniffed, 'it's got really crap compared to how it used to be.'

Her hand made a dismissive circle in the air. One of the problems with Keisha doing so great at *Up and Running* was she now thought she was an expert on TV. I couldn't drool over George Clooney without her saying, 'God, that shot is really badly put together,' or 'God, don't they *have* a continuity expert?'

This time, however, the only thing I noticed was a big fuck-off ruby sparkling in the lamplight.

'That's nice, is it Butler and Wilson?' Bronwen said innocently.

Keisha arched one eyebrow sneeringly. 'As if. This is bona fide, honey, the real thing.'

'But it's on the wrong finger,' Bronwen went on blithely, 'unless—'

We put down our bowls of Kettle Chips, which is the greatest cop-out ever, to let you eat crisps and not feel twelve.

'Yeah, well, we're getting married next Saturday at Marylebone Registry Office,' said Keisha, and then pulled away when we tried to hug her. 'Jesus, I've just had this dry-cleaned.'

I felt an overwhelming sense of melancholy. I wanted to jump up in the air, to be thrilled and squealy and girly, but what I actually felt was, oh, shit.

It's like when you're a third-year girl at school and your best mate gets a new boyfriend. I mean, you've had it, haven't you? She's mooning over his picture in the yearbook and wondering if he's looking her way while he's hanging out with his mates at the bus stop. Only that usually breaks up, and then you can get your *Jackies* and your *Just Seventeens* and write in letters together asking why all boys are stupid.

Marriage. It had this big, clanging sound of gates clashing shut behind Keisha, and me never seeing her again.

'D'you want to be a witness, Alex?' Keisha was saying.

Or alternatively, the trumpets sounding at the Best Party In The World . . . Ever!, guest list, to which I was not going to be invited.

'Three times a bridesmaid, never a bride,' I said absently.

'Only twice a bridesmaid, I don't think you can count Charles Drummond's wedding,' Bronwen giggled.

'Just witness. I'm not going for any of that roses and lilies crap,' said Keisha romantically, 'fifteen minutes straight in straight out, it was tough enough to get the time off from work as it was.'

'Sure,' I said, trying to smile. I didn't want her to see I was as enthusiastic as Mary Whitehouse at a brothel.

'We might have a bit of a party after,' Keisha said modestly. Oh blimey, now we were getting it. I knew there would be some excuse for new TDOs somewhere in the equation. 'We could pop down to South Molton Street – anyway, come on, Alex, it'll be great to have the famous sculptor.'

'Famous my arse,' Bronwen giggled. She can always be relied to keep other people's feet on the ground, although her own are still suffering from altitude sickness.

'Well, Alex is a bit famous,' Keisha said judiciously. 'And she can afford to get some new gear.'

That was true. It's amazing, success comes along like buses in the cliché. Now Gordon was proudly showing my stuff in his gallery, and wealthy, annoying New Labour Bolinger Bolsheviks from Tufnell Park would ring and commission me for ever-increasing sums of money. You'd like to tell them to fuck off, you know they know nothing about what you're trying to do, but I was responsible these days. I had my own tiny flat in a smart building in Holloway. I had a mortgage. I had nice clothes and nice make-up, and Joel from John Frieda was doing my hair again. Sometimes Sunday supplements would do tiny features on me.

For the first few months I was wary, of course. I hoarded every penny. I waited furiously for the bubble to burst.

But amazingly enough, it hadn't. I was slowly, surely, picking up reviews, clients and profiles. Agents wanted to represent me. I was actually making a bit of money.

Once an eager young journo from the *Mail* rang me at home: 'We're doing a feature on the future being female. Would you say the future's female?'

'Yes,' I said bleakly.

My future was female, wasn't it? No nice men, only ever-increasing numbers of cats. I was going to get all eccentric and retire to a farm in Sussex with sixty cats, leaving my nieces and nephews to grind their teeth in fury when I left everything to the moggies. I could see it now.

I didn't actually have a cat yet, but it was inevitable.

'Hur hur,' she giggled, 'and what's the best thing about being rich?'

'The money,' I said.

I was joking. Of course I was joking. But the gossip columns loved it, and I got a bit of notoriety and a few more commissions. And my price kept going up.

Rich, though. I wasn't rich. I should have told her to ask Tom Drummond. He might know.

Tom was everywhere in my life. His new deal with Richard Branson had him all over the papers, the 'young tycoon', in the business sections, the gossip columns, inside *Hello!*, everywhere.

Except actually in my life.

He didn't call. He didn't write. He didn't even respond when I sent him my change of address card.

Once, on a pretext, I rang his office, and when he came on the line he was perfectly polite, but he bought ten books of the charity raffle tickets I was selling and then said goodbye. No tremors in the voice, I mean nothing.

Well, I wasn't going to take it lying down. Because I had taken it lying down, if you get my drift, and it had been so utterly wonderful. I couldn't let him go just like that.

My new book on *How to Hook a Rich Man: Thirty-six Steps to Total Commitment* said I should never call him, and on pain of death, never call a man twice in one week, he might work out you have feelings for him. But then I thought – hey – Girl Power, we don't hide around waiting for men to ask us out, I'll talk to Tom, he'll see reason, he'll quietly agree to see me, and everything will be OK.

I mean, I couldn't give him what he wanted. How could I? Gail was taking it hard enough as it was.

'You bitch, you ruined my life,' was about as friendly as it got. Before I moved out of the Belsize Park flat I was always finding acid notes in the bathroom. 'See if you can manage to keep your thieving hands off this.' 'Don't you touch this video, Alex, you'll break it like you broke my heart.' I wallowed in agonies of guilt. Gail used to lock herself in her room and cry for hours, and she wouldn't let me in. I used to pass the bathroom and see her shoulders shaking. I felt so bad, I couldn't deal with it, I had to get out of there.

'Gail's off her food,' my dad told me when Gail packed a small hempen suitcase and stormed home to recuperate. Off her food – what did that mean, one button mushroom instead of two for dinner? But it was enough to get my skin all dry and flaky from stress.

I had had so much misery in love. When Hannah stole Justin, I remember just wanting to die. But at least Hannah hadn't been my own sister.

'Don't you think it's *sick*?' Gail squealed at me down the phone. 'Going out with two sisters? Urgh, he's probably writing about it for *Playboy*, he's such an utter bastard!'

And don't let's even talk about my success.

'Oh, I always knew it,' Gail wailed, 'I always knew you would do this, you're such an ambitious bitch, you've just been waiting for a chance to show me up.'

'But I didn't mean to,' I said humbly.

'Well, I'm writing about it in the nature novel,' Gail said, terribly triumphant. 'You won't like it when it comes out.'

'Ooh, please tell us what's in the nature novel,' Keisha wheedled, 'please, Gail.'

'No. It's a—' Then she caught sight of Keisha's mocking grin and ran off crying again.

I felt lower than a piece of worm dirt. 'How can you be so mean?'

'Oh please, Al,' Keisha said briskly, 'nothing's wrong with that girl except her pride. You should marry Tom if you want to, she'll get over it.'

But I couldn't do it. Even when I moved out. The thought of

Gail's tear-streaked face at the wedding, as she sat there in some little pink twinset knitted in organic wool.

So I ignored my *Commitment!* manual and rang Tom.

'You're being silly, I think you should go out with me,' I said confidently.

'You mean sneak around behind your sister's back?' Tom said, after a nasty moment during which I thought he might ask who was this?

'Until she finds someone else,' I replied, a bit less self confidently.

'Alex.' Tom sighed. Even his sighs turned me on, my God, my nipples were as hard as Keisha's ruby. 'I've waited too long to sneak around. If you really want to be with me, you'll stop making excuses.'

'Excuses?' I said, indignantly.

'Yes, excuses. You know Gail didn't really love me. You're just hiding again; hiding from commitment like you always do.'

I started to laugh. '*Me* hide from commitment? It's men that hide—'

'Why don't you have a good look at the men you chose?' Tom said softly, 'You, Alex, nobody else, and then tell me you're not truly hiding from love.'

'So you won't go out with me,' I snarled.

'I'll marry you,' Tom said simply, 'or I'll start dating someone else and try to forget you. The trouble with you, Alex, is you want everything your own way.'

He hung up on me.

The selfish, arrogant little fucker! He actually hung up on me.

So you'll forgive me if I wasn't too thrilled at the wedding announcement. Love hurts, as John Wayne Bobbit is no doubt fond of telling the world. Weddings should be banned from inviting single people, hateful torture sessions that they are. Standing around with all the old parents and parents' mates comparing who's been paired off to whom: score one for boyfriend, four for engaged and a clear six for married. Even worse are the actual young couples, sneaking their arms through each other's in such a way that you look, and then they blush and pretend to have been caught out. And say patronising things about how great it must be to have a career. Uuurgh, they make me sick.

I said this to Keisha on our way to the registry office. Bronwen came dressed in peach leather trousers and a matching silk jersey with thigh-high boots. Keisha wore her normal black trousers. I put on a long floaty dress, which they all laughed at, so maybe it was better that I did forget the hat.

'Oh yeah, weddings, they suck,' Keisha snarled, then grinned at Bronwen. 'OK, but this isn't a wedding, I'm just getting married.'

'I want to marry Dan like this,' Bronwen said, 'it's so romantic, just walk off the street in your jeans and just do it.'

'What about you, Al?' Keisha demanded.

I sighed. 'Tom says I've got fear of commitment.'

'You have,' Bronwen said serenely.

'Well, of course she has,' says Keisha, as if that was an obvious truism, 'but I bet she still thinks about getting married.'

I tried to banish the vision of me, in the full monty, long, white dress, floating down the aisle, trumpets sounding, orange blossoms wreathed in my hair. I just wasn't postmodern like these two. I wanted the whole thing, the real deal.

What scared me was that the guy in this fantasy – usually faceless – was now possessed of features. Tom's features.

'You should talk to Tom,' Keisha said, when we got out of the car.

I shook my head. 'That's over.'

Keisha shrugged. 'OK. But I tell you, honey, stop going on about Gail. You know perfectly well it's got nothing to do with her.'

'It has,' I protested, 'it's all about Gail.'

'Alex,' Bronwen said, dragging me aside before it was our turn to go in, 'can I give you some advice?'

'If you must,' I said, sneering haughtily and keeping my eyes fixed on the bottom of my champagne glass.

'You do refuse to face reality a bit. You are running from love. It's always about some unsuitable bloke, or some man you can't have, because of his wife or whatever – you always look at other women, not yourself. You refuse to see how great life is. Maybe it's a British disease – postmodern cynicism,' Bronwen said, in irony-free tones. 'No, I'm serious. You've got Venus Envy. You're just afraid to let yourself be happy.'

'What nonsense,' I said weakly, but I felt like I was going to cry.

Keisha allowed herself a bit of a smile when she actually got married, I'm sorry to report. Even Keisha lets her standards slip sometimes.

They held the part at the Lancaster Gate Hotel. Just a small, intimate affair for five hundred of Keisha's closest friends and family.

Gail arrived, carrying an organic yoghurt maker for the happy couple.

'Cheers,' Keisha said. 'It'll do for a garden ornament.'

'How are you?' I asked nervously.

'No better for seeing you,' Gail replied, stomping away with a toss of her lovely blonde head.

I slunk off miserably, but Bronwen wasn't having any of it. 'Look at that,' she said, pointing out Jeremy and Keisha kissing in a corner. 'Look at how happy they are. That could be you, you know.'

'For the last time, Tom's not interested in going out,' I said. 'And even if he was, I wouldn't talk to him. He's such an arrogant git.'

'That's a pity,' Bronwen said with a sly grin, 'because he's coming this way.'

I looked up with a start, but it was too late. Unless I was seeing a very handsome, very determined mirage, Tom Drummond was indeed coming towards me, threading his way through the crowd and looking like it would take a charging rhino to stop him.

I felt total panic. Fluttery stomach, wanting to puke, the works. 'Who invited him?'

'It's Keisha's guest list. Anyway, gotta go, Dan's waiting for me,' Bronwen said cheekily, and legged it, leaving me on my own.

'Alex,' Tom said when he arrived on the spot a second later.

I looked up at him. I felt a thrill of desire between my legs. I looked away, I couldn't hold his gaze.

'Gail's here,' he said, putting his hand out and tipping up my face so that I had to look into his eyes. It was pretty sexy, I have to tell you. He looked like he was in no mood to argue. 'I'm going over there to talk to her. I'm going to explain that she can't come between us any more.'

'You can't – er – you'll really upset her,' I muttered.

Oh, I want to fuck you. Oh, get me out of here. Oh, help.

No man had ever made me feel this way in my whole life.

'I doubt that,' Tom said dryly, 'look over there.'

I looked. Gail was doing some energetic tongue wrestling with a stocky frame I'd seen somewhere before.

'That's Tony Meadows!' I gasped. 'Her old boyfriend!'

'Her new boyfriend, if you ask me,' Tom pointed out. 'So tell me. What's your excuse now?'

'Er . . .' I gasped.

'Why are you looking around the room?' Tom asked softly. 'Need time to think? To get another reason why you can't be happy?'

'Well . . .'

'I'm not going to wait around for ever,' Tom said firmly. 'You know me inside and out, Alex. You're going to have to make up your mind.'

I wanted him. I loved him. But I was still panicking. What if I said yes? What if it was a mistake? How would I know? Tom might not be the one after all.

Gail walked past us, saw what Tom was doing and gave me the death stare from hell. But I finally realised I couldn't care less.

'What do you think you're doing?' she screeched.

'Piss off, Gail,' I replied wittily.

'Tony will be missing you,' said Tom.

He winked at me. And then, before I could protest, or struggle, or play for time, he kissed me.

And then I knew.